FROM HYDASPES TO KARGIL

A History of Warfare in India
from 326 BC to AD 1999

FROM HYDASPES TO KARGIL

A History of Warfare in India
from 326 BC to AD 1999

KAUSHIK ROY

MANOHAR
2004

First published 2004

© Kaushik Roy, 2004

ISBN 81-7304-543-7

Published by

Ajay Kumar Jain for
Manohar Publishers & Distributors
4753/23 Ansari Road, Daryaganj
New Delhi 110 002

Typeset at

Digigrafics
New Delhi 110 049

Printed at

Lordson Publishers Pvt. Ltd.
Delhi 110 007

To
Suhrita
and
My Parents

Contents

8   *Contents*

Maps

Preface

Since my childhood, for reasons unknown, I have been obsessed with the history of warfare. None of my family members or relatives were ever in the army and nor was any member killed by the army or in military action. Nevertheless, military history captured my imagination. I used to badger my father to tell me war stories before going to sleep. And I used to steal money from my mother's safe for buying war comics.

During the last ten years, while studying Indian history, the thought often came to my mind that 'war makes state and state makes war'. None the less, decent books on Indian military history are a rarity. My book is a modest attempt written in the hope that its very inadequacies will provoke academic historians to write serious works on Indian military history.

Besides the civilian practitioners of military history and the military buffs, is there any necessity for the 'men in uniforms' who had experienced the 'face of battle' to go through this volume? The necessity of military history for men of action is put forward most succinctly by Clausewitz's 'God of War' Napoleon who, in his *Military Maxims*, urges his fellow military men to understand the contributions made by the great generals in history:

Read over and over again the campaigns of Alexander, Hannibal, Caesar, Gustavus, Turenne, Eugene and Frederick. Make them your models. This is the only way to become a great general and to master the secrets of the art of war. With your own genius enlightened by this study, you will reject all maxims opposed to those of the great commanders [Brigadier General Thomas R. Phillips (ed.)].

Nehru Memorial Museum & Library, KAUSHIK ROY
Teen Murti, New Delhi
March 2003

Acknowledgements

My thanks to Professor Rudrangshu Mukherjee and Ms Kamini Mahadevan for encouraging me to write this book. Thanks to Prof. I. Kamtekar for reading part of the draft. I am indebted to the anonymous referee for his critical comments regarding my handling of the sources. The usual disclaimers apply. I also express my thanks to my sister for tolerating my idiosyncrasies. Finally, I wish to express my gratitude to Mr Ramesh Jain for his interest in publishing books on Indian military history.

Nehru Memorial Museum & Library,   KAUSHIK ROY
Teen Murti, New Delhi
March 2003

Abbreviations

AAC	Army Air Corps
ASR	*Asian Strategic Review*
ATJS	Advanced Trainer Jets
C3I	Command, Control, Communications and Intelligence
C4I	Command, Control, Communications, Computer and Intelligence
C4I2	Command, Control, Communications, Computer, Intelligence and Information. C4I2 represent the command apparatus of the post-Cold War armies
COAS	Chief of Army Staff
DRDO	Defence Research and Development Organization
EIC	East India Company
IAF	Indian Air Force
IAS	Indian Administrative Service
IB	Intelligence Bureau
IESHR	*Indian Economic and Social History Review*
IPS	Indian Police Service
JCS	Joint Chiefs of Staff
JSS	*Journal of Strategic Studies*
JUSII	*Journal of the United Service Institution of India*
LCA	Light Combat Aircraft or Interceptor meaning fighter planes
LoC	Line of Control along the India-Pakistan border
MoD	Ministry of Defence
NAI	National Archives of India
NAM	Non Aligned Movement, which constituted the core of Nehru's foreign policy in the era of the Cold War
PAF	Pakistan Air Force
PLA	Peoples Liberation Army or the Chinese Army
PLAAF	Peoples Liberation Army Air Force, i.e. the Chinese Air Force
PLAN	Peoples Liberation Army Navy, i.e. Chinese Navy
RMA	Revolution in Military Affairs
SA	*Strategic Analysis*
SMA	Synthesis in Military Affairs

Glossary

Ahimsa	Non-violence
Akhbarat	Mughal newspapers
Akhbar nawis	Mughal news writers
Altmash	Tactical reserve for supporting the vanguard of the Mughal army
Amir	High-ranking Muslim commander
Amir-ul-Umara	Commander-in-chief of cavalry in the medieval Muslim army
Arquebusier	Firearms-equipped infantry of early modern Europe
Arthashastra	Political text of the ancient Hindus
Auftragstaktik	German concept of mission-oriented command system, opposite of *Befehlstaktik*
Baniya	Hindu businessman
Banjaras	Grain dealers who supplied the armies operating in India till the nineteenth century; they were the near equivalent of the *munitionnaires* of the pre-modern French army.
Bans	Hand-held rockets used by the Mughal infantry
Bardic literature	Folk literature produced by the roving *bards* (poets) of medieval India. *Bards* were mostly prominent in Rajasthan
Batta	Extra pay given to the personnel of the Sepoy army while campaigning
Battalion	See regiment
Bazar	Market
Bazar-i-Lashkar	Persons in change of supplying the medieval Muslim army
Befehlstaktik	German concept of a centralized top-down hierarchical command, opposite of *Auftragstaktik*

Bhagavad Gita	Religious text of the Hindus
Blitzkrieg	German concept of lightning warfare, somewhat similar to the fast mobile campaigns of manoeuvre warfare
Brigade	An assortment of regiments
Caliphate	Empire of the Arab emperors *Caliphs*
Caltrop	Iron ball with spikes used by the European infantry for breaking up a cavalry charge
Caracole	Skirmishing tactics employed by the firearms-equipped medieval European cavalry
Cassid	Ruuner who carried information for the army. The introduction of the telegraph resulted in his demise
Cataphract	See *Cuirassier*
Chaturanga-Bala	Four-limbed army of the ancient Hindus, composed of chariots, elephants, infantry, and cavalry
Chakra	Iron discuss thrown at the enemy personnel by the infantry of ancient India
Chakravartin	Hindu emperor in ancient India
Chakravyuh	Ancient Hindu concept of encircling the enemy
Chi	Chinese equivalent of *ahimsa,* emphasizing spiritual forces
Chuppoo	Boat used by the Khalsa Army for crossing rivers
Cuirassier	Armoured cavalryman, i.e. heavy cavalry
Dagh wa Chihra	System of branding war horses in medieval India to prevent fraud by the chieftains supplying cavalry contingents to the ruler
Dak	Postal system
Dhammavijaya	Conquest through *ahimsa,* somewhat similar to winning the hearts and minds of the people, opposite of *Kutayuddha*
Diwan-i-Arz	Military bureaucracy of the Delhi Sultanate
Dvandvayuddha	Sanskrit for heroic warfare which involves a duel between warlords
Feranghi	Indian term for European, especially the British
Festung	German for fortress

Feurkampf	German concept of firefight on the battlefield
Field artillery	Artillery used on the battlefield.
Furusiya	Training exercise of the *Mamluks*
Ganimi kava	Guerrilla war with an emphasis on a scorched-earth policy practiced by the Maratha light cavalry
General-Feldmarschall	Field Marshal in the German Army
Ghee	Clarified butter
Ghulam	Warrior slave of a Muslim chief
Gomastah	Hindu official in charge of the commissariat department
Gotterdammerung	Twilight of the Gods
Horse artillery	Light artillery drawn by horses
Iltimish	Tactical reserve of the Mughal army
Imperium	Empire
Iqta	Grant of land revenue to a Muslim chief for maintaining cavalry contingents. The *iqta* system which was introduced by the Delhi Sultanate was the precursor of the *jagir* system
Jagirdar	Holder of a *jagir*
Jagir	Land revenue granted to a holder of a *mansab*, i.e. the mansabdar for maintaining troopers
Janissaries	Ottoman infantry
Jawan	Indian infantry
Jehadi	Men conducting *jehad*
Jehad	Religious war waged by fanatic Muslims
Kafir	Impure Hindu in the eye of the *jehadis*
Kaianian bow	Bow made from the poplar tree and used by the mounted soldiers of Central Asia
Kesselschlacht	German concept of 'pocket battle' or 'battle of encirclement'
Khalsa army	Army of the Khalsa Kingdom, also known as *Dal Khalsa*
Khalsa Kingdom	Sikh Kingdom established by Maharaja Ranjit Singh
Khan	Commander of a *tumen*. The khan was assisted by ten *amirs*.

Khatri	Hindu trading class of Punjab
Khud Kasht	Rich peasantry of Mughal India. They occasionally also functioned as infantry of rebellious chieftains
Kleinkrieg	German for limited war or small war
Kotwal	Mughal police official
Kshatra Dharma	Code of conduct of Rajput warriors
Kshatriya	Warrior caste of pre-modern India. Rajputs belonged to this caste.
Kutayuddha	Ancient Hindu concept of covert warfare involving intrigues and commando operation, opposite of *Dhammayuddha*
Lal Paltans	Sepoys
Lambardar	Hindu village headman
Lance	Long spear used by a cavalryman
Lashkar-i-Islam	Army of Islam
Lashkar	Armed tribal of Afghanistan and the North-West Province of Pakistan conducting *jehad*
Light cavalry	Non-armoured cavalry usually noted for its mobility
Mahabharata	Epic of ancient India
Mahajan	Hindu moneylender
Mamluk	Mounted slave soldier of medieval Muslim armies
Mandala	Kautilya's grand strategy of surrounding the enemy state with buffer and satellite states.
Mangonel	Medieval siege engine used either for throwing stones or as a battering ram. These engines were used by both Mongols and Turks. Mangonels were similar to the trebuchets and catapults of the Greek and the Roman armies, respectively.
Mansabdari system	Military system of the Mughals. Under this system, the semi-autonomous nobles were granted ranks of office, which were known as *mansabs*. In return for the grants of revenue, i.e. *jagirs*, they supplied cavalry to the Mughal emperor.
Mars	Roman god of warfare

Maskirovka	Russian concept of tactical deception
Matchlock	Primitive musket, a modified form of the *tufeng*
Materialschlacht	German concept of attritional warfare in which the side with superior material resources is bound to win, opposite of *Blitzkrieg*
Moksha	Hindu religious concept of personal salvation
Mujahideen	See *lashkar*
Namakharami	Indian concept of lack of loyalty to or betrayal of the salt giver, i.e. the employer
Naukri	Liternal meaning job. In medieval India this term denoted temporary jobs taken up by the armed peasantry who functioned as mercenaries.
Nawab	Autonomous *subadar*
Nawabi	Rule of the *Nawab*
Padshah	Mughal emperor
Paik	Indisciplined infantry of pre-modern India
Pandy	A *Purbiya* soldier who rebelled against the British in 1857
Parganah	Administrative division
Parwanah	Order issued by the Mughal court
Pasee	Low caste of Awadh
Phalanx	Heavy infantry of the ancient Greeks
Pharaoh	Emperor of ancient Egypt
Pike	Long spear used by the pre-modern European infantry
Pindari	Mercenary light cavalry hired by the Marathas
Pir	Muslim holy man
Porte	Ottoman Sultan
Purbiya	High-caste soldier from Awadh and Bihar; many joined the Sepoy army in large numbers till 1857
Qighaz shot	Turkish tactic of shooting arrows while riding horses at full gallop
Qizilbash	A Turkish group settled in Central Asia. This group provided cavalry contingents to Nadir Shah's army.
Raj	Term denoting British rule in India

Rajput	Warrior *Kshatriya* chief of medieval India. Around AD 700 the Rajputs spread from Rajasthan to other parts of north India.
Rao	Hindu chief
Ratha	War chariot of ancient India
Rathin	Driver of a *ratha*
Realpolitik	German term for power politics
Regiment	An unit of 1,000 to 2,000 soldiers. A regiment was composed of one or more battalions
Resaldar major	Indian cavalry officer of the Sepoy army
Rohillas	Inhabitants of Rohilkhand in Uttar Pradesh The Rohillas provided contingents to the Indian armies during the eighteenth and the nineteenth centuries
Sadhanika	General in charge of cavalry of the Gupta army
Samanta	Hindu hereditary chieftain of early medieval India
Sangar	Stronghold of stones made by the Pathans at the tops of mountains
Sardar	Indian chieftain
Sari-i-Khail	Commander of ten horsemen in medieval Muslim armies
Sarissa	Long pikes of Alexander's infantry
Sayid	High-class Muslim
Schwerpunkt	Literal meaning centre of gravity. Actually this term denotes Clausewitz's concept of the concentration of the enemy's armed forces
Senapati	Commander-in-chief in the *Chaturanga-Bala*
Sepoy	Infantry of the Sepoy army
Sepoy army	Army of British India. While the officer corps was British, the rank and file was Indian
Shaikh	See *Sayid*
Siege artillery	Heavy artillery used in siege or positional warfare (for taking or defending forts and cities)
Sipahi	Cavalry provided by the *iqtadar,* i.e. the holder of the *iqtas*
Sipah salar	Commander of ten *Sar-i-Khail*
Sowar	Cavalryman of the Sepoy army

Sreni	Corporation of mercenary soldiers which flourished in late ancient and early medieval India
Strategos	General of the ancient Greek army, equivalent to *senapati*
Subadar	Mughal provincial governor. In the nineteenth century, the term was used for an Indian infantry officer of the Sepoy army However, officers such as the resaldar major of the cavalry, subedar and subedar major of the infantry had no authority over the youngest British officer
Subah	Mughal province
Sultan	Muslim ruler
Sultanate	Kingdom of the sultan
Suta	Commander in charge of the contingent of *rathas* in the *Chaturanga-Bala*
Tao	Chinese concept of methods or ways of warfare
Tehsil	See Parganah
Thanedar	See *Kotwal*
Timar	*Iqta* of the Ottoman Empire
Topiwalah	European commander of the Westernized Maratha infantry
Topkhana	Mughal artillery department
Tufeng	Hand-held firearm used by the Muslim infantry in medieval India
Tulghama	Flanking attack by mounted bowmen
Tumen	Battle group of 10,000 Mongol soldiers
Ulema	Religious teacher of Islam
Zamburak	Light gun mounted on a camel, used by the Persian, the Afghans, and the Khalsa army

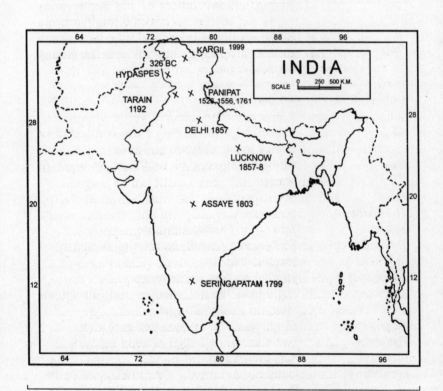

Map 1: Famous Battles and Sieges in Indian History

The Ride of the Fourth Horseman of the Apocalypse in India

On the field of Truth, on the battlefield of life, what came to pass, Sanjaya, when my sons and their warriors faced those of my brother Pandu?

When your son Duryodhana saw the armies of the sons of Pandu he went to his master in the art of war and spoke to him these words:

See there, master, the vast army of the Pandus well set in order of battle by the son of Drupada, your own wise pupil.

There can we see heroic warriors, powerful archers, as great as Bhima and Arjuna in battle: Yuyudhana and Virata and King Drupada of the great chariot of war. ...

And many other heroic warriors ready to give their lives for me; all armed with manifold weapons, and all of them masters of war. ...

Stand therefore all firm in the line of battle.

Bhagavad Gita (500 BC)[1]

When the Lamb opened the fourth seal, I heard the voice of the fourth living creature say, "Come!" I looked, and there before me was a pale horse! Its rider was named Death, and Hades was following close behind him. They were given power over a fourth of the earth to kill by sword, famine and plague, and by the wild beasts of earth.

Book of Revelation, Bible.[2]

The opening stanza of the *Bhagavad Gita*, the most powerful text of ancient India's philosophy, as well as the Book of Revelation refer to Warfare. The horrible consequences of warfare are more prominent in the Bible when it refers to the deathly ride of the fourth horseman of doom. This is because armies and warfare have determined the fate of this subcontinent in particular and the world in general from the dawn of history. The battles of Panipat and Plassey are like household names, since they have altered the course of South Asian history. Feeding Mars in the subcontinent also influenced the evolution of state and society. The army has always been one of the biggest government employers in employment-scarce Indian society. The Mauryas and the Mughals maintained huge armies which numbered more than a million. In British India, the biggest government employer was the Sepoy army which in peacetime annually enlisted 20,000 peasants. In post-1947 India, though the railway service has overtaken the army in the annual intake of personnel, still the million-strong armed forces, a legacy of ancient India, provide a means of alternate livelihood to many from the country's predominantly agrarian society. Again, throughout history, the military constituted the principal item of expenditure for the state. Both the Mughals and the British extracted about 50 per cent of the agricultural produce, which constituted the principal source of their income. About 80 per cent of the Mughal budget, 50 per cent of the revenues of the Gupta Empire, and 46 per cent of the British Indian Empire's budget went to finance Mars.

Nevertheless, military history remains marginal within the current academic discourse. This is due to the stance of political correctness fashionable among the academicians who are mostly swayed by the current of post-modernism. Studying 'marginal' groups like women and tribals seems to be the order of the day. In the age of 'feminism' and 'liberalism', military history is regarded as irrelevant at best, male chauvinistic and obnoxious at worst.[3] Strangely, armies and warfare do not appear within the ambit of the theory of 'power' propounded by Michel Foucault,[4] the cult figure of the post-modernist approach.

Before the 1990s, when Marxism ruled the roost of Indian academia, military affairs were relegated to the footnotes of academic monographs. This was in tune with the orthodox tenets of the teachings of Karl Marx for whom the armed forces were agents of exploitation of the poor and instruments of class dominance by the ruling class. Though Engels wrote about military history,[5] he failed to influence the Marxist pundits of India. In a way both the Marxist and the post-modernist perspectives overlook the fact that armies and warfare are worthy of attention since women and the economically underprivileged suffered worst during organized violence.

The net result of this sort of historiographical oversight is that there is no single volume which deals with warfare in India from the beginning of Indian civilization to recent times. Some military officers after retirement have tried to fight the battle against the marginalization of military studies. Their output has resulted in chronological narratives of the Indian army that highlight the glamour and glory of the soldiers and of particular valorous regiments.[6] Memoirs of retired generals are also a successful publishing industry in India. However, it seems that Indian generals throughout history have lost most of the battles but are on the point of winning the 'battle of the memoirs' by placing all the blame on the shoulders of the vulnerable politicians.[7]

Among the academicians a few important exceptions prove the rule. In recent times interdisciplinary approaches have become a part of historical research methodology in India. So political sociologists in their attempt to study the Indian social system have approached the analysis of warfare as part of the subcontinent's social structure. Stanislav Andreski first propounded the assumption that the military system is shaped by the host society which spawns it.[8] This approach as applied in the Indian scenario by the American scholar Stephen P. Rosen was subsequently termed as the new military history.[9] The basic tenet of the school as represented by Rosen is to link up India's military backwardness with the most characteristic element of the subcontinent's social structure, the caste system. Ironically, the study of the linkage between the caste system and the evolution of the various militaries in India was the concern of many scholars even before 1947.[10] Hence, the so-called new military history does not seem to be all that new. Again, the problem with this sort of writing is that the votaries of this school tend to establish a sort of reductionist determinism between society and military culture. As a result, to their way of thinking, the part played by military hardware, leadership, training, doctrine, strategy, and tactics in systematizing warfare remains in the background and occupies a secondary place.

In this volume of about 80,000 words the aim is not to give a comprehensive and chronological account of all aspects of warfare in India. The focus in this volume remains on land warfare, because aerial warfare has been of secondary significance in Indian history. Again, despite India's long coastline, the country remains a subcontinental landmass. And history shows that without a strong land force, even a power that enjoyed naval supremacy in the Indian Ocean was able to do little.

Instead of dividing the history of Indian warfare into the traditional periods of the ancient, medieval, and modern eras, a better approach for mapping the contours of the history of warfare would be to analyse South Asian history with the aid of the concept of 'military synthesis'. This idea is used as a heuristic tool for understanding the military landscape of India. The notion of military synthesis has two dimensions. It is assumed that technology (military hardware) and managerial expertise (which includes both intangible and tangible factors such as military theory, generalship including the art of war, and organization of the army) are the two driving forces behind warfare. Advanced technology without managerial adaptability could neither be absorbed nor assimilated by an army.[11] A proper amalgamation of these two disparate elements gives rise to a superior war machine. This phenomenon is one side of the military synthesis.

The litmus test of a proper military synthesis is achieving success in battle. Despite the study of battles being accorded a secondary position in the current military historiography (both Indian and international),[12] battles are not neglected in this study. It is difficult to disagree with Carl von Clausewitz, the Prussian military philosopher of early nineteenth century, who asserts '... so to speak of the strategic budget, while important battles and other operations comparable in scale may be considered its gold and silver'.[13] And battle means the Clausewitzian concept—the destruction of the enemy's armed forces in a pitched encounter.[14] However, unlike earlier historians like Jadunath Sarkar, who analysed each battle separately,[15] here the attempt is to bring out the crucial features of battles fought at various points of time and space against the broader backdrop of technological and organizational changes.

What are the factors that shape the managerial expertise, i.e.

the absorptive and assimilative capacities of the various armies as regards new technologies? Using the approach propounded by 'organizational theory', I would like to posit that the army is a bureaucratic and hierarchical organization engaged in a continuous dialogue with the host society and its culture. For example, the feudal society and its ethos of 'chivalry' prevented the Rajputs from absorbing radical new technologies during their struggle against the Turks. In addition, ecology is a crucial factor in shaping the scope and mode of warfare. A *longue duree* approach along with cross-cultural comparisons is a must for understanding the specificity of South Asian politico-military history and the managerial capacity of the different armies separated spatially and temporally from each other. To give an example, due to the large manpower resources of South Asia, conscription was never necessary as it was in Europe. The absence of conscription discouraged the growth of an authoritarian state bureaucracy among the polities of India. Hence, compared with the European polities, the Indian states remained 'soft states' throughout history. In addition, the presence of a dynamic military labour market probably explains the occasional collapse of the armies of the Indian states against foreign invaders.

I argue that several military revolutions have occurred outside India since the dawn of history. The term military revolution signifies a quantum leap in military lethality due to structural breakthroughs and technological advances within the organization of war machines.[16] None the less, military revolutions by themselves were unable to guarantee military success to the foreigners due to certain conditions within the Indian theatre of warfare. Only those powers that were able to integrate the elements of military revolutions within the traditional Indian system of warfare were able to dominate the subcontinent. And those Indian states, that were able to blend foreign innovations with traditional elements survived. A balanced blend of foreign ways of warfare (steppe warfare till AD 1600 and then the western way of warfare) with the Indian system of warfare constitutes the second aspect of military synthesis. And this is a long-drawn-out process extending over several centuries.[17]

An analysis of the two dimensions of military synthesis is the principal thrust of this study. Though the nature of the book

demands viewing warfare from the top-down, occasional
glimpses of the experiences of the soldiers caught in the midst of
a firefight are included to give the readers a feel of the 'face of
battles'. I begin with the Battle of Hydaspes (326 BC) and end
with the Battle of Kargil (AD 1999) because both these battles
show the limited military effectiveness of the Indian armies due
to an incomplete blending of advanced foreign military techniques with the traditional systems of warfare. Such a perspective
is not only useful from a strictly academic perspective but is also
of interest to policy makers and military buffs.

This volume is divided into seven chapters, and each chapter
constitutes a self-contained analysis of a specific theme. The
length of the chapters depends on the significance of the
technological and managerial changes covered. As we move into
the twenty-first century, the pace of technological and managerial changes has increased considerably.

The first chapter discusses the failure of the Greeks to
dominate the subcontinent. Alexander's victory was ephemeral.
His successor Seleucus was defeated by Chandragupta. This was
due to the successful amalgamation of war chariots with
elephants, *paiks* (infantry), and cavalry by the Mauryas. These
four elements together constituted the *Chaturanga* army, and
this balanced force proved adequate for the military security of
India till AD 800.

This case of the successful military synthesis of the Mauryas
should be contrasted with the failure on the part of the Rajputs
to accommodate a state-of-the-art technology within a flexible
managerial format. The social and cultural ethos of the Rajputs
was partly responsible for this failure on their part. By AD 800, a
military revolution had occurred on the Central Asian steppes
due to the introduction of the stirrup. This technological
innovation raised the lethality of a fast-moving cavalry against
infantry soldiers by giving the troopers a stronger grip over their
horses. As a result, the mounted bowmen from the Oxus–
Jaxartes–Altai region started moving out, and attacked the
agrarian bureaucratic civilizations like the Byzantine Empire in
Europe, the Persian Empire, the Chinese Empire, and the Rajput
kingdoms in Asia. Due to their superior mobility, the steppe
nomads were able to alter the 'speed of battle', and they practiced
'manoeuvre warfare' against the 'positional warfare' conducted

by the infantry armies of the agrarian states. The Mongols, the most dangerous representatives of the mounted horse archers, were unable to annihilate the Indian potentates. This was because the climate and physical geography of the subcontinent presented a constraint to the steppe model of warfare. The Indian climate was too hot for the Central Asian horses and the absence of grasslands prevented these foreign invaders from maintaining a large contingent of operational cavalry. But the Turks were able to conquer India and establish the Delhi Sultanate by properly incorporating elements of the steppe nomadic warfare model with certain indigenous elements within a coherent military system. Chapter 2 analyses this process.

Military synthesis is an ongoing and dynamic process and not a static one. Since technological progress is multidimensional and continuous, the selection and accommodation of certain technological devices and managerial innovations that had succeeded in the past might prove to be a failure in the future. Hence, it was imperative to rejuvenate and re-evaluate the military structure by absorbing fresh elements and innovations with new techniques. This is evident in the failure of the Delhi Sultanate against the Mughals. Chapter 3 argues that the Mughals were not only able to Indianize their Central Asian war machine by partly absorbing the requirements of the South Asian theatre of operation but were also able to update their military machine in accordance with the gunpowder revolution that occurred in Europe from AD 1450 onwards. The Mughals introduced the latest military hardware of the day, i.e. siege artillery. Further, they used the elephants, another age-old Indian military carrier, to pull their siege artillery. Thus, mobile siege artillery provided the Mughals with adequate firepower to demolish the fortresses of the Indian chiefs. Military synthesis also influenced the trajectory of the process of state formation. The Mughals also absorbed the lance-wielding Rajput cavalry as unlike the Central Asia horse archers, the former were suited to India's hot climate. However, this military measure forced the Mughals to give political power to the semi-autonomous Rajput nobles. And this in turn prevented the growth of a centralized gunpowder empire under the Mughals.

The dominance of hand-held firearms and quick-firing field artillery ended the supremacy of the cavalry composite bow combination of the steppe nomads. The Mughal failure to develop a disciplined infantry equipped with hand-held firearms and supported by horse artillery proved to be their Achilles heel. These two weapon systems emerged during the military revolution that occurred in Western Europe between AD 1650-1750. The British imported this combine into India around AD 1740. By itself it was inadequate to destroy all the forces of Indian opposition. The British infantry just could not tolerate India's heat and dust. Moreover, British horses were too heavy for conducting reconnaissance and outpost duties. Chapter 4 surveys the British attempts to develop solutions to these problems. The East India Company started recruiting Indian troopers as sowars. Indian peasants were given Western-style infantry training, and they became sepoys. On the other hand, the modernizing Indian princely states and powers like the Marathas, Mysore, and the Khalsa kingdom failed to balance their traditional Indian military system comprising feudal cavalry and matchlockmen with the imported Western military hardware. So, while the Indian powers represented cases of unbalanced military synthesis, the British in India were able to balance properly the western way of warfare with selected Indian military elements. And this balanced military synthesis won India for the British.

After the collapse of the Khalsa kingdom of the Sikhs, the greatest military challenge for the Raj came from the rebel *Purbiya* soldiers of the Bengal army in 1857. For some months the fate of India hung in the balance. This issue is considered in Chapter 5. The failure of the rebels to synthesize Western military elements (in the form of field artillery, Enfield rifles, etc.) with indigenous military practices (mobile guerrilla war tactics in the tradition of the Marathas) against the Company's loyal troops resulted in their military collapse. The British were once again able to pull off a case of a successful military synthesis by absorbing India's military manpower within the regiments manned by the Western-trained officer corps.

The classic British synthesis of India's military manpower within the Western regimental format commanded by British officers broke down during the Second World War. This war which involved mass armies equipped with industrial-age weapons destroyed the under-equipped cavalry-heavy Sepoy army of the Raj. Nor were the Indian officers allowed any upward mobility by the British. The resentment of the Indian soldiers and officers was expressed in the creation of the *Azad Hind Fauj* by Subhas Chandra Bose. As the British lost the loyalty of the sepoys and the sowars, a process that coincided with the rise of nationalist fervour in India, the process of decolonization gathered pace. The post-independent government tried to catch up with the advanced nations by aiming to equip the Indian army with industrial-age weapons like heavy artillery, tanks, etc. Towards the end of the 1990s, the American military experienced another revolution in military affairs. This involved the advent of information warfare in the form of digitalized battlefields. The shift was from firepower to C4I (Command, Control, Communications, Computer, and Intelligence). As the Battle of Kargil shows, the industrial age Indian army was caught in the process of transition towards the information age force. This is the theme of Chapter 6.

Chapter 7 attempts to answer the million-dollar question: why military coups did not occur in post-1947 India? Civilian supremacy is not merely the product of British Indian political culture, as political scientists seem to believe. In fact, the roots of civilian supremacy may be traced back to classical antiquity. The marginalization of the army within the entire structure of the state machinery was the chief characteristic of ancient Indian political philosophy. After 1947, Indian politicians, unlike their Pakistani counterparts, further strengthened the structure of civilian supremacy by synthesizing ancient India's politico-military culture with certain elements of Western organizational culture. And this resulted in innovative techniques for establishing a bureaucratic stranglehold over the 'men in uniform'.

The Conclusion sums up the prospects for military synthesis in the near future. My historical analysis shows that the mere application of advanced technology is inadequate for securing a battlefield victory. Technology has to be in tune with managerial agility (proper doctrine or theory of warfare and a flexible organizational format) in accordance with the varying demands posed by specific regional conditions. For example, unlike the US army, the Indian army has to give serious thought to counter low-intensity warfare conducted by regional dissenting and secessionist groups armed with precision weapons within its geographical boundaries. Thus, proper military synthesis, and not merely an imitation of the Western models would ensure success. The big question before the Indian military is to decide what traditional weapons and doctrines they need to retain and what sort of state-of-the-art technology they need to procure in order to meet the challenges of the twenty-first century.

Historians who during their research construct a molehill from the mountain-like database of information are obviously going to find fault with my approach and will criticize me for running roughshod over two thousand years of Indian military history. Since this study is a work of synthesis, the principal dependence is on translated printed documents. For Chapter 1 the *Artha-shastra* and the various *Vedas* are crucial texts. As regards the Turko-Mughal period (Chapters 2 and 3), some of my principal sources are the *Babur Nama,* the *Akbar Nama,* the *Humayun Nama, Riyaz-us-Salatin,* etc. There is a wealth of data for Chapters 4, 5, 6, and 7 available in the form of Military Department Proceedings, regimental records, general orders by the commander-in-chief, etc., all available in the National Archives of India, New Delhi, along with the service journal of the Indian army (*Journal of the United Service Institution of India*), and numerous memoirs published by British and Indian military officers. Since Chapters 6 and 7 spill into recent times, I have drawn upon contemporary newspapers and magazines. Major works dealing with Eurasian military history have also been consulted to give a comparative perspective to India's military experience. Although by no means a definitive account, it is hoped that this volume will stimulate further serious academic research on the fourth horseman of the apocalypse. But first let us witness the origin of the fourth horseman of doom.

NOTES

1. *The Bhagavad Gita,* tr. from the Sanskrit and with an Introduction by Juan Mascaro, London: Penguin, 1962, pp. 3-4.
2. *New International Version of The Holy Bible containing The Old Testament and The New Testament,* 1973 rpt, Colorado Springs: International Bible Society, 1984, p. 1219.
3. For this approach to history writing, see the relevant volumes of *Subaltern Studies* published by Oxford University Press, New Delhi from

1982 onwards. The latest volume is published by Permanent Black, New Delhi.

4. For Foucault's 'power' philosophy, see Michel Foucault, *Politics, Philosophy, Culture: Interviews and Other Writings, 1977-1984*, ed. and with an Introduction by Lawrence D. Kritzman, 1988 rpt, New York: Routledge, 1990.

5. For Engel's military writings and the general framework of Marxist military writings of Russian and Chinese scholars, see *Marxism and the Science of War*, ed. and with an Introduction by Bernard Semmel, Oxford: Oxford University Press, 1981.

6. The latest in this genre is Lieutenant General S.L. Menezes, *Fidelity and Honour: The Indian Army from the Seventeenth to the Twenty-First Century*, New Delhi: Viking, 1993.

7. A typical representative of this sort of autobiography is General K. Sundarji, *Of Some Consequence: A Soldier Remembers*, New Delhi: Harper Collins, 2000.

8. Stanislav Andreski, *Military Organization and Society*, 1954, rpt, Berkeley: University of California Press, 1968.

9. An example of this genre of writing is Stephen Rosen, *Societies and Military Power: India and Its Armies*, New Delhi: Oxford University Press, 1996.

10. P.C. Chakravarti was one such historian. See his *The Art of War in Ancient India*, 1941, rpt, Delhi: Low Price Publications, 1989, especially pp. 189-91.

11. Some historians dealing with European warfare accept that advanced technology by itself does not lead to victory. See Martin S. Alexander, 'The Fall of France, 1940', in John Gooch (ed.), *Decisive Campaigns of the Second World War*, London: Frank Cass, 1990, p. 34. Recently an attempt has been made to link technological innovations with the dynamics of warfare in India. Jos J.L. Gommans and Dirk Kolff (eds), *Warfare and Weaponry in South Asia: 1000-1800*, New Delhi: Oxford University Press, 2001.

12. John Gooch, 'Introduction', in idem, *Decisive Campaigns*, pp. 1-4. For an analysis of the historiography of Indian warfare, see Kaushik Roy, 'The Historiography of the Colonial Indian Army', *Studies in History*, vol. 12, no. 2, 1996, pp. 255-73; Roy, 'Mars in Indian History', *Studies in History*, vol. 16, no. 2, 2000, pp. 261-75.

13. Carl von Clausewitz, *On War*, ed. and tr. by Michael Howard and Peter Paret, 1976, rpt, Princeton: Princeton University Press, 1984, p. 244.

14. Clausewitz, *On War*, p. 596.

15. Jadunath Sarkar, *Military History of India*, 1960, rpt, New Delhi: Orient Longman, 1970.

16. For the concept of military revolution, see Geoffrey Parker, *The Military Revolution: Military Innovations and the Rise of the West, 1500-1800*,

Cambridge: Cambridge University Press, 1988. The concept of military revolution is also applied in the case of ancient history. Arthur Ferrill, *The Origins of War: From the Stone Age to Alexander the Great*, 1985, rpt, London: Thames & Hudson, 1986, pp. 149-86.

17. The time span of military synthesis is similar to that of military evolution. For an evaluation of the concept of military evolution, see Jeremy Black, *A Military Revolution?: Military Change and European Society, 1550-1800*, London: Macmillan, 1991.

ONE

The Chaturanga Armies of India: 500 BC-AD 600

Strength is power; happiness is the objective [of using power]. ... Augmenting one's own power is preparing for war. A King with special advantages shall make preparations for war. Active hostilities is waging war. A King superior to his enemy in power shall attack him.

KAUTILYA in *Arthashastra*[1]

A group of chariots wheeling back and forth, manoeuvring against each other and jostling for advantageous positions, threw up a dust storm. The noble warriors riding the chariots, clad in shining armour, tried to kill their opponents by throwing spears and shooting arrows. Around the chariots, the ordinary soldiers collided with each other, confused and terrified, and attempted to kill their opponents with swords. Pushed from behind a soldier fell forward over the trampled bodies of his dead comrades whose flesh had become jelly like. Suddenly a mace landed on his head with a bone-shattering impact. And then there was darkness.

Thus does Dronaparva of the *Mahabharata* convey the feel of war in ancient India. The quotation from Kautilya's *Arthashastra* points to the importance that warfare had achieved by 300 BC in Indian political philosophy. Due to innovations of certain military elements and the absorption of selected foreign military techniques, ancient India had produced a fourfold military organization. Thanks to this long-drawn-out and complex process of military synthesis, the resultant Indian military was able to protect the subcontinent till AD 800. How did it all begin?

THE GENESIS OF THE *CHATURANGA-BALA*:
600 BC-300 BC

By the third millennium BC, the agricultural communities of Asia
produced enough surplus for maintaining armies, which were
primarily composed of foot soldiers (infantry). They specialized
in various aspects of combat and their duty was to check the
nomads who carried out predatory raids. Raiding the rich
agriculturists was necessary due to the operation of the deficit
economy in the Eurasian steppes[2] that stretched from the
Chinese border in the east to southern Russia in the west. Around
2500 BC, a military encounter between the nomadic Aryans
occurred along the banks of the river Ravi. This conflict is known
as the Battle of Ten Kings.[3] Such conflicts were quite frequent.
What was the nature of the armies involved in such conflicts?
How were they equipped? How did they fight?

   By 500 BC, a transition occurred from heroic warfare to
interstate warfare, which continues to dominate the military
landscape in India even today. This transition occurred in Greece
a bit earlier, i.e. around 700 BC, when with the rise of the polis
(city state) collective fighting became common. Leaders of
opposing clans and tribes fighting each other characterized
heroic warfare. Individual duels between the leaders of opposing
camps constituted the chief feature of this sort of warfare. The
best description of single one-to-one combat between heroes in
ancient Eurasia is found in Homer's *Iliad*, especially the climactic
duel under the walls of Troy, between Achilles, representing the
Greeks, and Hector, representing the Trojans.[4] The common
soldiers were not supposed to challenge the aristocratic warlords.
Homer describes this socially sanctioned practice in the following
words: 'Achilles had been signalling to his men by movements
of his head that they were not to shoot at the quarry, for fear that
he might be forestalled and one of them might win renown by
striking Hector with an arrow.'[5]

   Heroic warfare (known as *dvandvayuddha* in Sanskrit literature) among the Indians[6] is best exemplified in the combat between Arjuna and Karna, the chief lieutenant of Duryodhana.
The clan leaders advanced towards the front lines and then show-
ered spears and arrows on the opposing leaders. As the
Bhagavad Gita tells us: 'The flight of arrows was now to begin
and Arjuna, on whose banner was the symbol of an ape, saw

Duryodhana and his warriors drawn up in their lines of battle. He thereupon took up his bow.'[7] There were two kinds of arrows: one was poisoned and the other was tipped with copper.[8] The bows made of bamboo had originated in Africa. However, the light composite bows meant for use from horseback, made of the horn and sinews of animals, first appeared in India along with the Scythian steppe nomads in Alexander's service around 330 BC. Such bows first originated in the region between Siberia and Central Asia.[9] The spears were made of bronze and copper. The origin of the spear could be traced back to the Indus Civilization which flourished on the banks of the river Indus between 2500 BC and 1200 BC. Slingers (stones thrown by soldiers with the help of a sling at enemy soldiers from a distance) also emerged in the Indus Civilization.[10] Slings were the first missile weapons in the history of warfare.

In contrast to heroic warfare, interstate warfare meant large conglomerations of warriors fighting collectively against each other. The new form of warfare demanded that the soldiers should stand shoulder to shoulder with their comrades providing mutual support instead of displaying acts of individual bravery. In Greece this gave rise to hoplite warfare. The soldiers of the opposing armies lined up shoulder to shoulder behind their line of hollow round shields, each one metre in diameter, and then ran at each other trying to force their opponents from the field. Victory was dependent on the cohesion of the line of troops. There was no room for the display of individual daredevil acts. If anyone stepped out of his linear formation, it weakened his side by opening up a gap in the line.[11] Fighting collectively was the legacy of human males hunting together. The teamwork and unity required for hunting big game also constituted the core of interstate warfare.[12]

While the chief requirement for military leaders practicing heroic warfare was individual bravery, the principal skill required from the leaders of interstate warfare was managerial talent. This does not mean that the virtue of personal courage became unnecessary. Managerial skill was necessary since the principal objective of interstate warfare was the permanent annexation of enemy territory instead of raiding for merely animals (especially cows in India) and booty.[13] Till 900 BC, for the Aryans, as is evident from the hymns of the *Rig Veda*, cattle raiding remained the principal objective of war. The hymns depicting combat between the Gods (Aryans) and the Demons (non-Aryans) are as follows:

Panis/Demons: These are the cows which you desire, lovely Sarama, having flown beyond the ends of the sky. Who would release them to you without a fight? And we have sharp weapons.

Sarama/God's Agent: Your words, O Panis, are no armies. Your evil bodies may be proof against arrows, the path that goes to you may be impregnable, but Brhaspati will not spare you in either case.

Panis: Sarama, this treasure room full of cows, horses and riches is set firm in the cliffs of rock. Panis who are good sentinels guard it. You have come in vain on this empty path.[14]

This shift in the objectives of warfare from raiding to annexation occurred because of the shift in the nature of the economic structure. The Aryans were initially pastoral nomads, whose economy was geared to cattle rearing. They gradually evolved to living in settled agricultural communities.[15] Since the annihilation of the enemy forces became the aim of interstate warfare,[16] continuous combat among large groups became necessary, which in turn gave rise to new strategies and tactics and to the raising of bigger armies; all these developments in turn required managerial abilities.

This paradigm shift from heroic warfare to interstate warfare was not merely due to economic changes but also occurred due to certain technological advances, which in turn gave birth to more complex militaries. The agrarian societies of Asia became adept in using iron from 1200 BC onwards. Iron weapons replaced bronze weapons. This was one of the imperatives behind the emergence of collective warfare. Since iron weapons were much cheaper, a greater number of soldiers could be equipped.[17] Till 600 BC, the armies in India were composed of two divisions: the foot soldiers and the charioteers (those who fought from chariots). The integration of the infantry with the chariots first occurred in Egypt around 2000 BC.[18] For close-quarter combat, the Indian infantry used the *chakra* (discus), a revolving weapon made of iron[19] and thrown towards the enemy. The Sikhs in the first half of the nineteenth century revived the use of this weapon against the British. In addition, the infantry also used long swords made of iron, which spread from Europe to Asia around the second millennium BC.[20] After 500 BC, horses and elephants were incorporated into the fighting machine in India, and the term used to describe the fourfold military organization was *Chaturanga-Bala.*[21]

The principal component of the *Chaturanga-Bala* was the horse-drawn chariot (known as *ratha* in India) which first emerged in Mesopotamia around 2500 BC, following the invention of the wheel around 3000 BC.[22] This event could be marked as the first military revolution in world history because the chariot was a definite technological breakthrough as it provided the warriors with a higher and mobile platform from which to attack the enemy foot soldiers from a distance. Around 1500 BC, the chariot had spread in all the agrarian civilizations starting from Egypt in the west, up to India and China in the east. The Egyptian *pharaoh* (emperor) used chariots with decisive effect at the Battle of Megiddo against the Syrians in 1485 BC. These chariots were made of wood planks tied together with straps of leather. Each chariot had only one person who acted both as the driver of the vehicle as well as a warrior. Each wheel of the chariot had six spokes. Attached to each side of the chariot were two quivers containing arrows and javelins.[23] Further specialization in chariot warfare occurred when, around 1200 BC, the chariots in Greece began to carry a warrior as well as a charioteer. Due to the rocky terrain of Greece, the chariots often broke down. So the Greeks started using iron axles for their chariots.[24]

In India, the spoked-wheel horse-drawn chariot was an advance in transportation over the ox-drawn carts.[25] Later the chariots in India were accommodated within the battle order by the military. This was a case of the successful absorption of a foreign technological innovation, initially used in the subcontinent for civilian purposes but later extended to war-making purposes. Near about 500 BC, Magadh (present-day Bihar) invented chariots fitted with long knives around their wheels[26] to scare away the enemy infantry. This was similar to the scythe chariots which Alexander's army had encountered at the Battle of Arbela (or Gaugemela) against the Persians in 331 BC.[27] This technological innovation was one of the primary factors behind the expansion of Magadh, which finally became the seat of the Nanda Empire in the fourth century BC and then the core of the Maurya Empire in the third century BC. With the passage of time, the size of the chariots continued to increase. By 400 BC, the chariot had become bigger, and carried initially one and then two warriors besides the driver of the chariot (*rathin*). India probably borrowed the concept of the bigger chariot from Assyria where it was developed around 900 BC.[28] Unlike the Europeans who fought with spears and swords from the vantage point offered by the elevated platform of the chariot, the Indians and the Egyptians mainly fought with bows. The Indian bowstrings made of cowhide thong were a deadly long-range weapon indeed. While two horses pulled a small chariot, the bigger chariot was yoked to four horses.[29]

The bigger chariot was somewhat similar to the armoured personnel carrier of the twentieth century as the former was covered with armour for protection against enemy spears and arrows and transported the soldiers to the battlefield. Thus, the troops were able to reach the frontlines quickly and instead of being fatigued due to long marches, they arrived at the battlefield relatively fresh. Hence, they fought better.[30]

Besides chariots, the cavalry was the second component of the *Chaturanga-Bala*. The advent of the Aryans resulted in the introduction of horse warfare in India. Some of the hymns of the *Rig Veda* which were composed between 1200 BC-900 BC emphasize the importance of horses. One sacrificial hymn is as follows: 'Keep the horses happy and you will win the stake.' Again, Indra is regarded as the lord of horses, grown and aided in battle by the priests.[31] Between 1500-1000 BC, use of cavalry on the battlefield became common. The troopers (soldiers riding on horses) fought with swords and lances (long spears with iron heads used by the soldiers from the horseback).[32] The troopers armed with lances (known as lancers) continued to be used by both the British Indian and the European armies till the First World War.[33]

By 750 BC, the Assyrians tried to imitate the system of mounted archery followed by the nomads of Central Asia. For shooting arrows from horseback while the horse was moving at high speed, the nomads used the composite bow effective up to 300 yards. Arrows shot from such bows could penetrate armour up to 100 yards.[34] However, the Assyrian mounted archers were not as good as the steppe nomads. The Assyrian mounted archers, unlike the nomads, could not shoot arrows while the horse was moving.[35]

The third component of the *Chaturanga-Bala* was the elephant. Induction of elephants into the army was an Indian innovation of far-reaching consequence. An elephant became ready for battle at the age of 12 years and reached the peak of its physical strength between the age of 20-5 years. The normal life expectancy of an elephant was up to 60 years but this was considerably reduced in captivity and ranged from 20 to 30 years. Further, elephants rarely mated in captivity.[36] For this reason, the Maurya Empire maintained an elephant forest. An official called the chief of elephant forester looked after these forest lands. He was also responsible for the capture and training of the war elephants. A large train of veterinary doctors assisted him. Special border guards were maintained for tracking wild elephants by following their footprints, dung, etc. All the elephants captured by the state officials were marked by the stamp of the *chakravartin* (Hindu emperor). The elephants were so highly valued that any one found killing an elephant was executed.[37]

The fourth, and also the weakest component, of the *Chaturanga-Bala* was the infantry. Kautilya advocated hunting as it kept the soldiers physically fit. Further, attempts to shoot fast-moving animals running for cover raised the target acquisition skill of the bowmen and the javelin men.[38] Hunting as a method for exercise continued even under the Mughals till AD 1700. However, unlike in the West, drilling the infantry with the aid of drums (a legacy of the war dance practiced by hunter-gatherers) so that they marched together in unison during combat never occurred in India. Drilling instilled a feeling of cohesiveness and *esprit de corps* among the infantry. Drill and discipline enabled the Greek infantry to operate as a con-centrated body of massed pikemen capable of pushing and thrusting without stumbling over and against each other in the chaos of the battlefield.[39] Thus, in close-quarter combat, the Greek infantry, due to their better integration and collective effort, fared better than their Indian counterpart. And this proved to be a telling factor during the climactic Battle of Hydaspes.

Around 1500 BC, the Assyrians attempted a sort of military synthesis by accommodating cavalry with war chariots.[40] The Indians organized more complex and integrated battle groups, which included the four components of their *Chaturanga* army. The lowest such battle group known as the *patti* was composed of one elephant, one chariot, three horses, and five foot soldiers.[41] The military theoretician of ancient India realized the importance of battle training for fighting in combined arms formation. Kautilya emphasized: 'Infantry, cavalry, chariots and elephants shall have their training outside the city at sunrise every day. ... The King shall take a personal interest in the training and make frequent inspections.'[42]

The *Chaturanga-Bala* was self-sufficient as regards its weapon systems. The Maurya *chakravartins* were able to pay wages to the armourers for manufacturing weapons for the empire's troops.[43] This was possible because the polity was able to skim off the agricultural surplus from its subjects. The peasants had to pay one-fourth of the produce to the state.[44] The Guptas who were the successors of the Mauryas spent 50 per cent of their revenue on the military department. The *senapati* (general), equivalent of the Greek *strategos*, commanded the *Chaturanga* army, and the *suta* was the commander of the chariot corps.[45]

THE *CHATURANGA-BALA* IN ACTION:
326 BC–301 BC

How did the *Chaturanga-Bala* fare in the 'heat of battle'? The ancient Indian military organization had to face their contemporary superpower—the Greeks—first under Alexander and then under his successor Seleucus.

THE BATTLE OF HYDASPES (JHELUM), MAY 326 BC

The Campaign

The *Chaturanga* army met its acid test when the world-conquering military genius Alexander entered India with an army of 75,000 men. The need to maintain the long communication lines with far-flung bases as well as to garrison the newly conquered territories tied down many Greek troops. So at the decisive Battle of Hydaspes, Alexander was able to concentrate only 6,000 cavalry and 15,000 infantry against the Indian King Porus (Paurava) who commanded 30,000 infantry, 6,000 cavalry, 300 chariots, and 200 elephants.[46]

How did Alexander decide to cross the Hydaspes? Arrian the Greek historian describes this in the following words:

Alexander accordingly sent Coenus, son of Polemocrates, back to the Indus with orders to cut into sections the boats which had been used at the crossing of that river and transport them to the Hydaspes; the order was carried out, the smaller vessels being cut in half, the thirty-oared galleys into three, and these sections carried in carts to the bank of the Hydaspes, where they were reassembled, so that the whole flotilla was once again to be seen, as it had been seen upon the Indus.[47]

But there was a problem. Alexander realized that he could not cross the river because Porus had lined its banks with his mighty elephants. The Greek cavalry could not face these beasts. The horses feared the smell of these animals as well as their thunder-like trumpeting. If the horses were forcibly packed on to the rafts, then they might jump into the river rather than face these ungainly Indian beasts.[48] So Alexander resorted to tactical deception. Arrian continues:

Alexander therefore publicly announced that he would remain where he was throughout that season of that year if his passage was for the present to be obstructed, but he continued as before waiting in ambush to see whether he could anywhere rapidly steal a passage to the other side without being observed. ... Leading out by night the greater part of his cavalry along the river bank in different directions, he ordered them to set up a loud clamour. ... Porus marched meanwhile along the opposite bank, in the direction of the noise. ... When this had been done repeatedly, Porus made no counter-movement.[49]

Then one night when a thunderstorm was brewing, Alexander silently crossed the river upstream with the flotilla gathered by Coenus. Quintus Curtius Rufus tells us about Porus' reaction:

He at first indulged the belief that this was his ally Abisares come to help him in the war as had been agreed upon. But soon after, when the sky had become clearer, and showed the ranks to be those of the enemy, he sent 100 chariots and 4,000 horses to obstruct their advance. ... Its main strength lay in the chariots, each of which was drawn by four horses and carried six men, of whom two were shield bearers, two archers posted on each side of the chariot, and the other two, charioteers, as well as men–at–arms, for when the fighting was at close quarters they dropped the reins and hurled dart after dart against the enemy.[50]

The advance guard sent by Porus under his son was numerically inferior compared to its opponents because Alexander had landed with his principal contingents. When the Indian forward detachment was eliminated, Porus advanced with his main army to meet Alexander. The fate of Punjab hung in the balance.

The Battle

Alexander placed his 5,000 heavy Macedonian cavalry on his right flank and 1,000 Scythian horse archers on his left flank. The centre was occupied by his *phalanx* (heavy infantry).[51] Porus stationed his 85 elephants at intervals of 15 m. each, and behind these beasts he deployed his 20,000 infantry. The infantry occupied a front of 1.3 km. On both sides of the infantry, he deployed 1,000 cavalry. In front of the elephants he deployed the chariots.[52] Diodoros Siculus in his *Bibliotheca Historica* provides an eyewitness account about the 'face of battle' on the bank of the Hydaspes:

The Macedonian cavalry began the action, and destroyed nearly all the chariots of the Indians. Upon this the elephants, applying to good use their prodigious size and strength, killed some of the enemy by trampling them under their feet, and crushing their armour and their bones, while upon others they inflicted a terrible death, for they first lifted them aloft with their trunks, which they had twined round their bodies, and then dashed them down with great violence to the ground.[53]

Alexander's heavy cavalry, which was fully armoured, functioned as shock troops[54] and smashed the Indian cavalry at Porus's left wing. The Scythian archers decimated the Indian cavalry at Porus's right wing. As the Indian cavalry fled from the battlefield, the Indian infantry was attacked from the rear by Alexander's cavalry. The *coup de grace* was delivered by the Greek *phalanx* following the tactic of the 'push of the pike'. The *phalanx's* charge collided with the indisciplined Indian infantry. Standing along one another, the *phalanx* presented an unbroken shield wall. With their long pikes, the Greeks stabbed and pushed at the Indian infantry, resulting in the collapse of the latter. The battle for Punjab was over after two-thirds of Porus's troops were killed.[55]

MILITARY EFFECTIVENESS OF THE *CHATURANGA-BALA*:
A COMPARATIVE ANALYSIS

Let us pose a theoretical question. Would it have been a better option for Porus if he, instead of meeting Alexander on the battlefield, had resorted to positional warfare by shutting himself inside the 300 cities within his realm?[56] The answer is no, because Alexander's army was equipped with sophisticated siege weapons against which the Indians had no antidote. The fortifications of Indian cities were quite inferior by contemporary world standards. Jungles, streams, and earthen walls protected Indian cities. The walls were made of baked bricks which were first used by the people of the Indus Valley Civilization.[57] These obstructions would have been unable to stop the Greek siege engines such as catapults which threw heavy stones up to 300 yards and wooden towers equipped with ladders for scaling walls. The Macedonian army had the engineering capacity to break up these heavy siege engines into very small pieces, and then carry them up on the backs of soldiers and animals on very high mountains, and then reassemble them at the required spot.[58] After all, the Macedonian conqueror had been able to conquer cities like Tyre, which had been protected by more advanced fortifications and a huge naval fleet.[59]

Could Porus then have retreated to the jungle-clad mountains of Punjab and conducted a guerrilla war against the Greeks from mountain forts? Even in this situation it is most probable that Alexander would have fared better because he possessed light infantry known as *peltasts*. Armed with javelins, they were specially trained for mountain warfare. Credit is due to the Athenian General Iphicrates who first invented the *peltasts* at the beginning of the fourth century BC.[60] The tribes which inhabited the region around the Indus tried to conduct guerrilla warfare from the mountain forts against the Greeks but the result proved disastrous for them. Alexander easily conquered the mountain fort of Massaga near the bank of the Indus which was protected by walls made of stone and sun-dried bricks.[61] Again, it was impossible to starve Alexander's soldiers by severing their supply lines. This was due to Alexander's managerial expertise; the Greek army had the most advanced logistical apparatus at its disposal. The Greek army carried 14 days' supplies with them. Again, Alexander did not blunder into a region with his main army. He first constructed a base camp with well-stocked supplies. Then he sent a forward detachment to collect supplies from a region within a radius of about 80 miles. With these supplies another forward base camp was set up, and only then did the main army advance.[62]

In fact, the only option open to Porus was to challenge the Greeks on the battlefield. For Porus, it was the gambler's last throw of the dice. However, an Indian defeat was not altogether inevitable. Except in the case of siege warfare (the art of capturing cities and forts), as regards a land battle, Alexander's Greeks enjoyed no technological advantage over the Indians. The quality of metals produced by the Indians met contemporary international standards.[63] What then went wrong? The secret of the Greek victory lay in the Greek superiority in tactics and training and in the practice of operational deception. Alexander's genius lay in crossing the Hydaspes unobserved, and Porus's greatest mistake was in thinking that only a minor detachment of the Greeks had landed. So Porus sent his son with a small contingent. Had Porus marched with his main army then he could have attacked the Greeks while they were on the point of making landfall. The course of Indian history might then have been different.

Luck was with Alexander because the slippery ground made the Indian chariots useless. The Indian bows were made of wood[64] and were very heavy. The size of the bows was about five feet each. While discharging the three-foot-long arrows that could penetrate any armour, the bowmen had to press the bows with their left feet. The huge size of these bows proved to be a hindrance for Porus because it had rained heavily before the day of the battle. And in the slippery banks of the Hydaspes, the bowmen could not get a grip on the ground and hence the bows could not be used for the accurate discharge of arrows. Further, these bows, due to their massive size, were very heavy, and hence not easily manoeuvrable against Alexander's fast-moving cavalry. If Porus had used the light bows deployed by the Assyrians that had a range of 650 m.,[65] things might have been much more difficult for Alexander.

As regards close-quarter combat, Porus's indisciplined infantry was no match against the disciplined Macedonian *phalanx*. The Indian infantry was armed without any attention paid to uniformity. Besides bows, they were armed with heavy swords whose use required both hands and carried shields made of raw oxhide.[66] Nor was the Indian infantry divided into any tactical subunits. On the other hand, the *phalanx* was divided into *taxeis*, which were further subdivided into *chiliarchies* (units of 1,000 men). They carried a *sarissa*, a huge pike about 6 m. long and with a leaf-shaped blade. Since it weighed about 7 kg., this weapon had to be handled with both hands.[67] The pike originated from the hoplite spear, which was 2.5 m. long. After the end of the Peloponnesian War in the fourth century BC, the size of the hoplite spear continued to increase till it eventually became a pike.[68] In the ancient world, till the emergence of the Roman legions, no infantry had succeeded in breaching the bristling wall of the Macedonian pikemen.

The Indians had never experimented with horse archery before AD 300. Horse archery was also a novelty for the Greek cavalry. Even under Alexander, the Greek cavalry, like the Indian cavalry, fought without stirrups. But the Greek cavalry had an edge in the fields of tactics and training. Hence, Porus's cavalry though armed with javelins, swords, and shields failed to vanquish Alexander's elite Companion Cavalry. The latter had thrusting lances of cornel wood (cornel trees grow in the Mediterranean region and the wood is very tough) and shields with helmets. Alexander's cavalry was trained for attack in close columns and in dense formation. The cavalry attacked in squadrons of 300 troopers each, in a wedge formation.[69]

However, the Indian main battle tanks, the elephants, worried the Macedonian world conqueror. Alexander said before the crossing, 'The only real danger to our horses, as we put them ashore, is the elephants. Nothing else will worry them.'[70] Thanks to these elephants, Alexander could not cross the Hydaspes in front of the Indian army while the Greeks, in 334 BC, were able to cross the river Granicus in Asia Minor (present-day Turkey) with impunity even though the Persian army was deployed along its bank.[71] In the Battle of Hydaspes, due to inadequate collective training, Porus' infantry and cavalry failed to support the elephants. Hence, devoid of integral support from both infantry and cavalry, the elephants could not achieve victory, just as the wars in the 1940s have shown that tanks without organic infantry support could achieve little.

The Indians were no easy target for Alexander. The biggest battle fought by Alexander against Darius, the Persian emperor, was at Arbela (also known as Gaugemela) in 331 BC. About 500 Greeks died in this encounter, while Porus's forces were able to kill about 930 Greeks.[72] And Porus was a small frontier king compared with the Nanda *chakravartin* who ruled over the Ganga Valley with 20,000 cavalry and 2,00,000 indisciplined infantry. Alexander's army could have tackled these two components of the *Chaturanga-Bala*. In addition, the Nandas maintained 3,000 elephants and 2,000 four-horsed chariots. And these were enough to scare away Alexander's battle-hardened soldiers.[73] Plutarch tells us that after the heavy fighting at the Hydaspes, the Greeks had no stomach for combat against the Nanda army which was much bigger than that of Porus.[74] For the above-mentioned reasons, the Indian army must be regarded as more combat effective than Darius' Persian army.

The *Chaturanga-Bala* under Chandragupta Maurya (313 BC-300 BC), the first *chakravartin* of the Maurya Empire that succeeded the Nanda Empire, was able to defeat Alexander's successor Seleucus, who ironically after taking the title of *Nicator* (the Victor), invaded India in 304 BC. The point to be noted is that the Seleucid army was the strongest military force beyond India. In return for ceding Kabul, Kandahar, Herat and Sind, to the Maurya *chakravartin*, Seleucus received about 500 elephants from Chandragupta. Since the Mauryas controlled a vast herd of elephants, they still retained considerable supremacy over the Seleucid Empire as regards the number of war elephants. Remembering the effect that Porus's elephants had had on the Greeks at the Battle of Hydaspes, Seleucus was eager to acquire these beasts for destroying his Greek opponents. In 302 BC, at the Battle of Ipsus, Seleucus deployed 400 elephants against Antigonus. Seleucus' elephants wiped out Antigonus's son Demetrius's cavalry. In response, Ptolemy, another general of Alexander, deployed African elephants in his battles against Seleucus. But these African beasts were no match against Seleucus' Indian elephants. Supplies of elephants from India to the Seleucids continued till the people of Bactria, the connecting kingdom between India and the Seleucid Empire, rebelled against their Seleucid overlords and the Maurya Empire started disintegrating around 200 BC.[75]

In general, the armies of the ancient Western world had no effective antidote against the military deployment of elephants. Hannibal's greatness lies in his military synthesis whereby he incorporated Numidian (Libyan) light cavalry with African elephants,[76] because he could not get hold of Asian elephants. Thus, his army which represented a blend of Eastern and Western military elements was able to defeat the greatest superpower of the ancient world, Rome, again and again.[77]

THE DECLINE OF THE *CHATURANGA-BALA*: 300 BC-AD 600

The seeds of decline had already been sown during the heyday of the *Chaturanga-Bala* under the Mauryas. The Maurya Empire was able to maintain a large army of 6,90,000 men[78] All the polities that ruled India till AD 2000 were able to recruit very easily for their armies. This was because of the enormous manpower resources of India. Recruitment was voluntary and there was no conscription. On the other hand, the European polities starting from the Roman Empire[79] onwards till today have had to resort to conscription. Just to maintain 3,00,000 infantry around 200 BC, the Roman Empire had to conscript 26 per cent of the male populace.[80] Like the present-day Indian army, the Mauryas and the Guptas easily managed to recruit infantry running into several lakhs from the marginal peasantry (share-croppers and landless labourers) who were armed. During poor harvests, the armed peasantry sold their services to the highest bidders. After the end of the fighting, they left the army, returned to their villages, bought land with the loot collected during the campaigns, and became farmers with a military tradition.[81] The Sikh and Jat peasantry who constitute the backbone of the present-day Indian infantry have descended from these sorts of martial agricultural communities.

Due to the presence of such a vast reservoir of armed manpower, the state did not enjoy a monopoly over the armed forces in the subcontinent. One such reservoir of manpower was Kalinga (preset-day Orissa). The mercenaries of Kalinga took part in many wars before the advent of the Mauryas.[82] To remove this thorn, in 261 BC, Ashoka, the grandson of Chandragupta, led a campaign to exterminate the free-floating

mercenaries of Kalinga. Ashoka's genocidal pogrom, which an-
tedated Hitler's 'Final Solution', resulted in the annihilation
of many lakhs of captives and the imprisonment of several thou-
sands of able-bodied men and women.[83]
   But not all the part-time militias of the subcontinent could
be exterminated. Even a modern totalitarian state is incapable
of doing such a thing. Autonomous corporations of soldiers
(*srenis*) existed and were hired during emergencies by the
warlords. The Maurya army also hired these mercenaries with
divided loyalties during emergencies.[84] This meant that the
control of the rulers over the armed military personnel of the
empire was limited. These hired troops were *Kshatriyas*, the
professional soldier caste, as noted by the Greek ambassador
Megasthenes.[85] Conditions worsened under the Gupta Empire in
the sixth century AD, when the state depended on the *samantas*,
hereditary landed chieftains, who were granted villages for
recruiting and maintaining hereditary soldiers.[86] Obviously,
troops raised by the *samantas* were more loyal to the latter than
to the *chakravartins*. The *samanta* system was the precursor of
the *iqta* system of the Delhi Sultanate.
   By AD 450, the *Chaturanga* structure had disintegrated, and
the Indian armies became tripolar: composed of horses, elephants, and infantry.[87] The chariots were no longer used in
battles. Elephants now took the central place previously occupied by the chariots.[88] This change in status became evident when we see that during Harsha's reign in the seventh
century AD, the ruler rode to the battlefield not on chariots but
on elephants.[89] This was because the chariots were defenseless
against manoeuvre warfare conducted by the steppe nomads in
the form of the Parthian horse archers who appeared on the
Indian horizon in large numbers from AD 100 onwards.
   From AD 450 onwards, the fearsome Huns, another branch of
the steppe nomads hailing from the borders of China, appeared
on the Indian military horizon.[90] The military collapse of India
does not necessarily mean the total inefficiency of the
Chaturanga-Bala. No agrarian polity was able to check the advance of the Huns. The Roman Empire also reeled under
the poundings delivered by the Huns. By AD 450, the Huns were
roving unchecked both along the Eastern Roman Empire (Byzantine Empire) and the Western Roman Empire.[91] The Romans

deployed the best heavy infantry of the world: the legionnaires. The legions (each composed of 5,000 legionnaires, the precursor of the Western infantry brigades) had evolved from the Greek *phalanx*. Nevertheless, the slow-plodding legionnaires failed to catch up with the Huns who using their mobility altered the 'speed of battle'. Against the fast-moving cavalry warfare of the Huns, the Romans had no answer. One of the factors behind rapid mobility of the nomads was the fact that the logistics of their armies was simple: their war horses ate grass and the soldiers ate the animals. The Parthians and the Huns, thanks to their skill in horsemanship and archery and better quality horses at their disposal, defeated the Roman legions several times. The Romans, like the Guptas, tried to revive their military fortunes by raising the number of cavalry.[92] However, both qualitatively and quantitatively, the cavalries raised by the agrarian bureaucracies were no match against these agile nomadic warriors.

Due to continuous military interaction with the Huns, the Guptas realized the military value of horse archery. Even the dress of the horse archers—tight trousers that were well suited for riding horses—were adopted by the Gupta soldiers.[93] Thus, trousers were not a Western invention. The steppe nomads of Eurasia—the Scythians, the Sakas, and the Parthians—introduced trousers to the agricultural communities of Eurasia. Due to the military encounters with the Huns, the Guptas also realized the importance of maintaining a light cavalry armed with bows. In the end, the man with the larger number of horse archers would win the day. In desperation the Guptas instituted a new post called the *sadhanika*, an official who was in charge of horses. But the Guptas failed to procure horses in large numbers. As a result, the Gupta Empire disintegrated under the onslaughts of the Hun chiefs, Mihirakula and Tormana.[94]

Despite, the attempts of the Gupta *chakravartins* to introduce mounted archery in India, the enterprise failed just as the Assyrian project to introduce mounted archers had failed.[95] Why was this so? Ecology shaped the culture of warfare. The nomads were expert horsemen due to their familiarity with horses; from infancy they had hunted on horseback with their composite bows. Due to this ecological and cultural gap, the peasant communities in India failed to absorb the techniques of mounted archery. India's hot and humid climate was not suitable for the breeding of good-quality horses. For that, an arid climate was required. Further, India lacked semi-arid pastoral zones required for grazing the horses. The peasants of India, like those of China, used the fertile river valleys (drained by the rivers) for intensive agriculture. Both the Chinese Middle Kingdom and the Indian polities had to depend on horses from Central Asia, which produced the best horses in the world. However, this supply line was tenuous and could be severed during times of political trouble. Hence, the Achilles heel of India and China's military defence systems till the eighteenth century, when the firearms-equipped infantry and quick-firing artillery pushed the horse archers into the margins of the battlefield, was lack of adequate numbers of war horses. So while the Chinese were forced to depend on extensive fortifications for protection against the horse-riding nomads of Central Asia, the Indian rulers relied heavily on elephants. Inadequate numbers of cavalry remained the bane of the Indian military from an early period. Even Chandragupta Maurya, the greatest Indian *chakravartin* of ancient India who had checked Seleucus, could muster 8,000 chariots and 5,00,000 infantry but could deploy only 30,000 cavalry.[96]

The Persian Empire reeled under the blows delivered by the Parthians and the Huns. However, the Huns and their fore-runners the Parthians failed to conquer all of India. This was because their light cavalry could not conduct siege war-fare.[97] Further, the hot climate and the absence of pasturage in north India prevented the steppe nomads from maintaining their cavalry. The Hun rule stabilized around west Punjab[98] (now in Pakistan) because that region was an extension of the Central Asian arid zone into India.[99] They were able to conquer Persia because of its extensive arid zones.

CONCLUSION

Use of elephants in warfare—which influenced strategy and tactics in Italy, Africa, and the Near East till the birth of Christ—was the greatest contribution made by the Indian *Chaturanga-Bala* to the art of war. Besides introducing war elephants into the military equation, ancient India also deserves praise for accommodating and assimilating foreign revolutionary technologies such as bows and chariots within its military system. Technology by itself does not mean anything. Rather, the secret lies in utilizing it properly by coordinating a particular hardware with other components of the armed forces and then perfecting its use by honing the skill of the soldiers through rigorous training. Alexander's victory over Porus brings out this salient feature.

Again, with the passage of time, as a particular piece of technology, i.e. the chariot became outdated, the re-evaluation and reformation of the military structure became necessary. One witnesses the growing weakness of the chariot from 300 BC onwards. Disciplined heavy infantry acting in conjunction with the cavalry of the Greeks could deal effectively with the chariot. The Indian rulers never attempted to develop a heavy disciplined infantry. The nomadic mounted archers from Central Asia who first entered India as mercenaries of Alexander now became a constant threat. They appeared on the fringes of the agrarian civilizations stretching from the Danube to the Indus under various names, the Sakas, the Parthians, and finally the deadly Huns. No amount of cavalry raised by any agrarian bureaucratic civilizations—whether Roman, Persian, Chinese, or Indian— could stave off the disaster. While Persia disintegrated under their assaults, India was saved thanks to her ecology.

By this time, the Indian *Chaturanga-Bala* had become a spent force. The Indian rulers were living on borrowed time. Instead of innovating, experimenting, and accommodating indigenous and new foreign military elements, Indian kings relied mainly on elephants and on an indisciplined infantry. India missed the stirrup revolution which made the steppe nomads more deadly. The fate of India was sealed when the steppe nomads equipped with stirrups, appeared in the guise of Islamic invaders, along the north-west frontier of India around AD 900.

NOTES

1. Kautilya, *The Arthashastra*, tr. and ed. L.N. Rangarajan, 1987, rpt, New Delhi: Penguin, 1992, pp. 559, 563. This work is dated between the fourth and third century BC. There is also a debate whether the

Arthashastra was written by Kautilya or whether it was produced by a group of scholars.

2. John Keegan, *War and Our World*, 1998, rpt, London: Pimlico, 1999, p. xii.

3. H.N. Verma and Amrit Verma, *Decisive Battles of India Through the Ages*, vol. 1, California: GIP Books, 1994, p. 3.

4. Homer, *The Iliad*, tr. E.V. Rieu, 1950, rpt, Harmondsworth, Middlesex: Penguin, 1986, pp. 397-401.

5. Homer, *Iliad*, p. 402; Graham Shipley, 'Introduction: The Limits of War', in idem, and John Rich (eds), *War and Society in the Greek World*, 1993, rpt, London: Routledge, 1995, p. 18.

6. V.R. Ramachandra Dikshitar, *War in Ancient India*, 1944, rpt, Delhi: Motilal Banarasidas, 1987, p. 159.

7. *The Bhagavad Gita*, tr. from the Sanskrit and with an Introduction by Juan Mascaro, London: Penguin, 1962, p. 5.

8. Lieutenant Colonel H.C. Kar, *Military History of India*, Calcutta: Firma KLM Pvt. Ltd., 1980, p. 12.

9. Stuart Piggott, *Prehistoric India to 1000 BC*, Harmondsworth, Middlesex: Penguin, 1950, p. 282.

10. Mortimer Wheeler, *The Cambridge History of India: The Indus Civilization*, Cambridge: Cambridge University Press, 1960, pp. 58, 60-1.

11. John Lazenby, 'Hoplite Warfare', in General John Hackett (ed.), *Warfare in the Ancient World*, London: Sidgwick and Jackson, 1989, p. 54; Hugh Bowden, 'Hoplites and Homer: Warfare, Hero Cult, and the Ideology of the Polis', in Rich and Shipley, *War and Society in the Greek World*, p. 53.

12. Robert L. O'Connell, *Ride of the Second Horseman: The Birth and Death of War*, New York: Oxford University Press, 1995, p. 111.

13. Romila Thapar, *From Lineage to State: Social Formations in the Mid-First Millennium BC in the Ganga Valley*, 1984, rpt, New Delhi: Oxford University Press, 1990, p. 113.

14. *The Rig Veda*, tr. and annotated by Wendy Doniger O'Flaherty, 1981, rpt, New Delhi: Penguin, 1994, p. 157.

15. Romila Thapar, *The Past and Prejudice*, 1975, rpt, New Delhi: National Book Trust, 1994, p. 23.

16. Shipley, 'Introduction', in idem and Rich, *War and Society in the Greek World*, p. 14.

17. Lazenby, 'Hoplite Warfare', in Hackett, *Warfare*, p. 54.

18. P.C. Chakravarti, *The Art of War in Ancient India*, 1941, rpt, Delhi: Low Price Publications, 1989, p. 2; John Keegan, *A History of Warfare*, New York: Vintage, 1993, p. 176.

19. Bimal Kanti Majumdar, *The Military System in Ancient India*, Calcutta: Firma KLM Pvt. Ltd., 1960, p. 38.

20. Trevor Watkins, 'The Beginnings of Warfare', in Hackett, *Warfare*, p. 25; Gordon Childe, *What Happened in History*, 1942, rpt, Harmondsworth, Middlesex: Penguin, 1946, p. 23.

21. Chakravarti, *Art of War in Ancient India*, pp. 1-2.

22. Keegan, *War and Our World*, p. 29; Childe, *History*, pp. 62-3.

23. John Warry, *Warfare in the Classical World*, London: Salamander Books, 1980, p. 14; Watkins, 'Beginnings of Warfare', in Hackett, *Warfare*, p. 31; Doyne Dawson, *The First Armies*, London: Cassell, 2001, p. 123.

24. Warry, *Warfare*, p. 15.

25. Thapar, *Past and Prejudice*, p. 25.

26. Thapar, *Lineage to State*, p. 113.

27. A.B. Bosworth, *Conquest and Empire: The Reign of Alexander the Great*, 1988, rpt, Cambridge: Canto, 1993, pp. 78-9.

28. D.J. Wiseman, 'The Assyrians', in Hackett, *Warfare*, p. 43.

29. Dikshitar, *War in Ancient India*, pp. 157-9; Piggott, *India*, p. 282.

30. Indra, *Ideologies of War and Peace in Ancient India*, Hoshiarpur: Vedic Research Institute, 1957, p. 20.

31. *Rig Veda*, pp. 67, 155. The quotation is from p. 67.

32. Sarva Daman Singh, *Ancient Indian Warfare with Special Reference to the Vedic Period*, 1965, rpt, Delhi: Motilal Banarasidas, 1989, pp. 55, 57.

33. Peter Young, 'The Horse in War', in James Lawford (ed.), *The Cavalry*, 1976, rpt, New York: Crescent Books, 1982, pp. 22-3.

34. Keegan, *History of Warfare*, p. 163.

35. James Lawford, 'Origins', in idem, *Cavalry*, p. 33.

36. B. Bar-Kochva, *The Seleucid Army: Organization and Tactics in the Great Campaigns*, Cambridge: Cambridge University Press, 1978, pp. 78-9.

37. Kautilya, *Arthashastra*, pp. 688-91.

38. D.R. Bhandarkar, *Asoka*, Calcutta: University of Calcutta, 1932, p. 18.

39. O'Connell, *Ride of the Second Horseman*, p. 112; Victor Davis Hanson, 'The Ideology of Hoplite Battle, Ancient and Modern', in idem (ed.), *Hoplites: The Classical Greek Battle Experience*, 1991, rpt, London: Routledge, 1993, pp. 6-7.

40. Singh, *Indian Warfare*, p. 56.

41. Indra, *War and Peace in Ancient India*, p. 21.

42. Kautilya, *Arthashastra*, p. 701.

43. Romila Thapar, *Asoka and the Decline of the Mauryas*, 1963, rpt, New Delhi: Oxford University Press, 1989, p. 72.

44. Romila Thapar, *The Mauryas Revisited*, 1987, rpt, Calcutta: K.P. Bagchi, 1993, p. 37.

45. Nagendra Singh, *The Theory of Force and Organization of Defence in Indian Constitutional History: From Earliest Times to 1947*, Bombay: Asia Publishing House, 1969, pp. 43, 80.

46. Arthur Ferrill, *The Origins of War: From the Stone Age to Alexander the Great*, 1985, rpt, London: Thames & Hudson, 1986, pp. 211, 213.
47. Arrian, *The Campaigns of Alexander*, tr. Aubrey De Selincourt, 1958, rpt, Harmondsworth, Middlesex: Penguin, 1976, p. 267.
48. Theodore Ayrault Dodge, *Alexander*, 1890, rpt, New York: Da Capo, 1996, pp. 545-6.
49. J.W. M'Crindle (ed.), *The Invasion of India by Alexander the Great*, 1896, rpt, New Delhi: Cosmo, 1983, pp. 95-6.
50. M'Crindle, *Alexander*, p. 207.
51. Jadunath Sarkar, *Military History of India*, 1960, rpt, New Delhi: Orient Longman, 1970, p. 19.
52. Albert Divine, 'Alexander the Great', in Hackett, *Warfare*, p. 124.
53. M'Crindle, *Alexander*, p. 275.
54. Nick Secunda, 'Hellenistic Warfare', in Hackett, *Warfare*, p. 130.
55. Hanson, 'Hoplite Battle', and John Lazenby, 'The Killing Zone', in Hanson, *Hoplites*, pp. 4, 92-5; Stephen Peter Rosen, *Societies and Military Power: India and its Armies*, New Delhi: Oxford University Press, 1996, p. 81.
56. Hemchandra Raychaudhuri, *Political History of Ancient India: From the Accession of Parikshit to the Extinction of the Gupta Dynasty*, 1927, rpt, Calcutta: University of Calcutta, 1972, p. 220.
57. Udai Narain Roy, 'Fortifications of Cities in Ancient India', *Indian Historical Quarterly*, vol. 30, no. 3, 1954, pp. 237-44; Mortimer Wheeler, *My Archaeological Mission to India and Pakistan*, London: Thames & Hudson, 1976, p. 82.
58. J.F.C. Fuller, *The Generalship of Alexander the Great*, 1960, rpt, New York: Da Capo, 1989, pp. 246, 253.
59. Devine, 'Alexander', in Hackett, *Warfare*, pp. 116-17, 120.
60. Nick Secunda, 'The Persians', in Hackett, *Warfare*, p. 99.
61. Fuller, *Alexander*, note 3, p. 245.
62. Donald W. Engels, *Alexander the Great and the Logistics of the Macedonian Army*, Berkeley: University of California Press, 1978, pp. 1-10, 107-22.
63. Bridget and Raymond Allchin, *The Birth of Indian Civilization: India and Pakistan before 500 BC*, Harmondsworth, Middlesex: Penguin, 1968, p. 286.
64. Majumdar, *Military System*, p. 38.
65. Sarkar, *Military History*, p. 13; Wiseman, 'Assyrians', in Hackett, *Warfare*, p. 45.
66. Dodge, *Alexander*, pp. 542-3.
67. Bosworth, *Alexander*, pp. 259-60.
68. Secunda, 'Persians', in Hackett, *Warfare*, p. 100.

69. Bosworth, *Alexander*, pp. 262-3; I.G. Spence, *The Cavalry of Classical Greece: A Social and Military History*, 1993, rpt, Oxford: Oxford University Press, 1995, pp. 43-5; Rosen, *India and Its Armies*, p. 79.
70. Arrian, *Campaigns of Alexander*, p. 270.
71. Bosworth, *Alexander*, pp. 41-4.
72. Devine, 'Alexander', in Hackett, *Warfare*, pp. 123, 127.
73. R.K. Mookerji, *Chandragupta Maurya and His Times*, 1943, rpt, Delhi: Motilal Banarasidas, 1960, p. 34.
74. Bhandarkar, *Asoka*, p. 259.
75. Bar-Kochva, *Seleucid Army*, pp. 76-7; Harry Saggs, 'Seleucus I', in John Canning (ed.), *100 Great Lives of Antiquity*, London: Methuen, 1985, pp. 68-9; R.C. Majumdar, H.C. Raychaudhuri and Kalikinkar Datta, *An Advanced History of India*, 1946, rpt, Madras: Macmillan, 1991, pp. 93-4.
76. Lawford, 'Origins', in idem, *Cavalry*, pp. 38-9, 41.
77. Colonel Theodore Ayrault Dodge, *Great Captains: Hannibal*, vol. 1, 1891, rpt, New Delhi: Lancer International, 1992, pp. 23-4, 266-77.
78. Mookerji, *Chandragupta Maurya*, p. 165.
79. Secunda, 'Hellenistic Warfare', in Hackett, *Warfare*, p. 133.
80. John Patterson, 'Military Organization and Social Change in the Later Roman Republic', in John Rich and Graham Shipley (eds), *War and Society in the Roman World*, 1993, rpt, London: Routledge, 1995, pp. 95-6.
81. D. Devahuti, *Harsha: A Political Study*, Oxford: Oxford University Press, 1970, pp. 187-8.
82. S.B. Chaudhuri, *Ethnic Settlements in Ancient India, Part-1, Northern India*, Calcutta: General Printers and Publishers, 1955, pp. 71-2.
83. Verma and Verma, *Decisive Battles*, pp. 43-4.
84. Thapar, *Asoka*, pp. 74-5.
85. Thapar, *Mauryas Revisited*, pp. 33-4.
86. Brajadulal Chattopadhyay, *Aspects of Rural Settlements and Rural Society in Early Medieval North India*, Calcutta: K.P. Bagchi, 1990, p. 49.
87. Kar, *Military History*, p. 15.
88. Singh, *Theory of Force*, p. 63.
89. Devahuti, *Harsha*, p. 186.
90. Raychaudhuri, *Political History*, p. 515.
91. Warren Treadgold, *Byzantium and Its Army: 284-1081*, Stanford: Stanford University Press, 1995, p. 13.
92. Treadgold, *Byzantium*, p. 93; John Rich, 'Introduction', and Brian Campbell, 'War and Diplomacy: Rome and Parthia, 31 BC-AD 235', in Rich and Shipley, *Roman World*, pp. 2, 213-18; Christopher Coker, *Waging War without Warriors? The Changing Culture of Military Conflict*, Boulder, Colorado: Lynne Rienner, 2002, p. 89.

93. B.P. Sinha, 'Art of War in Ancient India (600 BC-AD 300)', in Guy S. Metraux and Francois Crouzet (eds), *Studies in the Cultural History of India*, Agra: Shiva Lal Agarwal, 1965, pp. 142-3.

94. Lieutenant Colonel Gautam Sharma, *Indian Army Through the Ages*, Bombay: Allied, 1979, pp. 3-4; Chattopadhyay, *Rural Settlements*, p. 49.

95. Sinha, 'Art of War', in Metraux and Crouzet, *Cultural History*, pp. 136-7.

96. Sharma, *Indian Army*, p. 19; *The Seven Military Classics of Ancient China*, tr. Ralph D. Sawyer, Boulder: Westview, 1993, pp. 367-8; Arthur Waldron, *The Great Wall of China: From History to Myth*, Cambridge: Cambridge University Press, 1990, pp. 1-51.

97. R. Crosbie-Weston, 'The Huns', in Lawford, *Cavalry*, p. 46.

98. Chaudhuri, *Ethnic Settlements*, pp. 109, 116.

99. R.G. Bhandarkar, *Early History of the Dekkan Down to the Mahomedan Conquest*, 1895, rpt, Calcutta: Chakravarty, Chatterjee & Co. Ltd. 1928, pp. 58-9.

TWO

Cavalry and Chivalry: The Men on Horseback, 700-1520

The river bank was lined with horses, mules, elephants, and various sorts of soldiers clad in shining armour. The Rajput host on horseback was nervously waiting for the deadly nomads of Central Asia (they accepted Islam and came to be known as Turks) who had come in through the north-western passes into India. Suddenly the horizon darkened. On a signal from the leader of the Rajput Confederacy, the soldiers blew conchshells from the backs of elephants. In response, the Turks struck their kettledrums carried on the backs of camels and sounded their trumpets. The Turks on their Central Asian chargers rode down on their adversaries. Chants of '*Din Din*', '*Allah ho Akbar*', and '*Yaa Ali*', along with the neighing of horses and the clank of armour, echoed across the battlefield. Amidst swirling dust columns, the confused soldiers tried to find their antagonists. In the midst of this chaos, the Turkish Sultan launched his reserve composed of iron-clad troopers. They carried everything in front of them, and the Rajput army was scattered like chaff in the wind. How to account for this turn of events?

THE DEMIGODS ON HORSES

The stirrup was invented in Central Asia near the Chinese border, by AD 690. From there, this device (which had a far-reaching influence on the evolution of military tactics and strategy) travelled westward and finally reached western Europe by AD 750 by way of Iran and the Byzantine Empire.[1] The introduction of the stirrup ushered in the age of horse warfare by raising the combat effectiveness of the troopers. However, cavalry tended to evolve in the opposite direction in the East and the West. While the European cavalry evolved as a battering ram for close-quarter combat, the Asian nomadic cavalry refined their tactic of long-distance horse archery.

From the eighth century onwards, the West Europeans experimented with massed charge by heavy cavalry, with knights using long lances while sitting in a couched position for the maximum impact.[2] This couched lance technique known as jousting was able to completely shatter enemy infantry formations. Thanks to saddles and stirrups, the knights could thrust their lances at their opponents with more pressure. And without stirrups, the knights would have been unhorsed if they had tried to gallop at their opponents by holding the long heavy lances with both hands. The stability offered to the riders by the stirrups not only made it difficult for the infantry to unhorse the knights but also enabled the latter and their chargers to put on heavier armour, thus raising the protective capability against the spear-wielding infantry.[3] The mounted men wore mail shirts which covered their whole body till the knees and also carried a kite-shaped shield. Similarly, in the Byzantine Empire there emerged the heavily armoured cavalry men armed with swords and lances who were known as the *cataphracts.*[4]

Heavy armoured cavalry was not an entirely European innovation. The attempt to charge the enemy with the aid of long spears wielded by the troopers, who wore breastplates and whose horses were also covered with armour was practiced by the Sarmatians. They were a nomadic tribe who around AD 300 migrated from southern Russia and attacked the Roman Empire. However, due to the absence of saddles and stirrups, these Sarmatian troopers were unsteady on their mounts and could not deliver strong blows like the medieval knights of western Europe.[5]

Unlike the medieval European knights, who were rulers of settled agrarian communities, the Eurasian steppe people were pastoral nomads. They lived in felt-covered tents which could be packed and carried from one place to another.[6] By nature they were hardy, and had spent most of their time from childhood on horseback. The necessity of moving away from exhausted pasture and the requirement of searching for new pasture resulted in development of excellent horsemanship among the nomads. No amount of training could transform the troopers of sedentary civilizations to that pitch of expertise and mastery. The stirrup, by providing additional stability to the rider, made the nomadic horse archer even more deadly. After the introduction of the stirrup, the nomads, by bending their waists, could shoot arrows in all directions even when their horses were at a gallop. The most deadly was the so-called *qighaz* shot when the rider, half standing on his stirrups with a slight forward lean, loosened off arrows. Though both his hands were off the reins, still by exerting pressure on the saddle and the stirrup, he could keep the horse running at a high speed in a particular direction.[7]

The steppe horse archers due to their inadequate armour never engaged in close-quarter hand-to-hand combat. Instead, utilizing their mobility, they attempted 'hit and run' plus 'swarming' tactics by outflanking, outmanoeuvring, and encircling the enemy. At times they practiced the Parthian shot (this tactic was initially practiced by the Parthian branch of the steppe nomads around AD 100) which meant feigning retreat, and when the enemy cavalry rode after them, the nomads shot at their rear from horseback.[8] If anything, the use of stirrups made the Parthian shots more effective. And all these developments had disastrous consequences for the agrarian societies of Eurasia.

Among the Inner Asian steppe nomads, the most dangerous were the Mongols, and the Turks learnt a lot from them. The Mongols' secret weapons were their mastery over archery and mobility. To sustain mobility, each Mongol trooper would bring to the battle between 5 to 18 steppe horses. Both during the longer campaign and during the battle they changed their mounts several times in order to maintain mobility. This was necessary to meet the requirements of the Mongol strategy, operational art and tactics. The Mongol strategy of covering several hundred miles in a few days and attacking at diverse points far into the rear of the enemy required the possession of many mounts. The possession of so many mounts gave the Mongols speed, range, and mobility. They could choose the place and time of battle, ambush their prey, overcome his strong points,[9] and go to his rear for over-turning his position and severing his lines of communications. Chingiz Khan occasionally detached battle groups, each of which was composed of 30,000 troopers, for conducting strategic raids deep inside the enemy territory. It was a case of 'deep operations', adopted long before the Europeans re-invented this concept in the twentieth century. Simultaneously, the Mongols sent advance parties, which were equivalent to the Soviet forward detachments of the twentieth century, for reconnaissance and to test the enemy strength. Behind the reconnaissance parties, advanced the main Mongol battle groups, equivalent to the follow-on second-echelon force of the twentieth-century Warsaw Pact forces.[10] The Mongol tactic of sending unit after unit galloping towards the enemy and shooting arrows, turning back, and again attacking the enemy tired the horses very quickly. By bringing additional mounts, the Mongols were able to keep up a sustained pressure on their adversaries continuously by circling and shooting at them till the latter collapsed.[11] The Turks imitated these techniques in their wars against the Rajputs in India as well as against the West Europeans in Middle East during the Crusades.

TURKISH STEPPE MOBILITY VERSUS RAJPUT CHIVALRY: A COMPARATIVE ANALYSIS, 900-1200

Between 900 and 1200, the Turks were able to smash the Rajput kingdoms which had arisen on the ashes of Harshavardhan's empire in north India. During the twelfth and the thirteenth centuries, the battles fought in India between the Rajputs and the Turkish invaders were much bigger affairs than the battles that were fought between the Muslim states and the Europeans in the Middle East. The size of the Muslim armies of West Asia at that time varied between 22,000 to 40,000 men. And the force that could be deployed by the Crusaders varied between 1,500 heavy cavalry and 9,000 infantry.[12] The greatest battle that the Turks fought against the Europeans was at Manzikert in 1071, and the Turkish Sultan deployed 40,000 soldiers against the Byzantine Empire.[13] In comparison, Sultan Muhammad Ghori invaded India in 1192 with a cavalry force of 1,20,000.[14] The Rajput force against him was much bigger.[15]

How can one explain the repeated defeats of numerically superior Rajput forces by these foreign invaders? In the spheres of military organization, logistics, tactics, and technology, the Rajputs lagged far behind. The point to be noted is that the Turks enjoyed no absolute technological superiority over the Rajputs. Rather, the Turks used certain technological devices (that were then unknown among the Indians) within a certain tactical format that rendered Rajput technological superiority in other fields useless. By the tenth century, the Turks were using stirrups made of leather, and by the twelfth century they came up with iron stirrups. In response, around the twelfth century, the Rajputs came up with wooden stirrups. The wooden stirrups being circular in shape, the rider could not stand on them to shoot arrows while riding at high speed. But this was made possible by the use of the iron stirrups due to their narrow flat footrest.[16] Further, the horseshoe raised the effectiveness of horses in warfare. The horse's hoof was a constantly growing horny structure like the human nail and was susceptible to breaking or splitting. Hence, regular trimming was necessary. Again, climate affected the horse's hoofs. In semi-arid desert areas like Iran and Central Asia the ground was rough and stony, so the hoof remained tough. But due to the moist climate in some parts of India, the horse's hoofs got damaged and then the horse could merely limp. And limping horses were useless as far as covering great distances and charging the enemy were concerned. Shoeing not only protected the hoofs but also enabled the horse to get a firm grip on the ground. The Turks brought the technique of horseshoeing to India; the Hindus had no knowledge of this. In fact, the practice of horseshoeing was confined among the Muslim artisans.[17]

Worse, the Turks used the crossbow, which not only outranged the Indian bow but was also very handy for using from horseback. Indian bows were made of cane and the bow-strings were made of the bark of the cane. Arrows from such bows did not travel far. The Turkish bow-strings were made of horses' hides, and in addition the Turkish archers used the thumb ring. All these devices raised the range and effectiveness of the Turkish bows.[18]

The Turks' utilization of the iron stirrup, the horseshoe, and the crossbow functioned as force multipliers on the battlefield because the Turks also controlled areas like Afghanistan, Iran, and Central Asia which produced superior breeds of horses. The plateaus and plains of India were not conducive to horse breeding.[19]

From the perspective of battlefield tactics, the Rajput battle plan was inferior compared with that of the Turks, which made the Rajputs' technological edge in certain weaponry useless. On the other hand, the Turks were able to mesh their technological advantages within a coherent battle plan. Indian metallurgy enjoyed a global reputation in the manufacture of swords. Iron ore of exceptionally high grade was mined in Gwalior and in south India. From it, damascened steel was produced. India produced the strongest swords in the world, and both the Arabs as well as the Turks knew about it. The sword blades produced in India were harder than the sword blades produced in Iraq and Central Asia.[20] The fame of Indian swords was such that even the stories of the *Arabian Nights* refer to the fame of the swords from Hind among the soldiers of the Abbasid *Caliphate* that came into existence in the ninth century.[21] So the Turkish cavalry always avoided close combat with the Rajputs, preferring to fight from a distance which permitted them to exploit the advantages of the longer range of the crossbow. The Rajputs concentrated their armoured heavy cavalry equipped with swords and spears into one densely packed body and, like the western European heavy cavalry, made one massed charge towards the Turkish cavalry. However, unlike the western European cavalry, the Rajput cavalry were without iron stirrups, and hence they lacked lateral stability; also, the impact of the shock delivered by the Rajput cavalry was much less than that delivered by the knights of medieval Europe. The Rajput cavalry armed with straight swords for thrusting never got a chance to engage in close combat with their mobile adversaries because of the superior horsemanship, the horseshoe, and the stirrups of the Turks. Thus, the latter were easily able to avoid the Rajput cavalry's frontal charge and returned to attack by circling around the Rajput force. Further, the Rajputs had no conception of a reserve which could be thrown at a critical moment either to retrieve a disaster or to turn the scales in their favour. The Turks always maintained the picked troops as a reserve to be thrown into battle at the decisive moment.[22] Besides the reserve, the Turkish cavalry was divided into three bodies, and while the Turkish centre engaged the Rajputs by making a show of a frontal attack, the other two wings encircled and enveloped the whole Rajput force from the sides and the rear. From the eleventh century onwards, Islamic military theorists like Kai Kaus Ibn Iskander emphasized the tactics of putting the veteran troops on the flanks for attacking the enemy at its sides and rear. The three wings encircled the Rajput cavalry and harassed it with their deadly arrows till the enemy was on the point of collapse. Then the final *coup de grace* was delivered by the Turkish reserve, composed of heavy armoured cavalry armed with lances. The emergence of heavy armoured cavalry armed with lances occurred under the Abbasid *Caliphate*, and the Turks were quick to absorb this element within their military system.[23] All these developments resulted in the repeated victories of the Turks, some of which are described below.

In 978, Subuktagin, the ruler of Ghazni in Afghanistan, attacked the Rajput ruler of Lahore; the battle was fought on the banks of the Kabul river. The Rajput rulers deployed a disorderly mass of 1,00,000 cavalry and infantry armed with swords and spears. Subuktagin divided his cavalry archers into several bodies of 500 troopers each. These independent agile cavalry groups by coordinating their actions surrounded the near-static Rajput mass and continuously pounded them from a distance with arrows. When the panic-stricken Rajput army was on the point of dissolving, Subuktagin delivered the death-blow by charging at the chaotic Rajput mass with his heavy cavalry reserve.[24]

In September 1001, Mahmud of Ghazni invaded India with 15,000 cavalry and was opposed by Jayapala, the ruler of Punjab, at Peshawar. Jayapala deployed 12,000 cavalry, 30,000 infantry, and 300 elephants. On the morning of 28 November 1001, Mahmud attacked by using the above-mentioned tactics, and by noon the battle was over, leaving 15,000 Hindus dead on the battlefield.[25]

Nevertheless, the Rajputs had one trump card: the elephants. And the Turks were afraid of them. The Turkish military chronicler Taj-ud-Din Hasan Nizami had written:

In the open space of the battlefield, the elephants, fitted with litters and covered with armours stood in a row—like a mountain of steel. The huge elephants, each one as big as a patch of cloud, ran across the battlefield like wind and fire, and with their crystal-like tusks caused the molten cornelian of the blood of the warriors to flow on the ground. With this blood their emerald-like trunks were dyed red like ruby and coral. Every now and then the lasso-like trunk would show beneath the armour to demonstrate anger and bitterness.[26]

But, as we have seen in the ancient period, the elephants by themselves could not win battles. When, in 1003, Biji Rao of Bhera attacked Mahmud with elephants on the banks of the Jhelum, the right and left wings of Mahmud's horse archers harassed the elephants and at noon, with heavy cavalry, Mahmud attacked Bhera's demoralized centre and broke it.[27]

Again, the Parthian tactics of attack and retreat were unknown to the Rajputs. During the Second Battle of Tarain in 1192, Muhammad Ghori, the ruler of Ghur in Afghanistan, relied mainly on a cavalry army. He divided his force into four divisions—right and left wings, centre, and a reserve. Each division was composed of 10,000 cavalry archers. These divisions were ordered to advance again and again and to shoot the Rajputs from a distance. But when the Indians advanced to engage them, these divisions feigned retreat. The right and the left wings attacked the two flanks of the Rajput army. When the Rajput centre advanced towards Ghori's centre with their elephants, Ghori's centre made a tactical retreat. During the advance, the indisciplined Rajput host lost all cohesion. Then Ghori's centre turned back and practiced Parthian shots; standing on their stirrups, the Turkish archers loosed arrow after arrow on the Rajputs. Due to such continuous attacks throughout the afternoon, the Rajputs were harassed and tired. And then Ghori with his 12,000 heavy cavalry, which constituted his tactical reserve, charged the Rajput centre and broke it.[28]

The medieval Europeans, unlike the Rajputs, were successful in stopping the Turkish drive both in the eastern Mediterranean as well as in Central Europe. It was possible due to the Western evolution of a chain of command and an anti-horse archery tactical system. In comparison with the West Europeans, the Turks were quicker and more flexible in manoeuvres on horseback. However, the Europeans adopted heavier lances and shields. Hence, the Turks always fought from a distance.[29] In response to the classic Turkish tactic of conducting 'hit and run' operations at a distance with crossbows, the West Europeans developed the tactic of combining disciplined infantry and heavy cavalry into one cooperative venture. The West European army that landed in the Middle East in the eleventh century to recover the Holy Land (Jerusalem) from the Muslims during the First Crusade organized several battle groups, each composed of mutually supporting horse and foot, which were then deployed in the line of attack. To advance without breaking ranks under the shower of Turkish arrows required discipline and strenuous training for achieving a high level of unit cohesion. The infantry spread caltrops (iron balls with protruding spikes) in the ground ahead of them which made a frontal assault by the cavalry useless. In addition, the infantry was armed with pikes to deter the Muslim cavalry from charging. The average ratio of infantry and cavalry in a mixed European battle group was 5:1. This composite tactic was successful during the First Crusade in 1099.[30]

Again, the West Europeans made their cavalry effective by imitating and absorbing the technologically innovative components of horse warfare. By the twelfth century, the West European cavalry was using the horseshoe.[31] Around fourteenth century, the Europeans came up with the collar, the breast strap, and the nailed shoe for the horse.[32] All these developments raised the manoeuvrability and shock effect of the European heavy cavalry. However, the West Europeans enjoyed no absolute advantage over the Turkish horse archers. During the Battle of Manzikert fought in 1071, the Turkish horse archers rode down a Western army. While trying to pursue the Turks who feigned retreat, the Byzantine army became disordered and was then cut to pieces by the Turkish counterattack.[33]

Unlike the Europeans, the Rajputs failed to absorb and assimilate new technological devices and tactical forms due to their cultural ethos and the nature of their military structure. The Rajput warriors who constituted a hereditary caste of soldiers were devoted to the ideal of chivalry, which was an essential element of the *Kshatra Dharma*. The growth of *bardic* literature, a product of chivalry, was fostered by a dialectical process of action and reaction. For the Rajputs, warfare was a form of sport rather than a life-and-death struggle. Since they cherished the concept of chivalry, the Rajputs looked down upon the tactic of surprise attack. Operational deception was regarded as going against the virtues of honesty and decency which defined the warrior's code of conduct. Further, the concepts of tactical retreat and following a beaten foe were regarded as going against the ethos of *Kshatra Dharma*. Due to their strong devotion to the *Kshatra Dharma*, the Rajput troopers emphasized acts of personal valour which went against the concept of teamwork, an essential element of collective manoeuvre on the battlefields. Hence, unlike the Muslim cavalry, each Rajput trooper tried to fight his own personal duel. So the Rajputs failed to coordinate the actions of their various contingents that included cavalry, infantry, and the elephant corps.[34]

Along with their peculiar social ethos, the chaotic nature of the Rajput military system also militated against conducting manoeuvre warfare with advanced tactical concepts and new technology. After AD 600, the Hindu rulers did not maintain any disciplined permanent standing force as the Mauryas had done. The spread of the *samanta* system worsened the situation. The armies became a loose aggregate of raw untrained levies raised by the feudatories. Cultivators, artisans, and carters were recruited on an *ad hoc* basis just before a campaign. Most of the infantry comprised marginal peasants who were attracted to the army by the prospect of booty and plunder. The Indian infantry was an under-equipped and indisciplined rabble armed without any attention to uniformity and standardization. They lacked both combined training with the cavalry and with the elephants, and were further weakened by the absence of any unity of command.[35] So the Rajput infantry fell an easy prey to the long-distance horse archery of the Turks. The Rajputs also lacked a chain of command to control the levies assembled for a campaign. In 1009, when Mahmud of Ghazni attacked the Rajput Confederacy under Anandpal, the battle was initially going against the Turks. About 30,000 Jat infantry in the Rajput army attacked Mahmud's cavalry and killed about 4,000 of them. Then suddenly Anandpal's elephant took fright and ran away from the battlefield. Since there was no designated deputy to take over the command, the victorious Rajput host dissolved just as the Muslim army was on the point of collapsing.[36]

Unlike the Rajputs, the Turks imparted a thorough training to their military manpower. The core of the Turkish forces consisted of *ghulams*. The *ghulams* were males bought at tender ages from the slave markets of Central Asia and then trained for warfare. Due to continuous exercises and training, they became military veterans. They were converted to Islam and when they reached adulthood, they were freed and functioned as elite warriors. Since they were rootless and lacked local connections, they remained very loyal to the sultans.[37]

Finally, superior logistical apparatus increased the size of Turkish cavalry's operational field, and this in turn enabled them to conduct sustained strategic manoeuvres deep inside the enemy territory. The Turkish armies included the *bazar-i-lashkar* who had the responsibility of supplying the troops.[38] Hence, Mahmud could march from Multan to Somnath, a distance of a thousand miles as the crow flies over the desert in Rajasthan, fight a battle near the city of Somnath, and then march back to Multan.[39]

ECOLOGY AND THE NECESSITY OF MILITARY SYNTHESIS: 1210-1520

Why were the Turks and not the Mongols, who were militarily the most powerful in Eurasia during the thirteenth and the fourteenth centuries, able to establish a stable polity in India that lasted till the 1520s? The Mongols had destroyed bigger and more powerful empires compared to which the Turkish Delhi Sultanate was an infant. But the Mongol steamroller came to an abrupt halt along the banks of the river Indus. The Mongols decided not to cross the Indus in 1221 because the heat of the subcontinent was too much for the men from the chilly steppes of Central Asia.[40]

The Sultanate's greatest achievement was to blend the nomadic way of warfare with the components of the Indian way of warfare and also to tap certain foreign elements. The result was a hybrid super war machine. One important factor which explains the failure of the Arabs—who possessed siege engines, stirrups, and naphtha fireballs—to conquer India during the eighth century[41] was that, unlike the Turks, they failed to utilize Afghan military manpower. From the eleventh century onwards, the Turkish rulers encouraged the large-scale migration of the Afghans from deep in Afghanistan to the banks of the Indus, and they were assured jobs in the army.[42] This was probably the first historical example of long-distance migration for *naukri* (military jobs). There was a special recruitment department for inducting the Afghan tribes, and the latter's kinship and loyalty to their own chiefs were utilized to build up a tribal *esprit de corps*. Each tribe had a particular standard (a cloth attached to a lance and carried by the bravest man) for generating a corporate-cum-tribal identity, and this in turn preserved cohesion on the killing ground. In the Islamic military landscape, the Arab *Caliphate* first introduced the technique of incorporating tribes and families into units of 1,000 men and 100 men respectively. These were the Western equivalent of regiment and company. Later the Turks imitated this technique of organizing military manpower. From the fifteenth century onwards, due to the after-effects of political convulsions in Central Asia resulting from the Mongol conquests, the influx of Turks into India declined. Then the Afghans became a majority within the military of the Delhi Sultanate. In addition to the Afghan infantry, the sultans also recruited Hindu *paiks* (infantry).[43]

Why was infantry necessary? India was a land of fortified cities and villages, which could not be stormed by a cavalry army. For laying siege to Indian cities, infantry was necessary. The Hindu art of fortification did not advance much after the Mauryan age. Most of the fortifications were made of stones. In Kashmir, instead of stone, the forts were made of wood which was highly inflammable. And in Bengal, Sind, and Punjab, the walls of the forts were made of bricks. Along with the availability of infantry, thanks to the technological advantages enjoyed by the Turks as regards siege warfare engines, the Rajput fortified towns fell to the invading Muslim armies like ripe plums.[44] The Turks learnt the use of siege engines from the Mongols and the Arabs. When the Arab general, Muhammad Bin Qasim, invaded Sind in the eighth century, the Arab army used catapults each of which was worked by 500 men for throwing stones. In addition, the Arabs also used battering rams for destroying the walls of the forts.[45]

We have a vivid description of the use of mangonels (mechanical stone-throwing devices) by the Mongols against the heavily fortified city of Samarkand in Central Asia by Ata-Malik Juvaini, a historian in the service of the Mongols. He informs us:

First the discharge of mangonels and bows, arrows and stones were set in flight; and the Mongol army took up a position at the very gates and so prevented the Sultan's troops from issuing forth on to the field of battle. And when the path of combat was closed to them, and the two parties had become entangled on the chess–board of war and the valiant knights were no longer able to manoeuvre their horses upon the plain.... At length, when the Emperor of Khotan had let down the veil over his face, they closed the gates.[46]

Alauddin Khalji (1296-1316), one of the foremost sultans of the

Delhi Sultanate founded by the Turks, used mangonels which easily destroyed the walls and towers of the Rajput cities.[47]

And in the sphere of set-piece battles, the Rajputs had no chance against the Turks. The synthesis of Turkish horse archers with Indian elephants under the Sultanate proved to be a lethal combination. Like the Mauryas, the Sultanate's rulers paid great attention to maintaining the elephant herds which they termed *pilkhana*. The Sultans used to lead occasional expeditions to capture live elephants from the forests of Assam, Bengal, and Orissa. Later these elephants were trained for warfare. As long as the supply of elephants from eastern India and of horses from Central Asia continued, the Sultanate armies were unstoppable.[48]

The Sultanate army under Alauddin Khalji was able to conquer the eastern part of south India. Marco Polo, the world-famous globetrotter (1254-1329), gives an explanation for the Sultanate's victory. He writes about south India in the following words:

No horses being bred in this country, the king ... expends large sums of money annually in the purchase of them from merchants of Ormus, Diufar, Pecher, and Aden, who carry them thither for sale, and become rich by the traffic, as they import to the number of five thousand, and for each of them obtain five hundred saggi of gold. ... At the end of the year, in consequence as it is supposed, of their not having persons properly qualified to take care of them or to administer the requisite medicines, perhaps not three hundred of these remain alive ... the climate of the province is unfavourable to the race of horses, and that from hence arises the difficulty of breeding or preserving them.[49]

Thus, the inferior cavalry and the indisciplined infantry armed with lances and shields of the south Indian kingdoms sealed the fate of this region.[50]

In addition to Indian manpower, elephants, and Central Asian mounts, the Sultanate also absorbed Central Asian nomadic manpower for their exceptional horsemanship through the *mamluk* system, an institution which was imported from Egypt and applied to the Indian scenario. The *mamluk* system was a modification of the *ghulam* system. During military campaigns, young Hindu males were captured and were then converted to Islam. They got the best possible training and education and became warriors. They were heavy horsemen who wore mail shirts reinforced with lamellae of iron, and who functioned as shock troops. The core of the Sultanate army remained these *mamluks*.[51]

The *mamluks'* training on horseback was known as the *furusiya* exercises, which started in Egypt and which were then imported into India by the Sultanate. This professional military training gave the armies of the Delhi Sultanate an edge over their Hindu opponents. The *mamluks* were trained to shoot both upwards and downwards while riding. The upward shots were handy in killing the mahouts controlling the elephants and the downward shots were necessary for killing the enemy infantry. The training exercise for upward shots consisted of shooting from horseback at a pot tied to the top of a mast. This practice reached India from Egypt but it had originated in Central Asia, where the nomads had to practice such shots for hunting birds. The nomads practiced downward shots for hunting rabbits and other fast-footed animals. Excellence in marksmanship was achieved only through continuous practice.[52] The *mamluks* were coached in teamwork: how to fight in a group, how to join battle, how to disengage, etc. They were trained to attack, to encircle, and to flee.[53]

Sultan Balban (1266-87) emphasized the collective training of both cavalry and infantry. During winter, in the early hours of the morning, a thousand horse archers practiced together. The *paiks* underwent training in archery, fencing, and lance throwing. The game of polo and the sport of hunting were considered part of military training. The latter was a traditional Indian practice started by the Mauryas which the Sultanate rulers accommodated within the structure of their war machine. Hunting was a large-scale military exercise in which the ruler also participated along with the horse archers and the *paiks*. A hunting expedition was organized on the same lines as a military expedition. The soldiers went fully armed and marched in battle formations. The Mongols also conducted annual hunting expeditions, and the Sultanate absorbed some elements of the Mongol military hunting-cum-training exercises. Long distances were covered to keep the horses in form. The game was enclosed within a vast but steadily contracting circle. On reaching the hunting ground, the horse archers practiced their skill by targeting fast-footed animals and birds. The Sultanate reserved the region near Katehar, in present-day northern Uttar Pradesh, for annual hunting exercises.[54]

Among the Sultanate rulers, Alauddin Khalji maintained the largest number of soldiers. He had on his payroll about 4,75,000 cavalry. Following the Mongol tradition, the army was organized on the decimal system. The Delhi Sultanate by borrowing the military organization which had emerged on the Central Asian steppes was able to introduce a superior command system compared to the Hindu forces. The *mansabdari* system of the Mughals was also influenced by this system of organization. The lowest unit was 10 horsemen commanded by a *sar-i-khail*. Ten *sar-i-khails* were commanded by a *sipah-salar*. Above the ten *sipah-salars* was an *amir*, and above ten *amirs* was a *malik*, or khan. The biggest unit was about 10,000 horsemen, adapted from the Mongols' *tumen*, and the equivalent of a Western division was under a khan who commanded ten *amirs*. Each *tumen* was able to operate independently and was also able to coordinate its actions with the other *tumens*. Cavalry groups of about 10,000 men were able to operate independently deep inside the enemy kingdoms for carrying out surprise raids. Each *tumen* was subdivided into units of 1,000 men and these were the equivalent of the European regiment. Each such unit of 1,000 troopers commanded by an *amir* was able to operate separately but following a joint strategic aim of annihilating the enemy. The various components of the Mongol army like heavy cavalry, light cavalry, etc., under different commanders evolved a common battle plan for the smooth prosecution of a campaign to vanquish the enemy. The Mongols, long before the Americans and the imitative Indians who tinkered with this concept in the late twentieth century, had evolved the concept of 'jointness' in military operations. This enabled the Mongol force to spread widely over a region for surrounding the enemy force and then concentrating quickly at a particular point for delivering the death-blow to the enemy.[55] Hence, all the junior commanders under the *amirs* enjoyed much responsibility and independent initiative for making crucial decisions quickly in the midst of the chaotic nature of unpredictable battles.[56] This decentralized command system was the precursor of the German concept of *Auftragstaktik* (allowing freedom to the junior officers for making rapid decisions in the midst of a quickly changing battle scenario) which emerged only in the nineteenth century.

Alauddin's greatest innovation was that he maintained a

permanent army. Maintenance of a permanent army required a military bureaucracy. The formation of a military bureaucracy manned by literate people for administering and training a permanent army first evolved in the Muslim world of Eurasia under the Arab *Caliphate* in around the eighth century.[57] The Delhi Sultanate imitated this system. The military bureaucracy of the Sultanate's army known as the *diwan-i-arz* was manned by the *arz* and the deputy *arz*. Periodic reviews of the army both at the headquarters and in the camps were carried out by this department. In addition, the *diwan-i-arz* was in charge of supervising the level of skill attained by the soldiers. Further, he maintained registers which included information pertaining to the soldiers' physique, social background, as well as the type and quality of horses maintained by them. The practice of branding horses to prevent fraud by the troopers was also instituted. This was known as the *dagh wa chihra* (cauterization and descriptive roll) system,[58] and this was later continued by the Mughals.

Alauddin paid the army in cash regularly from the central treasury.[59] The idea of paying salary in cash from a central treasury was first propounded by Abu Hassan Ali, a scholar on the payrolls of the Seljuk Turks of Iran during the eleventh century.[60] In addition, Alauddin froze the prices of essential commodities so that the soldiers could buy food cheaply. In addition to their pay, the soldiers also received free rations and clothing during campaigns.[61] Hence, the troopers remained loyal and were motivated to fight for the Sultan. Alauddin was ahead of his times because at that time, even in Europe, soldiers were not paid in cash and nor were they given free clothing. Medieval Europe paid its soldiers through requisitions from civilians and by raiding the civilian population of the enemy areas.[62] The East India Company from the late eighteenth century onwards like Alauddin, followed the policy of regular payment in cash to the soldiers.

Unfortunately, Alauddin's successors depended on the *iqta* system. The *iqta* system, which emerged in West Asia around the eleventh century, was somewhat similar to the *samanta* system. Under this system land revenue was assigned by the ruler to an individual. The beneficiary collected the revenues and in return served in the army himself with a contingent. The size of the contingent depended upon the value of the *iqta* granted to him.[63] Further, the later sultans became dependent on the hereditary Afghan soldiers who were given land in present-day Uttar Pradesh.[64] With the passage of time, they became more interested in cultivating the land rather than in fighting. Further, *iqta* grants encouraged local attachments and gave rise to regional rebellions.[65]

Again, the Turkish rulers, like their predecessors the Guptas and the Mauryas, failed to control the vast free-floating mercenaries available in the dynamic military labour market of Hindustan. They remained a source of trouble for the Delhi Sultanate as these mercenaries sold their services to the highest bidder. All these factors led to numerous rebellions by the vassal Hindu kings and the Muslim *iqtadars*. Very often the *iqtadars* challenged the sultans by hiring mercenaries with the income generated by their lucrative *iqtas*. One example of how easily troops could be hired is evident from the fact that Sultan Balban was able to raise 2,00,000 men from Awadh (present-day central Uttar Pradesh) for conquering Bengal.[66] Under Sultan Firuz Tughluq (1351-88), it became customary for the Sultanate to hire troopers who came with their own horses and equipment.[67] Needless to say, their loyalty was suspect and they were willing to back any *amirs* who would pay them a higher sum of money.

As a result, the Sultanate's military strength started declining and this decline accelerated under the hammer blows delivered by the Central Asian nomadic warlord Amir Timur. As regards the Battle of Delhi in 1398, Timur's autobiography is our best source. His chief concern was the elephants of India, as he tells us:

I ordered the emirs of the right wing and the left wing, of the van and the centre, to take up their proper positions. ... It had been constantly dinned into the ears of my soldiers that the chief reliance of the armies of Hindustan was on their mighty elephants; that these animals, in complete armour, marched into battle in front of their forces, and that arrows and swords were of no use against them; that in height and bulk they were like small mountains, and their strength was such that at a given signal ... they could take up the horse and the rider with their trunks and hurl them into the air.[68]

Timur, who controlled the Central Asian and southern Russian steppes, enjoyed both qualitative and quantitative superiority as regards the horse archers. So he was able to defeat the Sultanate's dwindling and disloyal cavalry force. The Sultanate's elephants by themselves could not stave off the disaster.[69] However, with a purely horse archer-based army, Timur could not rule India. So he had to leave India while the Sultanate was bleeding white.

MISSING HELLFIRE

What options were then open to the Sultanate? Since Delhi had lost control over the supply of horses from Central Asia from the fourteenth century onwards due to the Mongol invasions and later Timur's conquest of Central Asia, the only way out for the Indian rulers was to integrate the firepower revolution within the gamut of their armed forces. The first mention of gunpowder appears in a Chinese treatise dated 1044. The formula for gunpowder was transmitted to the West by about 1267 through the Arabs and the Byzantine Empire. Around 1250, Roger Bacon described the manufacture of firecrackers.[70] By 1326, the Italians were using naphtha or liquid fire, and the next stage was the invention of firearms. The Europeans probably learnt the use of naphtha from the Arabs as well as the Mongols who used it during their campaigns in Central Asia. Each Arab corps of 10,000 men had a special unit of naphtha firemen attached to it for throwing fireballs at the enemy. By 1350, the Italians were using cannons on the battlefield. Towards the end of the fifteenth century, iron shots replaced stone shots and this in turn made the West European cannons more effective.[71] By 1410, both the Ottomans and their European opponents were using bronze cannons, which were made of 90 per cent copper, and 10 per cent tin. By 1462, standardization of the gun calibre occurred among the West Europeans. This facilitated the mass production of cannons and made their handling in the battlefield easier.[72] The point to be noted is that even in the seventeenth century, the Mughals in India failed to standardize their guns. As a result, the Indian rulers produced various sizes of guns which required different sorts of munitions. Supplying such different sorts of munitions was impossible in the battlefield. Europe had many foundries situated near iron and copper mines. The presence of skilled craftsmen and miners further aided the production of cannons on a large scale.[73]

Firearms and gunpowder were not entirely unknown in India. Sanskrit literature speaks of the *agni-bana*. This was an arrow which had a coating of lead and tin and was tied with fibre. The shafts of such arrows, made of metal, were called *naraca*. The composition of the inflammable material was ignited before the arrow was launched.[74] The *Sukra-Nitisara*, which may be dated to the eleventh century, gives a description of guns and cannons. The composition of the *agni-curna* (gunpowder) was laid down as 6 parts of saltpetre, 1 part sulphur, and 1 part charcoal which was burnt in a pit to exclude air. Then the mixture was dried in the sun.[75] In the 1360s, the two polities of south India, the Vijaynagar Empire and the Bahmani Kingdom, used firearms. They probably learnt this from the Ottomans.[76] In 1368, the Vijaynagar Empire deployed 300 guns against the Bahmani Sultanate.[77] At the beginning of the fifteenth century, Bengal emerged as the exporter of *ban*s (pyrotechnic and combustible materials) to the south Indian kingdoms. By the 1520s, siege artillery was playing an important role in the siege of forts in south India. During the second half of the fifteenth century, the kingdom of Gujarat also used cannons. This was possible probably due to Gujarat's connection with both the Ottomans and the Portuguese.[78] The failure to procure good horses from Central Asia as well as the dominance of the elephant-breeding areas by the Delhi Sultanate forced these regions to experiment with gunpowder weapons. This probably explains the failure of the Delhi Sultanate to annex these areas in the fourteenth century.

In the fifteenth century, the only option open to the Sultanate to check the cavalry superiority of the steppe nomads and the firepower superiority of the south Indian kingdoms was to induct an Ottoman-style infantry armed with hand-held firearms supported by cannons. During the thirteenth century, cannons were introduced in northern India by the Mongols who learned about them from the Chinese.[79] But the Sultanate failed to accommodate this element within their war machine due to the Turks' inability to produce gunpowder. Importing gunpowder from China was impossible since the Mongols had cut off the overland trade route to China. The use of gunpowder and hand-held firearms spread from China to Europe by the Mongols in the thirteenth century. From 1500 onwards, the Ottomans introduced a permanent infantry force armed with *tufengs* (hand-held firearms) known as *janissaries*. Due to their discipline, the *janissaries* were able to advance even under a shower of arrows. However, the infantry by itself was inadequate against the cavalry. After all, the Turkish archers could discharge arrows more quickly than the handguns could be fired.[80] Only in the eighteenth century did the infantry become the queen of the battlefield. The synthesis of the *sipahis* (feudal cavalry), raised by landholders from the revenues of the *timars*[81] (land grants, somewhat similar to the *iqtas*), with the Turkish horse archers and the *janissaries* was adequate to make the *Porte* (Ottoman ruler) the principal power in Eurasia. The *tufengs* spread from the Ottomans Empire to Persia and from there to the Uzbeks in Uzbekistan.[82]

It is ironic that the making of gunpowder, firearms, and cannons did not become a large-scale industry in India as in sixteenth-century Europe, despite the fact that India possessed all the essential ingredients for their manufacture. The point to be noted is that the thriving gun-making industry of Europe imported saltpetre from India for making guns.[83] All these failures on the part of the Delhi Sultanate had disastrous consequences since Babur, the Mughal warlord, used these techniques during the First Battle of Panipat.

CONCLUSION

Technological advances from 700 onwards resulted in the rise of the deathly horsemen. The Mongols were the best example of the war machine produced by the cavalry revolution. But raw cavalry strength was inadequate for dominating India. The failure of the Arabs and the Mongols to conquer India proves this point. The peculiarities of the subcontinent's physical geography demanded that the cavalry war machine needed to absorb diverse foreign and indigenous elements to establish a stable politico-military edifice. The Turks by combining the best elements of the cavalry revolution and by assimilating certain features of the Arabian and Indian military systems were able to achieve this.

However, with the passage of time, as the political calculus changed along with technological advances, the synthesis in the military machine had to be re-evaluated. And this the Sultanate failed to do, thus paving the way for its own doom. The supply of war horses from Central Asia was severed towards the end of the fourteenth century, and the Sultanate bureaucracy was in decline with the rise of hereditary office holders. Europe and the Middle East experienced a firepower revolution. Synthesizing the gunpowder revolution along with a disciplined infantry might have allowed the Sultanate to survive. But this was not to be the case. Babur assimilated the firepower revolution with horse archery. The result was Mughal victory at the First Battle of Panipat in 1526.

NOTES

1. Lynn White Jr., 'The Crusades and the Technological Thrust of the West', in V.J. Parry and M.E. Yapp (eds), *War, Technology and Society in the Middle East*, London: Oxford University Press, 1975, pp. 98-9.

2. John France, *Victory in the East: A Military History of the First Crusade*, Cambridge: Cambridge University Press, 1994, p. 372.

3. Philippe Contamine, *War in the Middle Ages*, tr. Michael Jones, 1980, rpt, Oxford: Blackwell, 1996, p. 181; Nicholas Hooper and Matthew Bennett, *The Cambridge Illustrated Atlas of Warfare: The Middle Ages, 768-1487*, Cambridge: Cambridge University Press, 1996, p. 154; Richard A. Preston and Sydney F. Wise, *Men in Arms: A History of Warfare and Its Interrelationships with Western Societies*, 1956, rpt, New York: Holt, Rinehart & Winston, 1979, p. 67.

4. Colonel Trevor N. Dupuy, *The Evolution of Weapons and Warfare*, 1984, rpt, New York: Da Capo, 1990, pp. 41, 43.

5. White Jr., 'The Crusades', p. 98; Ammianus Marcellinus, *The Later Roman Empire: A.D. 354-378*, Selected and tr. by Walter Hamilton with an Introduction and Notes by Andrew Wallace-Hadrill, 1986, rpt, London: Penguin, 1988, p. 132.

6. J.J. Saunders, *The History of the Mongol Conquests*, London: Routledge & Kegan Paul, 1971, pp. 11-12.

7. J.D. Latham, 'Note on Mamluk Horse-Archers', *Bulletin of the School of Oriental and African Studies*, vol. 32, 1969, pp. 262-5; Owen Lattimore, *Inner Asian Frontiers of China*, 1940, rpt, Oxford: Oxford University Press, 1988, p. 64.

8. Reuven Amitai-Preiss, *Mongols and Mamluks: The Mamluk-Ilkhanid War, 1260-1281*, Cambridge: Cambridge University Press, 1995, p. 215; Martin Van Creveld, *Technology and War: From 2000 BC to the Present*, London: Brassey's, 1991, p. 18.

9. Rudi Paul Linder, 'Nomadism, Horses and Huns', *Past and Present*, no. 92, August 1981, pp. 4, 8, 15.

10. Ata-Malik Juvaini, *Genghis Khan: The History of the World Conqueror*, tr. and ed. J.A. Boyle with an Introduction by David O. Morgan, 1958, rpt, Manchester: Manchester University Press, 1997, pp. 103, 118. For the twentieth-century Western concept of deep operation and the Soviet concept of forward detachments, see Shimon Naveh, *In Pursuit of Military Excellence: The Evolution of Operational Theory*, 1997, rpt, London: Frank Cass, 2000 and David M. Glantz, *The Soviet Conduct of Tactical Manoeuvre: Spearhead of the Offensive*, London: Frank Cass, 1991.

11. Amitai-Preiss, *Mongols and Mamluks*, p. 215.

12. Christopher Marshall, *Warfare in the Latin East: 1192-1294*, Cambridge: Cambridge University Press, 1992, pp. 147, 151, note 12.

13. J.F.C. Fuller, *A Military History of the Western World: From the Earliest Times to the Battle of Lepanto*, vol. 1, 1954, rpt, New York: Da Capo, 1987, footnote 3, p. 400.

14. Jadunath Sarkar, *Military History of India*, 1960, rpt, Delhi: Orient Longman, 1970, p. 34.

15. Lieutenant Colonel Gautam Sharma, *Indian Army through the Ages*, 1966, rpt, New Delhi: Allied, 1979, p. 57.

16. Irfan Habib, 'Changes in Technology in Medieval India', *Studies in History*, vol. 2, no. 1, 1980, pp. 17, 26.

17. A. Jan Qaisar, 'Horseshoeing in Mughal India', *Indian Journal of History of Science*, vol. 27, no. 2, 1992, pp. 134-5.

18. V.J. Parry and M.E. Yapp, 'Introduction', in Parry and Yapp, *War, Technology and Society*, p. 7; Simon Digby, 'The Problem of Military Ascendancy of the Delhi Sultanate', in Jos J.L. Gommans and Dirk H.A. Kolff (eds), *Warfare and Weaponry in South Asia: 1000-1800*, New Delhi: Oxford University Press, 2001, pp. 316-17.

19. Irfan Habib, 'Technology in Medieval India', p. 25; Gommans and Kolff, 'Introduction', in Gommans and Kolff, *Warfare and Weaponry*, p. 31.

20. Digby, 'Military Ascendancy', in Gommans and Kolff *Warfare and Weaponry*, p. 318; Irfan Habib, 'Non-Agricultural Production and Urban Economy', in Dharma Kumar and Tapan Raychaudhuri (eds), *The Cambridge Economic History of India: c. 1200-c. 1750*, vol. 1, 1982, rpt, New Delhi: Orient Longman in association with Cambridge University Press, 1991, pp. 77, 81.

21. *The Book of the Thousand Nights and One Night*, vol. 1, tr. into English from the French by Powys Mathers, 1962, rpt, London: Routledge, 1996, pp. 372, 468.

22. Major S.K. Bhakari, *Indian Warfare: An Appraisal of Strategy and Tactics of War in Early Medieval Period*, New Delhi: Munshiram Manoharlal, 1981, p. 211; Robert O'Connell, *Of Arms and Men: A History*

of War, Weapons and Aggression, New York: Oxford University Press, 1989, pp. 86-7; Taj-ud-Din Hasan Nizami, *Taj ul Ma'Athir,* tr. Bhagwat Saroop, Delhi: Said Ahmad Dehlavi, 1998, p. 56.

23. Lieutenant Colonel H.C. Kar, *Military History of India,* Calcutta: Firma KLM Pvt. Ltd., 1980, pp. 183-4; Jagadish Narayan Sarkar, *The Art of War in Medieval India,* New Delhi: Munshiram Manoharlal, 1984, p. 312; Captain B.H. Liddell Hart, *Great Captains Unveiled,* 1927, rpt, New York: Da Capo, 1996, p. 8; Gerard Chaliand (ed.), *The Art of War in World History: From Antiquity to the Nuclear Age,* Berkeley: University of California Press, 1994, p. 431; David Nicolle, *The Armies of Islam: 7th-11th Centuries,* London: Osprey, 1982, p. 15.

24. Mohammad Habib, *Sultan Mahmud of Ghaznin,* Aligarh: Aligarh Muslim University Publications, 1927, pp. 14-15.

25. Kar, *Military History,* p. 180.

26. Hasan Nizami, *Taj ul Ma'Athir,* pp. 56-7.

27. Habib, *Mahmud,* pp. 22-3.

28. K.A. Nizami (ed.), *Politics and Society During the Early Medieval Period: Collected Works of Mohammad Habib,* vol. 2, New Delhi: People's Publishing House, 1981, pp. 112, 114-5; Sarkar, *Military History,* p. 36.

29. R.C. Smail, *Crusading Warfare: 1097-1193,* 1956, rpt, Cambridge: Cambridge University Press, 1995, p. 77.

30. France, *Victory in the East,* pp. 371-2; Bernard S. Bachrach, 'On Roman Ramparts', in Geoffrey Parker (ed.), *The Cambridge Illustrated History of Warfare: The Triumph of the West,* Cambridge: Cambridge University Press, 1995, pp. 84, 87-8; Hooper and Bennett, *Warfare,* p. 91; Creveld, *Technology and War,* p. 19.

31. Marshall, *Warfare,* note 7, p. 49.

32. Parry and Yapp, 'Introduction', in Parry and Yapp, *War, Technology and Society,* p. 7.

33. Fuller, *From the Earliest Times to the Battle of Lepanto,* p. 402; Preston and Wise, *Men in Arms,* p. 63; Oliver Lyman Spaulding Jr., Hoffman Nickerson and John Womack Wright, *Warfare: A Study of Military Methods from the Earliest Times,* London: George G. Harrap & Co. Ltd. 1924, p. 295.

34. M. Habib, 'The Urban Revolution in Northern India', and B.N.S. Yadava, 'Chivalry and Warfare', in Gommans and Kolff, *Warfare and Weaponry,* pp. 46, 66-70.

35. Nizami, *Works of Mohammad Habib,* pp. 205, 207; Sarkar, *Art of War,* p. 312; Yadava, 'Chivalry and Warfare', in Gommans and Kolff, *Warfare and Weaponry,* pp. 74-6.

36. Ramesh Chander, 'Sultan Mahmud of Ghazni and the Khukhrain Kshatriyas of the Punjab', *Punjab Past and Present,* vol. 15, no. 29, 1981, p. 201.

37. C.E. Bosworth, 'The Army of the Ghaznavids', in Gommans and Kolff,

Warfare and Weaponry, pp. 153-9; Nicolle, *Armies of Islam*, pp. 14-15.

38. Bosworth, 'The Army of the Ghaznavids', in Gommans and Kolff, *Warfare and Weaponry*, p. 175.

39. Sharma, *Indian Army*, p. 53.

40. Saunders, *Mongol Conquests*. See especially p. 61.

41. Ameer Ali, *A Short History of the Saracens*, London: Macmillan, 1949, pp. 431, 433.

42. Jagadish Narayan Sarkar, 'Aspects of Military Policy in Medieval India', *Proceedings of the Indian History Congress*, 36th Session, Aligarh, 1975, pp. 243-56.

43. Hussain Khan, 'The Genesis of Roh (The Medieval Homeland of the Afghans)', *Journal of Asiatic Society of Pakistan*, vol. 15, no. 3, pp. 193-4; Ali Athar, 'The Role of Piyadah in the Sultanate of Delhi', *Journal of the Asiatic Society*, vol. 37, no. 2, 1995, p. 24; Olaf Caroe, *The Pathans: 550 B.C.-A.D. 1957*, London: Macmillan, 1958, pp. 127-8, 132; J. Wellhausen, *The Arab Kingdom and Its Fall*, tr. Margaret Graham Weir, Calcutta: University of Calcutta, 1927, p. 25; Philip Hitti, *History of the Arabs*, London: Macmillan, 1937, p. 173.

44. J. Burton-Page, 'A Study of Fortification in the Indian Subcontinent from the Thirteenth to the Eighteenth Century A.D.', *Bulletin of the School of Oriental and African Studies*, vol. 23, 1960, p. 514; M. Habib, 'Urban Revolution', in Gommans and Kolff, *Warfare and Weaponry*, p. 47.

45. Sharma, *Indian Army*, pp. 50-1; Hitti, *History of the Arabs*, p. 226.

46. Juvaini, *Genghis Khan*, p. 119.

47. Iqtidar Alam Khan, 'Early Use of Cannon and Musket in India: AD 1442-1526', in Gommans and Kolff, *Warfare and Weaponry*, p. 326.

48. Simon Digby, *War Horses and Elephants in the Delhi Sultanate*, Karachi: Oxford University Press, 1971; Ghulam Hussain Salim, *Riyaz-us-Salatin*, tr. Abdus Salam, 1903, rpt, Delhi: Idarah-i-Adabiyat-i Delli, 1975, pp. 104-5.

49. *The Travels of Marco Polo*, tr. William Marsden with an Introduction by Benjamin Colbert, Ware, Hertfordshire: Wordsworth, 1997, pp. 227-8.

50. *Marco Polo*, pp. 228-9.

51. R.C. Jauhri, *Firoz Tughluq*, 1968, rpt, Jalandhar: ABS Publication, 1990, p. 126; Gommans and Kolff, 'Introduction', in Gommans and Kolff, *Warfare and Weaponry*, p. 32.

52. Latham, 'Horse-Archers', pp. 258-9.

53. Hassanein Rabie, 'The Training of the Mamluk Faris', in Parry and Yapp, *War, Technology and Society*, pp. 156-7.

54. Ali Athar, 'Military Exercise and Training in the Sultanate of Delhi during the 13th and 14th Centuries', *Journal of the Asiatic Society*, vol. 37, no. 1, 1995, p. 19; idem, 'Role of Piyadah', p. 25; Peter Jackson,

The Delhi Sultanate: A Political and Military History, Cambridge: Cambridge University Press, 1999, p. 240.

55. Liddell-Hart, *Great Captains*, p. 8; Hussain Salim, *Riyaz-us-Salatin*, p. 64. For the concept of jointness in the late twentieth century, see Vinod Anand, 'Future Battlespace and the Need for Jointmanship', *Strategic Analysis*, vol. 23, no. 10, 2000, pp. 1623-40.

56. Anil Chandra Banerjee, *The State and Society in Northern India: 1206-1526*, Calcutta: K.P. Bagchi, 1982, p. 115; Bhakari, *Indian Warfare*, p. 208.

57. Wellhausen, *Arab Kingdom*, p. 120.

58. K.S. Lal, 'The Striking Power of the Army of the Sultanate', *Journal of Indian History*, Part II, vol. LV, August 1977, pp. 102-3; Ali Athar, 'The Ministry of War in the Delhi Sultanate', *Journal of the Asiatic Society*, vol. 37, no. 3, 1995, pp. 3-4.

59. Banerjee, *State and Society*, p. 112.

60. Chaliand, *Art of War*, pp. 438-9.

61. Lal, 'Army of the Sultanate', p. 104.

62. John A. Lynn, 'Medieval Introduction', Walter E. Kaegi, 'Byzantine Logistics: Problems and Perspectives', and Bernard S. Bachrach, 'Logistics in Pre-Crusade Europe', in Lynn (ed.), *Feeding Mars: Logistics in the Western World from the Middle Ages to the Present*, Boulder: Westview Press, 1993, pp. 35, 51, 70.

63. Smail, *Crusading Warfare*, pp. 64-5.

64. A.B.M. Habibullah, *The Foundation of Muslim Rule in India*, 1961, rpt, Allahabad: Central Book Depot, 1976, p. 221.

65. Jackson, *Delhi Sultanate*, p. 241.

66. Habibullah, *Muslim Rule in India*, p. 219.

67. Jauhri, *Firuz Tughluq*, p. 118.

68. Chaliand, *Art of War*, pp. 482, 484.

69. R.C. Majumdar, H.C. Raychaudhuri and Kalikinkar Dutta, *An Advanced History of India*, 1946, rpt, Madras: Macmillan, 1991, p. 328.

70. Thomas Arnold, *The Renaissance at War*, London: Cassell, 2001, p. 24.

71. Contamine, *War*, pp. 139-40, 143; V.J. Parry and M.E. Yapp, 'Introduction', in Parry and Yapp *War, Technology and Society*, p. 7; Juvaini, *Genghis Khan*, p. 106; Ali, *History of the Saracens*, p. 431.

72. Djurdjica Petrovic, 'Fire-arms in the Balkans on the Eve and After the Ottoman Conquests of the Fourteenth and Fifteenth Centuries', in Parry and Yapp, *War, Technology and Society*, pp. 179-81.

73. Petrovic, 'Fire-arms in the Balkans', pp. 184, 191.

74. Jogesh Chandra Ray, 'Fire-Arms in Ancient India: Part II', *Indian Historical Quarterly*, vol. 8, no. 2, 1932, p. 268.

75. Jogesh Chandra Ray, 'Fire-Arms in Ancient India: Part III', *Indian Historical Quarterly*, vol. 8, no. 3, 1932, p. 584.

76. Iqtidar Alam Khan, 'Origin and Development of Gunpowder Technol-

ogy in India: AD 1250-1500', *Indian Historical Review*, vol. 4, no. 1, 1977, p. 21.

77. Ray, 'Fire-Arms: Part III', p. 586.

78. V. Narayan Rao, David Shulman and Sanjay Subrahmaniyam, 'The Art of War under the Nayakas', in Gommans and Kolff, *Warfare and Weaponry*, pp. 139-40; Iqtidar Alam Khan, 'Coming of Gunpowder and the Response of the Indian Polity', unpublished paper (lecture delivered at the Centre for Studies in Social Sciences, Calcutta, 1980), p. 23.

79. Khan, 'Cannon and Musket', in Gommans and Kolff, *Warfare and Weaponry*, p. 321.

80. V.J. Parry, 'La maniere de combattre', in idem and Yapp, *War, Technology and Society*, p. 231; Alam Khan, 'Gunpowder Technology', pp. 22-3; Alam Khan, 'Coming of Gunpowder', p. 18; Steven Runciman, *The Fall of Constantinople: 1453*, 1965, rpt, Cambridge: Canto, 1990, p. 137.

81. Halil Inalcik, 'The Socio-Political Effects of the Diffusion of Fire-arms in the Middle East', in Parry and Yapp, *War, Technology and Society*, pp. 198-9.

82. Inalcik, 'Fire-arms in the Middle East', in Parry and Yapp, *War, Technology and Society*, pp. 203-4.

83. Arnold, *Renaissance at War*, p. 26.

THREE

The Chaghthai Compromise: Armies and Warfare in Mughal India, 1526-1739

Fight in the cause of Allah
Those who fight you
... And slay them
Wherever ye catch them
And turn them out
From where they have
Turned you out;
... And fight them on.[1]

The year was 1526. A young Chaghthai Turkish warlord named Zahir-ud-din Babur issued a call for *jehad* against the *kafirs* of Hindustan, which resulted in the raising of an army on the hoof followed by gun tumbrils, wagon carts, and double-humped Bactrian bullocks in north Afghanistan. Though the summer was yet to arrive in north India, the heat was already on the Central Asian nomadic warriors as they left the cool winding trails of mountainous Afghanistan for the sultry plains of Hindustan. Clad in Pishin overcoats and sheepskin boots, the sweating troopers of Babur were nevertheless eager to fight the 'infidels'. The world-shaking clash of arms which followed eventually resulted in the founding of the Mughal Empire.

The Mughal Empire has been rightly described as the 'Roman Empire of the East' by Jadunath Sarkar, the doyen of Indian historians. Babur established the empire in 1526. The empire, at its zenith under Aurangzeb in the late seventeenth century, encompassed the whole subcontinent, including Afghanistan in the west and Arakan in the east. Thus, Aurangzeb's writ ran over an area larger than that controlled by Lord Curzon, the most pompous Viceroy of British India in the first decade of the twentieth century. The financial health of the Mughal Empire was based on India's agrarian economy. The Mughals extracted about 40 per cent of the agricultural surplus and of this surplus about 80 per cent went for maintaining the Mughal army. This army was the biggest government employer as its ration strength ran into one million.[2] At that time in Europe, France maintained the biggest army whose size was about 4,00,000.[3] The genesis of this army—which played a crucial role in the establishment, consolidation, and final decline of the Mughal polity—may be traced back to Babur.

BABUR'S MILITARY SYNTHESIS AND THE
RISE OF THE MUGHALS, 1526-1539

Babur moved from Samarkand to Kabul in 1504 and made it a base for his operations against Hindustan. In 1524, Babur entered Lahore. After getting reinforcements from Badakhshan in 1525, Babur crossed the Jhelum. This campaign culminated in the decisive First Battle of Panipat, where he defeated Ibrahim Lodhi, the Sultan of Delhi. Babur not only won this battle but also all subsequent battles against the Afghans of Bihar and Bengal as well as the Rajputs of central India under Rana Sangha.[4] How can we explain this turn of events?

The military doctrines of the Mughals and their early opponents, the Delhi Sultanate, the Afghans, and the Rajputs were more or less similar. All these parties wanted to engage each other at a particular field, and their aim was to eliminate the enemy by a decisive stroke in a single afternoon. Thus, they pursued a strategy of fighting a decisive set-piece encounter battle for destroying the enemy at a single opportunity.

Let us compare and contrast three great battles fought in Mughal India (First and Second Battles of Panipat and Karnal) with three decisive contemporary West European battles (Lutzen, Dunes, and Oudenarde). In the First Battle of Panipat, on 21 April 1526, 25,000 Mughals (18,000 cavalry, 5,000 gunners, and 2,000 infantry) crossed swords with the Delhi Sultanate's Afghan army that numbered 32,000 (30,000 infantry and 2,000 men serving with the elephant corps). On 16 November 1632, at Lutzen, 20,000 Swedes (12,000 infantry, 7,500 cavalry, and 500 gunners) under the Swedish King Gustavus Adolphus clashed with 28,000 (8,000 of them cavalry) Germans under Count Wallenstein, General of the Holy Roman Empire. Compared with Lutzen, the Battle of Dunes was a smaller affair, just as the Second Battle of Panipat involved smaller forces than the First Battle of Panipat. On 14 June 1658, at Dunes, the French General Turenne's 14,000 French soldiers (8,000 infantry and 6,000 cavalry) matched swords with the Spanish General Don Juan's 14,000 Spanish soldiers (6,000 infantry and 8,000 cavalry). During the Second Battle of Panipat, on 5 November 1556, 10,000 Mughal cavalry fought against Hemu's 30,000 troops. Oudenarde fought on 11 July 1708 was a bigger affair, like Karnal. At Oudenarde, the 78,000 soldiers under the command of the British General, the Duke of Marlborough, fought and won against 1,00,000 French soldiers under Marshal Vendomme. On 13 February 1739, about 1,20,000 Persians (50,000 cavalry and the rest infantry and gunners) under Nadir Shah fought and won against 80,000 Mughals at Karnal. The outcome of all these battles was decided on a single day. In fact, the Battle of Dunes lasted merely four hours. The size of the armies that fought in India was comparable with the size of the European armies. While the Indian battles involved more cavalry, the European battles were mostly infantry affairs. What about the casualties (killed, wounded, and prisoner taken) suffered? In the First Battle of Panipat, the Sultanate army lost 20,000 men killed and the number of wounded and prisoners taken was another 10,000. Compared with it, Lutzen and Dunes were smaller affairs. At Lutzen, Wallenstein lost 4,000 killed and 6,000 wounded and taken prisoners. Lutzen was less devastating than the First Battle of Panipat, because while Ibrahim Lodhi's entire army was annihilated, Wallenstein was able to carry out a tactical retreat due to confusion in the Swedes' camp following the death of Gustavus Adolphus. While Hemu's entire army of 30,000 men was wiped out at the Second Battle of Panipat, Don Juan, the defeated Spanish commander, lost only 4,000 men at the Battle of Dunes. At Karnal, the Mughal loss was 12,000 soldiers, and the Persian loss was minimal. Similarly, at Oudenarde, the French lost 13,755 men, while the victorious Marlborough's loss, like that of Nadir Shah, was only 3,000. What about the tactical sophistication of the armies involved? Both the defeated com-

manders, Wallenstein and Hemu, divided their forces into three
groups—right, centre and left. Wallenstein at Lutzen, like the
defeated Padshah (Mughal Emperor) Muhammad Shah at Karnal,
entrenched his camp before battle.[5] The above account portrays,
if anything, that the battles fought in the subcontinent were more
lethal than the contemporaneous European battles.

The Mughals emerged supreme in the encounter battles
because Babur initiated a military synthesis in the Indian context
by integrating three distinct foreign weapon systems: mounted
archery, field artillery (guns used for blasting the enemy on the
battlefield), and handguns. His managerial expertise was evident
in amalgamating these three different weapon technologies
within his 'professional army'. The manpower of his army was
recruited from Afghanistan and Central Asia. He enlisted many
soldiers from the martial Yusufzai tribe around Kabul. Babur for
the first time used field artillery effectively in India. He borrowed
it from the Persians who in turn acquired it while fighting the
Ottomans. The use of artillery had both a physical and a psychological effect. Besides producing a high rate of firepower on
the battlefield, the artillery created adverse psychological
conditions for the enemies of the Mughals, since the Afghan and
the Rajput soldiers were overwhelmed by the strange noises
caused by the guns. The point to be noted is that till the fifteenth
century, cannons mostly had a psychological effect even on the
European battlefields. In addition, the mounted bowmen
recruited by Babur from Central Asia altered the pace of battle
due to their superior mobility and striking power. The shock
effect of the mounted archers of Persia and Central Asia was
mind-boggling during the sixteenth and the seventeenth centuries. Their *kaianian* bows were famous for the range and
precision of their shots. The mounted archers fired three times
faster than the musketeers of Europe. These archers used arrows
made of *khadang* (poplar) trees which could pierce both shield
and cuirass. Infantry armed with handguns supported the
mounted bowmen and the field artillery. These handguns
imitated from the Ottomans were metal tubes closed at one end.
These guns were held by the left hand and fired by a match
brought into contact with a touch hole. Since repeated firing
made them too hot to handle, they were supported on wooden
stocks.[6]

Possession of a single superior military technology by itself was not adequate to guarantee victory. It had to be properly absorbed and assimilated within a coherent tactical format by the military force concerned for its proper utilization on the battlefield. The Afghans of Bihar and Bengal at the Battle of Ghagra in 1529 used *bans* (rockets fired from hand-held tubes) against Babur. But the Afghans lacked mounted archers, field artillery, disciplined infantry, and any tactical theory for effectively coordinating the use of the *bans* with their elephant corps. Hence, the Mughals were able to defeat them.[7]

The Mughals' supremacy on the battlefield was due to their ability to coordinate the three distinct arms and this step resulted in a tactical breakthrough. The hand-held firearms, field artillery, and mounted archers had a multiplier effect because the Mughal army knew how to use them effectively and simultaneously, which in turn created a synergy. This was because due to superior training the Mughal force was adept in combined arms manoeuvres. Babur was an expert in simultaneously launching a *tulghama* charge (mounted archers attacking the enemy's flanks and rear at high speed) along with the opening of artillery fire against the enemy's centre and in using field artillery and infantry firepower together to check a frontal assault by the enemy. Babur's focus was to fight a battle in which a frontal assault was to be avoided and the focus was on encirclement. From the late nineteenth century onwards, the Germans termed such a battle *Kesselschlacht* (cauldron battle, i.e. double envelopment of the enemy from its flanks and the rear). The Mughals could implement such sophisticated tactics because, unlike the Sultanate, the Rajputs, and the Afghans of Bihar and Bengal, the former had a standing army. Babur's army comprised well trained and disciplined veterans. Their profession was soldiering, and they had fought several campaigns with Babur in Central Asia and Afghanistan.[8]

The core of the Afghan army was composed of chiefs commanding their unruly clansmen. When the news of the Mughal invasion came, Ibrahim Lodhi increased the size of his force by hastily recruiting men from the *bazars* of Delhi. They were mostly underemployed agriculturists who occasionally sought military service in order to supplement their income from their fields. Due to the massive demographic resources of Hindustan,

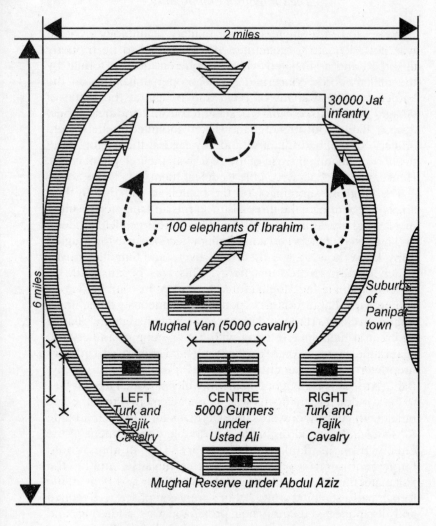

2 miles

6 miles

30000 Jat
infantry

100 elephants of Ibrahim

Suburbs
of
Panipat
town

Mughal Van (5000 cavalry)

LEFT
Turk and
Tajik
Cavalry

CENTRE
5000 Gunners
under
Ustad Ali

RIGHT
Turk and
Tajik
Cavalry

Mughal Reserve under Abdul Aziz

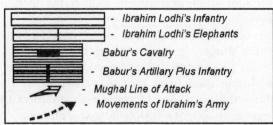

- Ibrahim Lodhi's Infantry
- Ibrahim Lodhi's Elephants
- Babur's Cavalry
- Babur's Artillary Plus Infantry
- Mughal Line of Attack
- Movements of Ibrahim's Army

Map 2: First Battle of Panipat

Ibrahim could raise a militia from among the underemployed marginal peasants before the campaign began. Being part-time militias, they were neither well equipped nor well trained like the Mughal soldiery. Hence, they could only launch frontal assaults, leading Babur to comment that the Indians know how to die but not how to fight. Moreover, due to arrears of pay, Ibrahim's soldiers became more indisciplined.[9] All these features of Afghan military backwardness were evident in Babur's classic victory at Panipat.

THE FIRST BATTLE OF PANIPAT, 21 APRIL 1526

The Campaign

When Ibrahim Lodhi heard that Babur had crossed into India, he moved out of his capital Delhi and crossed the Jamuna. Ibrahim had with him about 100 elephants which constituted his principal strike force, since he was weak in cavalry and lacked field artillery. The total strength of his force, including the non-combatants, was about 1,00,000. Ibrahim's infantry-heavy army had some chance of holding the narrow frontier passes against the invaders from Afghanistan. But while Babur's army moved at a fast pace, Ibrahim's ragtag army moved very slowly. The Delhi Sultanate's army moved about two miles every day and then halted at a place for two to three days.[10] Thus, any hope of checking the Mughals at the frontier passes before they debouched into the fertile plain of Punjab came to nought. The flat landscape of Punjab and the adjoining agriculturally prosperous Ganga-Jamuna doab region not only provided logistical support to the invaders from Kabul but the terrain was also suited for the wide encircling movement practiced by the Mughal cavalry. The Mughals and the Sultanate army finally met at the town of Panipat, 36 miles from Delhi.

The Battle

Generally, the Mongol-Turkish armies from which the Chaghthai Turks derived their military tradition were divided into four divisions: right, centre, left, and the reserve (*iltimish*).[11] Babur being a tactical genius added one more division. Thus, the Mughal army was divided into five divisions—van (advance guard), centre, right and left wings, and finally the reserve. Each division had its separate commander. For example, while Abdul Aziz commanded the reserve, Ustad Ali commanded the centre, and Babur remained the overall incharge of the five divisions. The buildings in the suburbs of Panipat town covered the right flank of the Mughal line. On the left flank ditches were dug and obstacles were constructed by felling trees. Thus, Ibrahim's army was denied any opportunity to envelop the Mughal flanks. In any case, the Sultanate's force lacked the tactical expertise to carry out any outflanking manoeuvres. The deployment of the Mughal centre showed that Babur had partly absorbed the Ottoman tactics. One feature of the Ottoman tactics was to connect the gun carriages with twisted bull hides and form a *laager* (a rectangular or square shaped fortification made of wagons for protecting the base. The steppe nomads under Attila first came up with this innovative tactical formation) in the battlefield. Between every two gun carriages the distance was 16 yards, and there were seven breastworks constructed by the infantry. The matchlock men discharged their muskets from behind them. This battle tactic was used by the Ottoman Sultan Selim against the Persian ruler Shah Ismail at the Battle of Kadrin fought near Tabriz on 23 August 1514. The Mughals copied this battle plan at Panipat.[12] There were about 5,000 gunners in the Mughal centre. The guns were surrounded by wagons to obstruct any enemy infantry breakthrough. Those guns, mounted on carts (each cart was drawn by four bullocks), discharged balls, each weighing 5.25 lbs. And 21 gun carriages had bigger guns which shot brass balls weighing 52 lbs. each.[13] However, to deceive the enemy, the Mughals set up dummy gun batteries all along the line. The Mughal van had 5,000 cavalry recruited from Punjab and these were armed with swords. Both the right and left wings of the Mughal army had *tulghama* (flanking party) contingents composed of 12,000 Tajik and Turkish mounted archers. The flanking party's job was to encircle, envelop, and eliminate the enemy army.[14] The horse-riding nomads of Uzbekistan and Kazakhstan from the time of Alexander had practiced this tactic.[15]

When Ibrahim's 30,000 strong Jat infantry armed with pikes and swords and supported by the elephants in front of them made a frontal assault, the guns in the Mughal centre opened fire with a defeaning roar. Ibrahim's soldiers and elephants had never seen such brass monsters before, and the sound of 'hell fire' unnerved them. The elephants turned back and then ran amok, wounding Ibrahim's soldiers. To add to the confusion, the matchlock men in the Mughal centre opened fire. Then the Mughal van advanced to engage the enemy. While the van 'fixed' Ibrahim's army, Babur's flanking parties composed of elite Central Asian mounted archers attacked both flanks of Ibrahim's force and closed upon them like the two horns of the crescent. Then the *iltmish* attacked the rear of Ibrahim's force. Thus, Ibrahim's army was tightly packed into a bag and slowly squeezed out. As the Mughal vice tightened, there was not enough space for the dust-caked soldiers of the Sultanate army to use their arms properly. Ibrahim's troops were encircled from all sides, like the Roman legions at Cannae. A perfect pocket battle or cauldron battle, i.e. *Kesselschlacht* developed. Since Ibrahim's soldiers could not break the steel cordon that the Mughals had thrown around them, there was no line of retreat available. Panic spread quickly among the men. Many died in the stampede that ensued. Babur won the battle by noon when, due to the total encirclement of the Sultanate army, it suffered 20,000 casualties and Ibrahim lay dead on the battlefield.[16]

Given the decisive military superiority of the Mughal field army, what other military options were open to Ibrahim Lodhi and Rana Sangha, the Rajput chief of Chitor? Speaking retrospectively with the advantage of historical hindsight, we may note that instead of fighting a pitched battle against Babur, Ibrahim Lodhi and Rana Sangha should have shut themselves in the fortresses of Delhi and Chitor respectively. Babur's forces were inept in mining and sapping the walls of a fort. Babur lacked sappers and siege artillery, and his ballistas and catapults would have been quite ineffective against the bastioned walls of Delhi and Chitor. It is possible that after besieging Delhi and Chitor for some months, Babur would have been forced to beat a hasty retreat, just as he did while attempting to take the fort of Kandahar in 1519-20.[17] Delhi was a massive fortress, and was taken for the first time in 1857 by the British with the aid of breaching batteries.

THE TEMPORARY DEMISE OF THE
MUGHALS: 1540-1554

Babur left an empire that extended from Kabul in the west up to
Bihar in the east. After Babur's death in 1530, his eldest son
Humayun succeeded him. However, Humayun's half-brother
Mirza Kamran, the governor of Kabul, refused to cooperate with
him. Taking advantage of the situation, the Afghans in eastern
India rallied under their warlord Sher Shah.

THE BATTLE OF KANAUJ, 17 MAY 1540

Humayun moved from Agra to Kanauj to meet the Afghan
challenge. Both the Afghans under Sher Khan (later he took the
title Shah) and the Mughals under Humayun decided to wage a
battle of annihilation. Like Babur, Humayun placed the artillery
at the centre. Each heavy cannon was drawn by eight pairs of
bullocks, while four pairs of bullocks drew each of the light
cannons. While the latter discharged shots of brass, the former
discharged stone shots which could travel about 3 miles. Mirza
Askari commanded the Mughal right wing and Nasir Mirza
commanded the left wing. The total combat strength of the
Mughals was 40,000 men. Sher Shah's army disposed of only
10,000 men. Sher Shah himself commanded the centre which
was composed of 3,000 men. The Afghan van was composed of
another 3,000 cavalry. To negate the enemy's numerical
superiority in cavalry, Sher Shah, like Wallenstein, made use of
field works. Deep trenches fortified the Afghan position. Sher
Shah was able to outflank and outmanoeuvre the Mughal left
wing and the centre, which in the end resulted in an Afghan
victory. This was possible due to lack of coordination between
the various Mughal divisions. The tactical superiority of Sher
Shah's military force was based on the fact that, unlike Ibrahim,
the former maintained a standing army paid in cash from the
central treasury. In addition, the superior tactical coherence of
the Afghan army vis-à-vis Humayun's Mughal army was the result
of a combination of religious fervour and organizational genius
on the part of Sher Shah. Not only did Sher Shah take care of the
soldiers' families but his soldiers also received the blessings of
the Sufi *pirs* (holy men). In the consciousness of the medieval
men who were believers in superstitions, the *pirs* could turn

defeat into victory. All these factors raised the morale of the Afghan soldiers, hence they fought with more spiritual strength and conviction. Moreover, while Sher Shah's troops were all veterans, most of the Mughal soldiers were newly raised and hence inexperienced troopers. Kamran, who had the battle-winning 12,000 cavalry archers with him for protecting the Mughal north-west frontier, refused to help the *Padshah* against the Afghan chieftain. Thus, Humayun was able to deploy only 400 experienced cavalry during the climactic battle. Due to the absence of a large number of horse archers, Humayun could not execute the deadly *tulghama* tactic against Sher Shah.[18]

After his defeat at Kanauj, Humayun escaped to Iran. When Sher Shah died in 1554, Humayun moved into India with 14,000 Persian reinforcements and re-established the Mughal Empire. After Humayun's death in 1556, his son Akbar succeeded to the throne. The Afghans under their Hindu general, Hemu, became a force to reckon with. Initially, the Mughals retreated to Kabul. But then at urging of the young Akbar and Bairam Khan, the Mughal army re-entered India.[19]

THE SECOND BATTLE OF PANIPAT, 5 NOVEMBER 1556

The Campaign

Hemu while campaigning in Bihar heard that the Mughals had moved into Punjab. He therefore started to concentrate his scattered troops. Hemu hastily ordered his artillery towards Delhi first, because if sent together with the infantry the heavy artillery would have slowed the advance of the foot soldiers. This was a tactical blunder because the Mughal van under Quli Uzbek was able to capture Hemu's artillery, which numbered 51 cannons and 500 falconets (for use by the infantry).[20]

The Battle

When Hemu arrived with his main body, he heard about the loss of artillery. At that time, Hemu had 30,000 combatants against 10,000 Mughals. So there was still a chance of victory. In addition to the usual five groups into which the Mughal Army was divided, Bairam Khan had introduced a new tactical body called *altmash* which was placed between the centre and the vanguard. Its duty was either to reinforce the van while it engaged the enemy or to cover the retreat of the centre in adverse circumstances.[21]

The Mughal left under Sikander Khan Uzbeg attacked Hemu's right wing and killed its commandant Rai Husain along with 3,000 of his troops. Hemu who was commanding the centre launched a charge with his fleet of elephants. At the trunks of these elephants were attached plates fitted with spears and knives, designed to drive away the infantry armed with swords and the lance-wielding cavalry. The Mughals who had initially migrated from Central Asia were as afraid of elephants as Alexander's Greeks and Timur's warriors had been in an earlier age. Abul Fazl, Akbar's court chronicler, has left a vivid description of Hemu's behemoths:

He took with him the mountain-like and dragon-mouthed elephants ... each of them a paragon for swiftness and dexterity. In might and courage they were exemplars. ... In truth each one of those famous elephants was capable of disordering a large force. They were especially calculated to confuse the onset of cavalry, as the horses had never seen such terrific forms.[22]

The Mughal left wing started retreating due to the shock effect created by these heavy beasts. However, Hemu did not pursue the Mughal left because he feared that the Mughals were feigning a flight in order to ambush his army at a later point. Again, the Mughal centre under Quli Khan had deliberately taken position behind a ravine which these elephants could not cross. At that critical moment the mounted bowmen of the Mughal army sprayed these beasts with arrows. The wounded elephants then trampled Hemu's infantry. Though Hemu's force was in difficulty, the battle was not lost by any means. While Hemu, sitting on an elephant (in order to make himself visible to his men amidst the dust raised by the horses), was trying to rally his disarrayed force, a chance shot proved fatal. An arrow shot by an unnamed Mughal trooper pierced Hemu's left eye and he died instantaneously. This was the turning point of the battle.[23]

It is generally believed by scholars that in Asian warfare the killing of the leader constituted the principal turning point in a battle since Asian armies had no clear hierarchy of command in place.[24] However, this was probably not an exclusive Asian military feature. Imagine what would have happened if an Austrian private had shot Napoleon while Soult's victorious

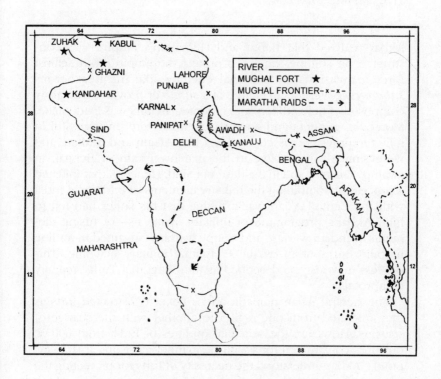

Map 3: Mughal India AD 1700

IV Corps were crossing the Pratzen heights at the battlefield of Austerlitz on 2 December 1805.[25] In the end, despite possessing numerical superiority, Hemu's army was vanquished due to a combination of superior field fortifications, the mobile cavalry tactics of the Mughals, and sheer bad luck.

CONSOLIDATION AND DECLINE OF THE EMPIRE: 1570-1740

THE AKBARI MILITARY SYNTHESIS

Akbar realized that Babur and Humayun's empire was constructed on shifting sands. To protect the empire both against foreign invasions and internal enemies like the treacherous *subadars* (governors in charge of a *subah* or province), an army composed of field artillery and mounted archers was inadequate. Moreover, gunners and mounted archers were unsuccessful in hilly terrain criss-crossed by rivers like Assam and Arakan, and were similarly ineffective in the marshy terrain of Bengal, in swampy Gujarat, and in the desert of Sind. Hence, Akbar initiated a process of combining the military elements of traditional India with the Central Asian war machine that his father had left to him. Akbar's programme of military synthesis—of fusing elements of Indian warfare and steppe warfare—resulted in trading mobility for solidity by the Chaghthai military machine. This process may also be described as the Chaghthai Turks' military compromise.

The Central Asian nomadic tribes never constructed forts as they migrated from one region to another with the change of seasons. However, the sedentary polities of India from 600 BC onwards constructed forts with permanent garrisons at strategic points. Akbar understood the necessity of forts for protecting the frontier. The Mughal scientific frontier as constructed by Akbar ran along the forts of Kabul, Kandahar, and Ghazni. Small forts like Attock surrounded these bigger forts and all of them were permanently garrisoned. This frontier was designed to save Hindustan from the incursions of the Persians and the Uzbeks of Central Asia. The forts protected the frontier, especially when the Mughal Empire was rocked by succession struggles. Against the Uzbeks, the Mughals won due to their superiority in artillery which they used to defend the forts. The Uzbek cavalry army lacked the technical expertise and siege materiel for taking forts. When, in early 1628, Jahangir (son of Akbar) died, Nazar Muhammad, the Uzbek ruler, attacked the north-west frontier with 16,000 cavalry. At the fort of Zuhak, the Mughal garrison with the aid of artillery drove away the Uzbeks. The Uzbeks then moved towards Kabul. Hearing this news, the imperial court reacted by mobilizing a relief army numbering 20,000 cavalry under Mansabdar Mahabat Khan. The relief army was supplied from the fort at Kabul. On the other hand, due to logistical difficulties, Nazar Muhammad's cavalry wasted away. After three months, in September 1628, his force numbered only 8,000 cavalry. Nazar Muhammad then decided to retreat.[26]

Though the Mughal army's size was massive, the cavalry component was barely adequate for all the tasks required of it. The necessity of meeting varying military demands and the imperatives of controlling the dynamic military labour market in Hindustan forced the Mughals to recruit infantry from India in large numbers. The subcontinent had vast numbers of armed peasantry and had to be garrisoned. In 1590, the size of the armed peasantry was about four million.[27] The local peasantry was powerful enough to attack small imperial contingents.[28] If the *subadar* happened to be militarily weak, no revenue would be forthcoming. To give an example, in 1710-11, when each and every trooper was required against the Marathas in south India, Ghazi Khan, the *subadar* of the backwater province of Gujarat, had to keep 4,000 cavalry for extracting revenue from the zamindars who were supported by armed peasantry.[29]

Deployment of a field army of 30,000 cavalry for operations at peripheral provinces was a routine matter till 1711, after which date the empire entered into the stage of terminal decline. However, even before 1711, this field army had failed in the peripheral regions of the subcontinent. In 1615, the Mughal sowars faced trouble in Assam when Sanatan (a tribal leader) supported by *paiks* (infantry) severed the imperial supply lines. The Mughal cavalry was decimated due to lack of forage and grain. Again, in 1662, 'General Flood' in Assam defeated the Mughal general, Mir Jumla. Due to continuous rain, rivers resembled oceans and streams looked like rivers. The Mughal cavalry was completely paralysed in the muddy and flooded terrain. In the damp humid climate of east India, the Mughal troopers and their horses met death very quickly.[30] The recalcitrant Bengal zamindars took full advantage of the local terrain. Amidst dense forests and numerous streams they ambushed the Mughal columns and conducted riverine warfare against the Mughal cavalry army.[31]

But Arakan, Assam, and Bengal were strategically vital for the Mughals because elephants were procured from these regions. Deployment of war elephants was an ancient Indina military tradition, which the Mughals amalgamated within their war machine and military strategy. Chandragupta, the Maurya emperor, first used elephants as both beasts of burden and as war animals. The Mughals needed elephants to drag their heavy siege guns used to destroy the forts of Indian chiefs.[32] The Mughal *Padshah* maintained about 5,000 elephants.[33]

Sind was strategically vital for the Mughals because this province constituted the lower part of the Mughal scientific frontier. The point to be noted is that the Arabs invaded India in the eighth century through Sind. Afghanistan formed the upper part of the scientific frontier. Also, from Afghanistan the Mughals derived manpower, horses, iron, and sulphur. The latter two items were required for their *topkhana* (artillery department).[34] But in the narrow defiles of Afghanistan, the Mughal cavalry could not be deployed effectively. Hence, they became easy targets of the recalcitrant Afghan and trans-Indus tribes, who ambushed them with arrows and by rolling down stones from the *sangars* (strongholds at the mountain tops fortified with stones).[35] Since Sind, Bengal, and Afghanistan were unsuited for fast-moving cavalry operations, Akbar initiated the process of absorbing indigenous military elements such as *paiks* armed with muskets, spears, and javelins into his force structure for fighting in these provinces.[36]

COMBAT INEFFECTIVENESS DUE TO MILITARY SYNTHESIS

The very process of military synthesis created several structural defects and weaknesses. Akbar organized the Mughal army around the *mansabdari* system in 1573-4. Political necessity forced Akbar to introduce this system. By giving *jagir* (the surplus extracted from a piece of land for maintaining armed contingents in accordance with the *mansab*, i.e. rank assigned) to the Afghan and the Rajput chieftains, the *Padshah* tried to integrate these chiefs and the armed retainers whom they commanded. The *jagirs* were somewhat similar to the *iqtas* of the Delhi Sultanate. After being granted *mansabs*, they along with their *paiks*, elephants, and lancers joined the Mughal military. The *mansabdari* system was a corrupted version of Chingiz Khan's military organization. Chingiz structured his army in units between 10 to 10,000. A Mongol tribal contingent composed of 10,000 troopers constituted a *tumen*. While the lowest *mansabdar* commanded 10 soldiers, the highest-ranking *mansabdar* commanded 10,000 soldiers. There were 33 grades between these two commands. After Chingiz, Timur introduced a mixed battle group composed of 1,000 infantry and cavalry. This was similar to the Roman cohort, a sub-unit of the legion. Similarly, in the Mughal army, many *mansabdars* commanded battle groups, each, composed of about 1,000 soldiers.[37]

However, in the long run the *mansabdari* system proved to be harmful for the Mughal army. Political necessity forced the induction of heavily-armoured Rajput lancers *(cuirassiers)* under the Rajput *mansabdars* in large numbers rather than the recruitment of Central Asian mounted archers. This step resulted in the decline of the combat effectiveness of the Mughal army against both the mounted archers of Nadir Shah's Persian army and the mobile Marathas. The slow-moving Rajput lancers were easy targets for the mobile steppe nomadic archers, and the plodding Rajputs were never able to catch up with the nimble and light Maratha cavalry, which conducted mobile guerrilla warfare.

Second, the *mansabdari* system did not encourage the growth of military professionalism. This was because no clear-cut distinction between civil and military officers existed in the Mughal Empire. The *mansabdars* were supposed to carry out both civil administration as well as military campaigns during emergencies.[38] Hence, this prevented them from honing their military expertise to a high degree.

Again, the *mansabdars* were not professional agriculturists. Due to political and military demands they had to remain at the *Padshah*'s court or away from their assigned *jagirs* during military expeditions. They increasingly acted as absentee landlords. Hence, they could not give their full attention to agricultural expansion. Even when agricultural expansion did take place, intermediary peasants like the *khud kashts* (high caste peasants owning land and capital) extracted the surplus and not the Mughal revenue officials who happened to be the *mansabdars'* agents. As a result, from the seventeenth century onwards, the *mansabdars'* real income from the land declined while the prices of commodities went up. This was termed an agrarian crisis. Thus, the number of cavalry that the *mansabdars* could maintain also declined to about one-fourth of the required number.[39] Hence, the effective cavalry strength of the empire declined substantially. In 1646, the theoretical strength of the *mansabdars'* contingents was 7,40,000. However, they could deploy only 1,85,000 cavalry.[40]

The principal defect of the *mansabdari* system was directly related to the emergence of centrifugal tendencies within the army. Due to the *mansabdari* system, the Mughals, unlike the European nation states, failed to build a permanent army governed by a centralized bureaucratic administration under the direct control of the state. The central government (*Padshah's* court at Delhi) failed to monopolize its hold over the coercive apparatus of the state, i.e. the army. In 1647, the Mughals possessed 2,00,000 cavalry and 40,000 gunners and infantry. Of them, only 7,000 cavalry and 10,000 gunners and infantry were under the *Padshah's* direct control. The rest of the troops were under the *mansabdars*.[41] Since the *mansabdars* had full control over the recruitment and wages of soldiers, the latter tended to become more loyal to their immediate commanders rather than to the more distant *Padshah*. The net result was the outbreak of frequent mutinies and desertions by the *mansabdars* and their retainers, which occasionally wrecked imperial campaigns. The army became a loose agglomeration of various chieftains along with their retainers. Hence, it was a friable instrument incapable of conducting attritional warfare. From the late seventeenth century onwards, faced with the daunting Marathas, several *mansabdars* along with their contingents deserted the Mughal banner and made separate peace pacts.[42]

For casting guns as well as for manning them, the Mughals were dependent on foreigners of dubious loyalty. This was because of the Mughal failure to keep pace with technological modernization due to the obstruction posed by the *mansabdars*. The latter feared that the rise of a technology-intensive artillery arm would result in the decline of their own status as leaders of the *paik*-cavalry-elephant force structure. Still, the *Padshahs* tried to induct the European deserters and travellers for purposes of casting and manning guns. Babur had with him some Persians for casting guns. But they were not very successful. In 1526, Babur's Persian chief of ordnance made an iron mortar that sent stone shots over 1,400 yards. This mortar was deployed against the Rajputs at the Battle of Khanwa in 1527, but burst after firing a few rounds. From the 1660s onwards, the Mughals were eager to enlist English gunners in their armies in order to exploit the Westerners' superior knowledge of technological matters.[43] Aurangzeb hired one Richard Bell for casting cannons and mortars. But these guns were crude and clumsy.[44] During the war of succession, in 1658, both Dara Shikoh, the eldest son of Shah Jahan, and his rival and brother Aurangzeb employed European gunners, who proved to be treacherous. Dara deployed about 200 European gunners. Niccolao Manucci, the Genoese traveller, enlisted in Dara's army as a gunner.[45]

The Mughals lagged behind not only in the case of field artillery but also in the case of hand-held firearms. The Mughal infantry continued to use long crude matchlocks and muskets supported on forks which could not be fired in rainy weather. However, from 1600 onwards, the European hand-held firearms became more handy as their length and weight were now reduced. They became more effective thanks to the innovation of paper cartridges and the introduction of the snaphance lock and the fusil in the seventeenth century. Thus, the firepower of the infantry increased. The battlefield effectiveness of the infantry became more lethal due to the drill and the use of volley firing. The Mughal infantry armed with all sorts of weapons, including bows and spears, remained a rabble without drill and training, and they failed to fire simultaneously. The achievement of tactical cohesion was out of the question for them.[46] The failure to develop a firearms-equipped, drilled, and disciplined infantry was also probably due to a conceptual failure on the part of the Mughal warrior aristocracy, i.e. the *mansabdars*, to realize the importance of infantry. Most of the *mansabdars* were Rajputs and Central Asian adventurers. The former were wedded to the culture of fighting from horseback from the ninth century onwards, while the Central Asian nomads were accustomed to the horse culture from the dawn of history. Hence, the *mansabdars* hated the foot-slogging infantry corps which were filled with low-caste people.[47] Due to this failure, the Mughals had to pay very heavily. When the Mughals could not use their armoured cavalry in inhospitable terrain as in Maharashtra, disciplined firearms-equipped infantry could have given them victory. Also, faced with the Persians who had better and more numerous mounted cavalry, the drilled infantry could have provided the Mughal army a chance to fight back.

In the sphere of gunpowder production too, the Mughals remained backward. Between 1420-30, western Europe began to use balled powder composed of small granules. This aided circulation of oxygen within the powder, which in turn permitted a more rapid combustion. The charge of such powder was three times more than ordinary powder.[48] The Mughals were never able to manufacture this sort of gunpowder.

Worse, after 1600 a shift occurred from an emphasis on manoeuvre warfare towards positional warfare. Positional warfare meant the construction and defence of fortresses and fortified lines against attack. Like Louis XIV,[49] Aurangzeb was obsessed with sieges. The shift in emphasis in the Mughal theory of warfare was due to the transition in the force structure of the Mughal army. This was necessary because Aurangzeb was campaigning against the two south Indian kingdoms—Bijapur and Golkunda—which were studded with forts. From being a force of principally mounted archers, the Mughal army became an amalgam of Rajput *cuirassiers* and musketeers.[50] Thus, the Mughals were in deep trouble against enemies like Nadir Shah and the Marathas who conducted high-speed cavalry warfare. With the passage of time, the Mughals developed very heavy guns for destroying the forts of Indian chiefs. Akbar's army deployed 60- to 120-pdr. static guns.[51] Between the reigns of Babur and Aurangzeb, the Mughal artillery became heavier, and these field pieces were useless for fluid situations on the battlefields. The lack of mobile field artillery in the shape of horse artillery was a handicap for the Mughals against the mobile Marathas and Nadir Shah's Persians. If the Mughals had some-thing like the 3-pdr. regimental guns of Gustavus Adolphus which, due to their mobility, provided emergency fire support to the infantry at crucial junctures,[52] then things might have been in far better shape for the Mughals. The induction of *paiks*, elephants, heavy artillery, and Rajput *cuirassiers* instead of Turkish mounted archers along with a focus on fortress defence made the Mughal army less mobile. The logistical support required for the elephants pulling siege guns increased the baggage of the Mughal military, thus further impeding its mobility.

GANIMI KAVA (LIGHTNING GUERRILLA RAIDS) OF THE MARATHAS
AND THE MUGHAL MILITARY COLLAPSE: 1650-1740

From the second half of the seventeenth century, the Marathas—first under Shivaji and then under his successors—posed a serious threat to Mughal military supremacy. Shivaji's army was composed of 50,000 cavalry. Unlike the Mughals, the Marathas did not use any beasts of burden, nor were the Maratha soldiers allowed to carry tents and women. Again, there was one spare horse for every two Maratha troopers. All these factors raised the mobility of Shivaji's force vis-á-vis the lumbering Mughal war machine. Hence, the Maratha cavalry was able to cover about fifty miles a day.[53]

With such a nimble cavalry, the Marathas conducted a sort of Fabian strategy of avoiding set-piece battles against the Mughals and succeeded in gradually wearing them down through attritional warfare. This was because, till 1707, the Mughals could deploy 65,000 cavalry and 45,000 infantry armed with match-locks for a single encounter battle.[54] The standard Mughal battle tactic was first to open a cannonade with the guns massed in order to soften up the enemy and then to launch a massive cavalry charge.[55] Shivaji's light cavalry would have been unable to withstand the shock tactics of the *cuirassiers* and the firepower of the heavy artillery.

The Maratha strategy was to conduct raids on Mughal territory. Nocturnal raids were favoured because the Mughal army was unprepared for this form of attack due to the prevailing norms of Mughal imperial culture. In 1573, when Akbar was campaigning in Gujarat, he refused to launch a night attack against the rebels. The reasons he advanced were the same as those advanced by Alexander on the eve of the Battle of Arbela. Akbar said, like Alexander, 'I will not steal my victory.' Akbar asserted that a night attack involved deception plus fraud and that this would not legitimize his victory among the public.[56] The point to be noted is that Babur had no such scruples and that he was a past master in the arts of deception (similar to *maskirovka* of the Red Army) and of deliberately misinforming and disinforming the enemy in order to surprise them.[57] The later-day Mughal army faced trouble when they encountered the Marathas, who practiced all sorts of deceptive manoeuvres, including nocturnal raids on the imperial camp.

Each Maratha raiding party was composed of about 3,000 light cavalry, and the bases of the raiding parties were the hill forts.[58] Due to the superior mobility of the Maratha cavalry, they could dodge the pursuing Mughal columns and vanish into the forts situated among the hills. Hence, Aurangzeb described the Marathas as 'mountain rats'. When Jai Singh, the Rajput *mansabdar*, was campaigning in the Deccan against Shivaji in the 1660s, the former's heavy cavalry and big ordnance pieces could not engage the light Maratha troopers on their hardy south Indian ponies who carried out skirmishes, ambushes, and forays. The most favoured Maratha tactics was to destroy the Mughal logistical infrastructure. The Marathas, like the British Parliamentary army in seventeenth-century Ireland, destroyed the economic base of the enemy by burning corn and killing farm animals, thus causing an artificial famine.[59] Further, the broken hilly tracts of Maharashtra were not conducive to the operations of the Mughal *cuirassiers*. The Deccan, being an agriculturally deficit area, could not provide adequate forage for the gun bullocks and elephants of the Mughals. All these constraints seriously hampered Jai Singh's military operations.[60]

After Shivaji's death, the Maratha resistance became dispersed and sporadic. Every chieftain fought along with his retainers. This struggle had the support of the peasantry. There was no Maratha state army or capital left to be conquered. But the Mughal army had to be present in strength everywhere in the Deccan, an impossible task.[61]

Aurangzeb then made an operational move to capture the forts in Maharashtra which functioned as bases for the Maratha raiding parties. Even in siege warfare, the Mughal siege artillery failed to perform effectively. Since the Maratha forts were protected by ravines, mountain ranges, etc., it was very difficult to breach them. More troublesome was the problem of how to transport the heavy siege guns over such difficult terrain. Generally, an enemy fort surrendered to the Mughals due to a lack of provisions, when the Mughal cavalry dominated the countryside from where the fort drew its supplies. Even then storming was impossible due to the heavy cost extracted in terms of casualties. The Mughals had no trained infantry to storm the forts, and the cavalry was not suited to perform this role. So the Maratha garrison was allowed to leave the forts with their arms under a truce. All these factors proved to be a hollow victory for the Mughals because the Maratha garrison survived with their equipment intact to fight another day. The moment the Mughal field army departed to mask another fort, the Maratha garrison immediately recaptured the fortress earlier vacated by them. The Mughal-Maratha conflict was characterized by military actions alternating with protracted negotiations and lengthy truces, much like the English army's operations in sixteenth-century Ireland.[62]

Another serious weakness of the Mughals was that they had no navy worth mentioning. Aurangzeb's attempt to land Mughal soldiers along the coast of Maharashtra with the aid of some crafts assembled by the Siddis of Janjira, who were originally pirates, failed due to the supremacy of the Maratha navy in the Arabian Sea.[63]

The war against the Marathas took on a religious colour which in turn alienated the Hindu subjects of the Mughals. To motivate the soldiers, Sufi saints accompanied the Mughal army which was called the *Lashkar-i-Islam* (Army of Islam). Senior Mughal commanders went to the saints, making offerings of large sums of money and requesting the holy men to use their supernatural power to ward off military disasters. In a way, the Mughal-Maratha conflict became somewhat a Muslim-Hindu tussle. The Marathas used it as a propaganda device to mobilize Hindu chieftains to rally to their support.[64]

THE PERSIAN CHALLENGE: THE BATTLE OF KARNAL,
13 FEBRUARY 1739

The Campaign

While the Mughal Empire was slowly bleeding to death under the continuous and harassing raids of the Marathas, a greater danger appeared along the north-western horizon. In November 1738, Nadir Shah, the ruler of Persia, invaded India. Before the

Mughals could think of organizing their frontier defence, Nadir
Shah's advance guard composed of 18,000 cavalry swept along
the frontier passes. About 20,000 ill-armed tribal soldiers of
Munim Khan, the *subadar* of Kabul, were easily brushed aside
by the 'heaven-born general'. The Persians were able to capture
Peshawar and Lahore, while the Mughal court was still planning
its course of action. With 11,000 tents and a great deal of
baggage, the Mughal army marched out of the capital and finally
reached Karnal, only 80 miles away from Delhi. Nadir Shah's
light cavalry destroyed the *banjaras* (grain dealers) who supplied the Mughal camp. The *banjaras* were roughly equivalent
to the *munitionnaires* (private contractors) who supplied the
French army during the seventeenth century. Thus, a food
crisis developed and it forced the Mughals to come out of their
entrenched camp at Karnal and fight the Persians.[65]

The Battle

Nadir Shah was a master in the game of bluff. He dressed 7,000
women of his camp as heavy cavalry troopers. Deceit, superior
armaments (in the form of mounted archers and camel-mounted
swivel guns) along with integrated all-arms manoeuvres (cavalry
archers plus infantry mixed together in a battle group and
provided with fire support by the artillery) won the day for Nadir
Shah. The total strength of Nadir Shah's army including the non-
combatants was 1,60,000 men. Unlike the Mughal army, Nadir
Shah's army's non-combatants had received combat training and
they were armed. Hence, they were able to fight in times of
crises. Each trooper of his army had three attendants. They were
armed and mounted on either camels or mules for battlefield
mobility. Nadir Shah had 40,000 cavalry archers. The Mughal
army was divided into four groups: right, left, centre, and rear.
Sadat Khan (the *subadar* of Awadh) who was commanding the
Mughal right wing of 20,000 ill-trained and ill-equipped cavalry
was attacked at 9 in the morning by the Persian van. The van
was a mixed battle group of 6,000 crack Qizilbash cavalry supported by 500 infantry armed with arquebusiers. Nadir Shah's
cavalry, skirmishing at high speed, misled the Mughals. The van
made a tactical retreat. Sadat Khan believed that the Persian
van was in full retreat, so he ordered a pursuit. At that critical
juncture, the Persian reserve ambushed Sadat Khan's contingent.

Meanwhile, the Persian centre composed of 10,000 Afghan cavalry and 500 arquebusiers kept *Khan-i-Dauran*, commanding the Mughal centre, busy and thus prevented any help from reaching Sadat Khan while the latter was overpowered. Nadir Shah's artillery was technically superior to that of the Mughals. So, in the ensuing *feurkampf* (firefight), the Mughal centre collapsed due to the rapid fire of the Persian *zamburaks* (camel-mounted swivel guns). These *zamburaks* were similar to Gustavus Adolphus' 3-pdr. leather guns. Internal jealousy among the Mughal nobles and the absence of an overall Mughal commander in charge of the various battle groups hastened the Mughal defeat. Nizam, the *subadar* of Hyderabad, came to the battlefield with only 6,000 cavalry and 3,000 infantry. Most of his best troops and artillery were left in Hyderabad to keep the Marathas in check. While the Mughal right and centre were disintegrating, Nizam commanding the Mughal left and Padshah Muhammad Shah commanding the Mughal rear remained inert.[66]

At Karnal, the Mughals lost 12,000 soldiers, and the artillery which was under the central government was completely decimated.[67] The loss of Kabul to Nadir Shah in the aftermath of Karnal was a death-blow to the Mughal Empire because the Mughals procured Central Asian horses from the horse dealers of Kabul. The Mughals annually imported about 25,000 horses from Uzbekistan and Iran.[68] Akbar exported slaves (prisoners of war) to Central Asia in return for horses. In exchange for 4,000 slaves at Kandahar and Kabul, the Mughals obtained about 500 war horses.[69] The loss of Kabul meant the loss of superior Central Asian horses for the Mughals. This in turn resulted in the loss of cavalry superiority on the part of the Mughals vis-á-vis the Marathas and the Afghans, the two powers who divided the empire between themselves by 1745.

CONCLUSION

Innovative technological and tactical inputs in the shape of field artillery, Central Asian horse archery, and the very concept of the *tulghama* charge gave Babur a string of victories over the Indians. The twin battles of Panipat show that the Mughal army was capable of conducting tactical manoeuvres like feints, counter-attacks, etc. Hence, the American scholar Stephen P.

Rosen's argument that the Mughal army was incapable of tactical manoeuvres due to the Mughal failure to overcome internal social divisions among the military personnel is erroneous.[70] As we have seen earlier that battles of Mughal India were deadly indeed. So, it is a bit difficult to sustain Jos Gommans' interpretation that Mughal Warfare was not geared to the annihilation of the enemy force, but to a great extent was 'flower warfare' a sort of sport aimed at negotiating with the enemy after some skirmishes.[71]

Babur's mounted archers were more effective than the slow-moving *cuirassiers* deployed by his grandson Akbar and the dragoons of Gustavus Adolphus who fought with swords and pistols.[72] The mounted archers would in all probability have crushed the pikemen of the early modern European armies. So, on a comparative basis, till the sixteenth century the military balance was in favour of the Mughals. However, the Mughals started to lag behind in the seventeenth century, when field artillery and handgun-equipped infantry became dominant due to rapid technical advances in these two arms. By the late seventeenth century, the global military balance of power started shifting away from the Mughals. The long-term effects of the Akbari compromise served to deepen this military obsolescence.

Akbar rightly realized that the reach of the Uzbek-Persian modelled war machine, the principal product of Babur's military synthesis of Central Asian and Ottoman techniques, was limited. Ecological factors made the mounted bowmen-field artillery combination useless in the deserts of Sind, in the marshy riverine tracts of Bengal and Assam, and in the rocky Deccan. The only solution was to integrate indigenous elements like elephants, *paiks*, and forts within the ambit of the Mughal military system. However, this very system of military amalgamation, which resulted in the perpetuation of the *mansabdari* structure, disrupted the coherence of the military machine and led to further technological backwardness. In the long run, this made the Mughal army less mobile and more disorganized. Instead of a centralized bureaucratic professional force, the Mughal army became a loose and unwieldy collection of chieftains, each with his own retainers.

The Mughal collapse was due to the slow ulcer eating into the military vitals caused by the continuous raids of the Marathas and the decisive defeat inflicted by the invader from the north-west. Fighting decisive battles remained the cornerstone of Mughal military strategy. The Mughals failed to evolve a viable strategic response to the Marathas' *ganimi kava*. Even in the sphere of pitched battles, the Mughals lost their tactical advantage due to a shift from an emphasis on mobile mounted archers to a reliance on the lancer-*paik* force structure. In the encounter battle against Nadir Shah, the Mughal military collapse occurred because the Persians not only possessed a larger number of mounted archers but also because they had better guns. Thus, the defeat at Karnal was inevitable. After this disaster, both the Mughal army and the Mughal Empire started disintegrating.

NOTES

1. *The Holy Quran*, English Translation of the Meanings and Commentary, Al-Madinah Al-Munawarah: The Ministry of Hajj and Endowments of Saudi Arabia, 1413 H, pp. 79-80.

2. Tapan Raychaudhuri, 'The Mughal Empire', in idem and Dharma Kumar (eds), *The Cambridge Economic History of India: c. 1200-c. 1750*, vol. 1, Delhi: Orient Longman in association with Cambridge University Press, 1982, pp. 172-4, 179.

3. Martin Van Creveld, *Supplying War: Logistics from Wallenstein to Patton*, 1977, rpt, Cambridge: Cambridge University Press, 1980, p. 5.

4. Stanley Lane-Poole, *The Emperor Babur*, 1899, rpt, New Delhi: Sunita Publications, 1988, pp. 158-60; Lieutenant Colonel Gautam Sharma, *Indian Army Through the Ages*, Bombay: Allied, 1979, pp. 73, 77-81.

5. For the European battles referred to here, see Anthony Livesey, *Battles of the Great Commanders*, 1987, rpt, London: Tiger Books, 1990, pp. 54-79; Major General J.F.C. Fuller, *A Military History of the Western World: From the Defeat of the Spanish Armada to the Battle of Waterloo*, vol. 2, 1955, rpt, New York: Da Capo, 1987, pp. 67-71; John Laffin, *Brassey's Battles: 3,500 Years of Conflict, Campaigns and Wars from A-Z*, 1986, rpt, London: Brassey's, 1995, pp. 151, 254, 318.

6. Olaf Caroe, *The Pathans: 500 BC-AD 1957*, London: Macmillan, 1958, pp. 151-62; Zahir-ud-din Muhammad Babur, *Padshah Ghazi, Babur-Nama*, vols 1 & 2, tr A.S. Beveridge, 1921, rpt, Delhi: Saeed International, 1989, vol. 1, p. 255; William Irvine, *The Army of the Indian Mughals: Its Organization and Administration*, 1903, rpt, Delhi: Low Price Publications, 1994, p. 91; Sharma, *Indian Army*, p. 72; Martin van Creveld,

Technology and War: From 2000 BC to the Present, London: Brassey's, 1991, p. 84; Philippe Contamine, *War in the Middle Ages*, tr Michael Jones, 1984, rpt, Oxford: Blackwell, 1996, p. 199; Ghulam Hussain Salim, *Riyaz-us-Salatin*, tr Abdus Salam, 1903, rpt, Delhi: Idarah-i Adabiyat-i Delli, 1975, pp. 241-2.

7. Iqtidar Alam Khan, 'Early Use of Cannon and Musket in India: AD 1442-1526', in Jos J.L. Gommans and Dirk H.A. Kolff (eds), *Warfare and Weaponry in South Asia: 1000-1800*, New Delhi: Oxford University Press, 2001, pp. 328-36.

8. For an account of Babur's campaigns in Samarkhand and Afghanistan, see Abul Fazl, *The Akbar Nama*, vol. 1, tr H. Beveridge, 1903, rpt, New Delhi: Saeed International, 1989, pp. 225-39. For the concept of *Kesselschlacht*, see G.D. Sheffield, 'Blitzkrieg and Attrition: Land Operations in Europe, 1914-45', in idem and G.D. Sheffield (eds), *Warfare in the Twentieth Century: Theory and Practice*, London: Unwin Hyman, 1988, p. 52.

9. *Babur Nama*, vol. 2, p. 470 including footnote no. 3. Dirk H.A. Kolff, *Naukar, Rajput and Sepoy: The Ethnohistory of the Military Labour Market in Hindustan, 1450-1850*, Cambridge: Cambridge University Press, 1990, pp. 1-26, 32-3.

10. *Babur Nama*, vol. 2, p. 470; Babur (1483-1530), in Gerard Chaliand (ed.), *The Art of War in World History: From Antiquity to the Nuclear Age*, Berkeley: University of California Press, 1994, p. 492.

11. Abdul Aziz, *The Mansabdari System and the Mughal Army*, Delhi: Idarah-i Adabiyat, 1972, p. 176.

12. Babur, in Chaliand, *Art of War*, pp. 493-4; Abul Fazl, *Akbar Nama*, vol. 1, footnote 2, p. 241; *History of the Regiment of Artillery Indian Army*, published under the authority of the Director of Artillery, Army Headquarters, Dehra Dun: Palit & Palit, 1971, p. 3; John Terraine (ed.), *The Decisive Battles of the Western World and their Influence upon History: 480 BC-AD 1757*, vol. 1, 1954, rpt, London: Granada, 1982, pp. 195-214.

13. Lane-Poole, *Babur*, pp. 161-2.

14. Abul Fazl, *Akbar Nama*, vol. 1, pp. 240-5; Douglas E. Streusand, *The Formation of the Mughal Empire*, New Delhi: Oxford University Press, 1989, p. 52.

15. Major General J.F.C. Fuller, *The Generalship of Alexander the Great*, 1960, rpt, New York: Da Capo, 1989, pp. 234-45.

16. Jadunath Sarkar, *Military History of India*, 1960, rpt, Bombay: Orient Longman, 1970, pp. 49-54; Lieutenant Colonel H.C. Kar, *Military History of India*, Calcutta: Firma KLM Pvt. Ltd., 1980, pp. 258, 261-6. For an account of Cannae see Sean McKnight, 'Cannae 216 BC—The Double Envelopment', in Richard Holmes et al., *The Hutchinson Atlas of Battle Plans: Before and After*, Oxford: Helicon Publishing, 1998, pp. 7-11.

17. For Babur's failure to lay siege to the fort of Kandahar, see *Babur Nama*, vol. 1, pp. 430-3.

18. Simon Digby, 'Dreams and Reminiscences of Dattu Sarvani: A Sixteenth-Century Indo-Afghan Soldier', *Indian Economic and Social History Review*, vol. 2, no. 2, 1965, pp. 178-9, 193; Gul Badan Begum, *Humayun Nama*, tr A.S. Beveridge, 1901, rpt, New Delhi: Atlantic Publishers, 1989, pp. 94, 137; Sarkar, *Military History*, p. 55; B.P. Ambashthya, *The Decisive Battles of Sher Shah*, Patna: Janaki Prakashan, 1977, pp. 129-63; Major P. Sensarma, *The Military Profile of Sher Shah Sur*, Calcutta: Naya Prokash, 1976, pp. 103-4.

19. Gul Badan Begum, *Humayun Nama*, pp. 138-200; R.C. Majumdar, H.C. Raychaudhuri and Kalikinkar Datta, *An Advanced History of India*, 1946, rpt, Madras: Macmillan, 1991, pp. 437-9.

20. Abul Fazl, *The Akbar Nama*, vol. 2, tr. H. Beveridge, 1903, rpt, New Delhi: Saeed International, 1989.

21. *Akbar Nama*, vol. 2, pp. 54-5.

22. *Akbar Nama*, vol. 2, p. 59.

23. *Akbar Nama*, vol. 2, pp. 47-51, 58-64; Streusand, *Mughal Empire*, pp. 52-3; H.N. Verma and Amrit Verma, *Decisive Battles of India through the Ages*, vol. 1, California: GIP Books, 1994, pp. 102-4.

24. Irvine, *Army of the Indian Mughals*, p. 299.

25. For an account of Austerlitz, see Brigadier Peter Young, *Strategy and Tactics of the Great Generals and their Battles*, London: Bison Books, 1986, pp. 16-17.

26. *The Shah Jahan Nama of Inayat Khan*, eds W.E. Begley and Z.A. Desai, tr A.R. Fuller, New Delhi: Oxford University Press, 1990, pp. 23-5; Irfan Habib, *An Atlas of the Mughal Empire: Political and Economic Maps with Detailed Notes*, 1982, rpt, Delhi: Oxford University Press, 1986, p. 3.

27. Gommans and Kolff, 'Introduction' in Gommans and Kolff, *Warfare and Weaponry*, p. 16.

28. Simon Digby, 'Dreams and Reminiscences of Dattu Sarvani: A Sixteenth Century Indo-Afghan Soldier', *Indian Economic and Social History Review*, vol. 2, no. 1, 1965, p. 58.

29. Muzaffar Alam, *The Crisis of Empire in Mughal North India: Awadh and Punjab, 1707-1748*, New Delhi: Oxford University Press, 1986, pp. 25, 28.

30. John F. Richards, 'The Seventeenth Century Crisis in South Asia', *Modern Asian Studies*, vol. 24, no. 4, 1990, p. 626; Gautam Bhadra, 'Two Frontier Uprisings in Mughal India', in Ranajit Guha (ed.), *Subaltern Studies*, vol. 2, Delhi: Oxford University Press, 1983, rpt, 1986, pp. 46, 48; Major P. Sensarma, *The Military History of Bengal*, Calcutta: Naya Prakash, 1977, pp. 97-105, 211-12; Jagadish Narayan Sarkar, *The Life of Mir Jumla: The General of Aurangzeb*, 1951, rpt, New Delhi: Rajesh Publications, 1979, pp. 315-16.

31. Jadunath Sarkar, *Studies in Mughal India*, Calcutta, 1913, pp. 119, 140-1.
32. Jadunath Sarkar, *Studies in Aurangzeb's Reign*, 1912, rpt, Calcutta: Orient Longman, 1989, pp. 119, 124, 129-30.
33. Vincent Smith, *Akbar: The Great Mogul, 1542- 1605*, rpt, Delhi: S. Chand & Co., 1962, p. 262.
34. Habib, *Atlas*, pp. 4-5, 13-16.
35. Rajiv Nain Prasad, *Raja Man Singh of Amber*, Calcutta: World Press, 1966, p. 71.
36. Sarkar, *Military History*, p. 55; Sunita Zaidi, 'The Mughal State and Tribes in Seventeenth-Century Sind', *Indian Economic and Social History Review*, vol. 26, no. 3, 1989, pp. 348-57.
37. Nicholas Hooper and Matthew Benett, *Cambridge Illustrated Atlas of Warfare: The Middle Ages, 768-1487*, Cambridge: Cambridge University Press, 1996, p. 62. For a detailed analysis of the ranks held by the *mansabdars* during the reigns of the Great Mughals, see M. Athar Ali, *The Apparatus of Empire: Awards of Ranks, Offices and Titles to the Mughal Nobility, 1574-1678*, New Delhi: Oxford University Press, 1985. For a description of cohorts, see Theodore Ayrault Dodge, *Caesar*, 1892, rpt, New York: Da Capo, 1997.
38. Jagadish Narayan Sarkar, *The Art of War in Medieval India*, New Delhi: Munshiram Manoharlal, 1984, pp. 76-80; S. Inayat Ali Zaidi, 'Ordinary Kachawaha Troopers Serving the Mughal Empire: Composition and Structure of the Contingents of the Kachawaha Nobles', *Studies in History*, vol. 2, no. 1, 1980, pp. 57-70.
39. M. Athar Ali, 'Organization of the Nobility: Mansab, Pay, Conditions of Service', in Gommans and Kolff, *Warfare and Weaponry*, pp. 241-2.
40. Athar Ali, *Apparatus of Empire*, p. xiii.
41. Jeremy Black, *Cambridge Illustrated Atlas of Warfare: Renaissance to Revolution, 1492-1792*, Cambridge: Cambridge University Press, 1996, p. 38.
42. Jagadish Narayan Sarkar, *The Military Despatches of a Seventeenth Century Indian General*, Calcutta: Scientific Book Agency, 1969, p. 137.
43. V. Longer, *Red Coats to Olive Green: A History of the Indian Army, 1600-1947*, Bombay: Allied, 1974, p. 5; *History of the Regiment of Artillery*, pp. 5-6.
44. *History of the Indian Ordnance and Clothing Factories*, Simla: Government of India Press, 1938, p. 8.
45. Niccolao Manucci, *A Pepys of Mogul India: 1653-1708*, tr M.L. Irvine, rpt, New Delhi: Srishti, 1999, pp. 50-2.
46. Trevor N. Dupuy, *The Evolution of Weapons and Warfare*, 1984, rpt, New York: Da Capo, 1990, pp. 130-1, 136-7; Aziz, *Mughal Army*, pp. 203-12.
47. Irfan Habib, 'Introduction: An Essay on Haidar Ali and Tipu Sultan',

and Barun De, 'The Ideological and Social Background of Haidar Ali and Tipu Sultan', in Irfan Habib (ed.), *Confronting Colonialism: Resistance and Modernization under Haidar Ali and Tipu Sultan*, New Delhi: Tulika, 1999, pp. xli-xlii, 4-5.

48. Contamine, *War in the Middle Ages*, p. 197.
49. John A. Lynn, 'Food, Funds, and Fortresses: Resource Mobilization and Positional Warfare in the Campaigns of Louis XIV', in idem (ed.), *Feeding Mars: Logistics in Western Warfare from the Middle Ages to the Present*, Boulder: Westview, 1993, p. 139.
50. Saqi Mustad Khan, *Maasir-i-Alamgiri*, tr. Jadunath Sarkar, 1947, rpt, Calcutta: Asiatic Society, 1990, pp. 2-3.
51. Lieutenant Colonel Rufus Simon, *Their Formative Years: History of the Corps of Electrical and Mechanical Engineers*, vol. 1, New Delhi: Vikas, 1977, pp. 57, 442.
52. Robert O'Connell, *Of Arms and Men: A History of War, Weapons and Aggression*, New York: Oxford University Press, 1989, p. 146.
53. David Kincaid, *Shivaji: The Founder of Maratha Empire*, rpt, New Delhi: Discovery Publishing House, 1984, p. 301, 305; S.N. Sen, *The Military System of the Marathas*, 1928, rpt, Calcutta: K.P. Bagchi, 1979, pp. 15-16; Jadunath Sarkar, *House of Shivaji*, 1940, rpt, New Delhi: Orient Longman, 1978, p. 174; Field Marshal Viscount Montgomery of Alamein, *A History of Warfare*, London: Collins, 1968, p. 405.
54. William Irvine, *Later Mughals*, 2 vols, rpt, New Delhi: Taj Publications, 1989, vol. 1, p. 23.
55. Jadunath Sarkar, *Anecdotes of Aurangzeb*, 1912, rpt, Calcutta: Orient Longman, 1988, pp. 34-5.
56. Abul Fazl, *The Akbar Nama*, vol. 3, tr H. Beveridge, 1903, rpt, New Delhi: Saeed International, 1989, pp. 17-19; Fuller, *Alexander*, p. 164.
57. The Soviet Army in the European context developed such deception techniques only towards the end of the Second World War. Christopher Duffy, *Red Storm on the Reich: The Soviet March on Germany, 1945*, 1991, rpt, New York: Da Capo, 1993, pp. 32, 36, 324-6.
58. Jadunath Sarkar, *History of Aurangzeb*, vol. 4, 1919, rpt, New Delhi: Longman, 1972, pp. 11, 23-4.
59. Jadunath Sarkar, *Shivaji*, 1919, rpt, Calcutta: M.C. Sarkar, 1961, pp. 107-8; Jane H. Ohlmeyer, 'The Wars of Religion: 1603-1660', in Thomas Bartlett and Keith Jeffrey (eds), *A Military History of Ireland*, 1996, rpt, Cambridge: Cambridge University Press, 1997, p. 168.
60. Jadunath Sarkar, *History of Aurangzeb*, vol. 5, 1924, rpt, New Delhi: Orient Longman, 1974, pp. 7, 11.
61. Jadunath Sarkar, *A Short History of Aurangzeb*, 1930, rpt, New Delhi: Orient Longman, 1979, p. 263.
62. Jadunath Sarkar, *Anecdotes of Aurangzeb*, pp. 46-7; Ciaran Brady, 'The

Captains' Games: Army and Society in Elizabethan Ireland', in Bartlett and Jeffrey, *Military History of Ireland*, p. 138.

63. Rahul Roy-Chaudhuri, *Sea Power and Indian Security*, London and Washington: Brassey's, 1995, p. 16; T.R. Raghavan, 'Admiral Kanhoji Angre', in K.K.N. Kurup, *India's Naval Tradition*, New Delhi: Northern Book Centre, 1997, pp. 72-7.

64. Simon Digby, *Sufis and Soldiers in Aurangzeb's Deccan*, New Delhi: Oxford University Press, 2001, pp. 1-72.

65. Irvine, *Later Mughals*, vol. 2, pp. 330, 334; Lynn, 'Early Modern Introduction', in idem (ed.), *Feeding Mars*, p. 106.

66. Satish Chandra, *Parties and Politics at the Mughal Court*, 1959, rpt, New Delhi: New Age, 1979, pp. 245, 250, 258; James Fraser, *The History of Nadir Shah*, MDCCXLII, rpt, New Delhi: Mohan Publications, 1973, pp. 152-8; Irvine, *Mughals*, vol. 2, pp. 337-8, 342-9; Van Creveld, *Technology and War*, p. 87.

67. Jadunath Sarkar, *Fall of the Mughal Empire: 1739-1754*, vol. 1, 1932, rpt, New Delhi: Orient Longman, 1988, pp. 2, 10.

68. *Babur Nama*, vol. 1, p. 202; Stanley J. Tambiah, 'What did Bernier actually say? Profiling the Mughal Empire', in Veena Das et al. (eds), *Tradition, Pluralism and Identity: In Honour of T.N. Madan*, New Delhi: Sage, 1999, p. 225.

69. Iqtidar Alam Khan, 'The *Tazkirat ul-Muluk* by Rafi'uddin Ibrahim Shirazi: As a Source on the History of Akbar's Reign', *Studies in History*, vol. 2, no. 1, 1980, p. 45.

70. S.P. Rosen, *Societies and Military Power: India and its Armies*, New Delhi: Oxford University Press, 1996, pp. 150-5.

71. Jos Gommans, *Mughal Warfare: Indian Frontiers and High Roads to Empire, 1500-1700*, London & New York: Routledge, 2002, pp. 204-6.

72. Fuller, *Military History*, vol. 2, p. 54.

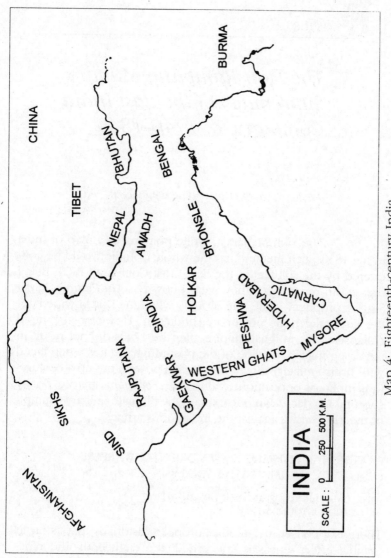

Map 4: Eighteenth-century India

FOUR

The Lion Rampant: Military Supremacy of the East India Company, c. 1740-1849

Sab lal ho jayega (Everything will become red.)

MAHARAJA RANJIT SINGH

The Sikh Maharaja, while pointing to a map of India in the 1830s, commented that the whole of India would be conquered by the soldiers of the East India Company (EIC). Being dressed in red jackets, they were known as *Lal Paltans*. Ranjit Singh's prophecy came true by 1849 when the British wiped out the last indigenous power in Hindustan. However, the rapid collapse of the Mughal Empire after the 1740s did not result in headlong military decline of the post-Mughal states when faced with British military might. The Indian powers put up a century-long military opposition against the *Feranghis* before finally succumbing. How can one explain the ultimate military triumph of the *Lal Paltans* against the indigenous armies?

OCCIDENTAL WARFARE *VERSUS* ORIENTAL WARFARE (1740-1790): A COMPARATIVE ANALYSIS

IMPORTING THE EUROPEAN INFANTRY-ARTILLERY REVOLUTION INTO INDIA

There is a consensus among European historians that as far as combat effectiveness is concerned, the eighteenth- and nineteenth-century European armies had a decisive edge vis-á-vis the Asian armies. This was because of the culmination of certain trends that had started emerging within the European armed forces in the preceding centuries. From the late sixteenth century onwards, north-west Europe experienced certain technological and organizational changes in the military sphere. This marked the genesis of post-feudal armies. Soldiers in uniform, regularly paid in cash by the central governments of the nation states, supported during military campaigns by a network of magazine systems, and directed by a technically skilled officer corps trained in the military academies became common.[1] The late seventeenth-century west European infantry witnessed the use of flintlock muskets and socket bayonets which replaced the pikes. This allowed the infantry to continue firing even when the bayonets were attached to their firearms. The bayonets gave additional security to the infantry against the cavalry that previously had been provided by the infantry armed with long pikes. The organization of the infantry in fixed tactical units like battalions, regiments, and brigades made continuous firing while manoeuvring on the battlefield a possibility. The standard infantry tactic was that after volley firing (infantry deployed in a linear formation firing simultaneously, which had greater killing power and psychological effect instead of troops firing at random), they made a bayonet charge on the enemy. Further, infantry got fire support from field artillery. The latter became effective due to the standardization of equipment and accuracy in shooting. Continued technological advancement made the artillery deadly. The invention of the screw in the early eighteenth century for elevating guns gave them greater precision and hence raised their lethality. All these factors increased the firepower of the infantry-artillery combine, and gave it an edge in close-quarter combat against the feudal cavalry.[2]

However, scholars disagree about the nature of these developments. One group of scholars who belong to what I call the 'military evolution school', and represented by Jeremy Black, asserts that west Europe experienced a series of slow and incremental developments in the art of warfare from the late Middle Ages onwards.[3] Another group of scholars, whom I characterize as the 'military revolution school', claims that northwest Europe witnessed radical and quick developments in the techniques of warfare from the early modern age. While Geoffrey Parker writes that Europe experienced a single military revolution,[4] one of his followers has modified his argument by claiming that Europe experienced a series of military revolutions from 1400 onwards. Between 1300-1400 there occurred the infantry revolution, which resulted in the rise of disciplined foot soldiers equipped with firearms. The artillery revolution between 1400-40 witnessed the advent of quick-firing field cannons.[5]

From the perspective of Indian history, it is noticeable that while in the seventeenth century the European powers were not successful in military encounters against the Indian powers, the military balance shifted drastically against the South Asians in the early eighteenth century. For example, in 1686 and in 1688, the Mughal cavalry defeated two British expeditions in Bengal.[6] But from 1757 onwards, the British went on winning a string of victories in Bengal and Bihar. The military success of the EIC in east India reached its culmination in 1764 at the Battle of Buxar, when 40,000 soldiers of the *Nawab* (Mughal *subadar* who had become independent of the *Padshah*) of Awadh (present-day central Uttar Pradesh) was defeated by 1,000 Europeans supported by 6,000 loyal Indian infantry.[7] Again, in 1746, 450 French infantry armed with muskets and supported by two guns capable of firing 15 shots per minute defeated the *Nawab* of Carnatic's huge host that comprised cavalry armed with badly-tempered swords and an indisciplined infantry armed with matchlocks.[8] The supremacy of European military techniques seemed increasingly evident.

So the Parker hypothesis that the Western armies which were products of the military revolution enabled the European powers to create empires in Afro-Asia[9] seems to hold water. Following Parker's line, some historians dealing with South Asia have developed an interpretation which I term the 'limited westernization school'. The adherents of this approach assert that the Indian rulers instead of totally Westernizing their armed forces pursued a policy of limited Westernization. And this resulted in the Indian military collapse against the British.[10]

However, by analysing the Indian military landscape, we will see that the imported European way of warfare was inadequate to meet the varied demands of warfare in the South Asian theatre. The EIC emerged supreme because the British were able to strike a balance between the European elements of war and certain indigenous military techniques. This I term the balanced military synthesis.[11] On the other hand, the Indian princes failed to combine the imported Western arts of warfare with the traditional

Indian elements of warfare. The armies of the indigenous powers represented cases that I characterize as the defective military synthesis. Still, British victory was not a linear, inevitable process. There was no British *Blitzkrieg*. There were many ups and downs in the fortunes of all the parties. The EIC's ponderous war machine took more than a hundred years to defeat the Indian rulers.[12]

THE INDIAN WAY OF WARFARE

The lethality of the European armies rose significantly in the early eighteenth century due to steady technological advancement. In contrast the combat effectiveness of the Indian armies underwent a drastic decline during the same period. In general, Indian armies after the Mughal collapse in the 1740s experienced frequent treacheries. This was because semi-autonomous chieftains raised most of the troops on the basis of *jagirs* (land grants made to the chiefs by the princes). As a result, the soldiers were more loyal to the *jagirdars* (holders of *jagirs*) rather than to the princes.[13]

These private armies of the *jagirdars* were without regular subdivisions and lacked a hierarchical command structure. Since arms, accoutrements, and clothing were provided by the soldiers themselves, there was no uniformity in their dress and equipment. Hence, these forces were incapable of conducting tactical manoeuvres. Since the cavalry lacked collective training, combat often degenerated into individual display of heroics.[14] Continuous drill and strict discipline were required for the effective use of matchlocks. Drilling gave the troops confidence and instilled a sense of unity which in turn enabled them to coordinate their actions under the enemy's firepower. For this a permanent army was required. Since Indian rulers maintained temporary military forces that were raised with the aid of the *jagirdars* during a crisis and demobilized after the emergency was over, their infantry though armed with matchlocks was neither drilled nor disciplined. Hence, they proved to be more or less useless against European armies on the battlefield.[15]

The Central Asian horse archers who were capable of waging high-speed manoeuvre warfare had vanished from the Indian order of battle because of the capture of the overland trade route to the horse markets of Central Asia by the Afghans after the collapse of Mughal authority in Kabul in the 1740s.[16] Still, cavalry remained the most prestigious branch of service till the mid-eighteenth century.[17]

The Marathas and the Sikhs made extensive use of light cavalry in the early eighteenth century. Though their equipment and tactics differed, both the Maratha and the Sikh cavalry followed an attrition strategy against their enemies. The Maratha light cavalry armed with spears conducted *ganimi kava* (predatory or desultory warfare). The troopers and their ponies lived on the country. Their operational aim was to avoid pitched battles with the enemy's army and to ravage the enemy's districts for a long period so that the economy would collapse. In the 1750s, Bhaskar, a general of the Maratha chief Bhonsle, the ruler of Berar in central India, invaded Bengal with 20,000 cavalry. They carried out night raids for pillaging the Bengal *Nawab's* camp. Then they destroyed those convoys which were bringing provisions to the *Nawab's* army. The Marathas followed a scorched earth policy burning the neighbouring villages to destroy the corn and thus prevent it from reaching the enemy. Thus, the *Nawab's* soldiers were denied food, clothing, and conveyance.[18] However, against artillery and walled posts defended by trained musketeers of the European powers, the Maratha cavalry was useless.[19]

As regards the equipment and tactics of the Sikh cavalry, George Forster, a civil servant of the EIC, wrote in 1783:

A Sikh horseman is armed with a matchlock. ... The predilection of the Sikhs for the matchlock musket, and the constant use they make of it, causes a difference in their manner of attack from that of any other Indian cavalry; a party from forty to fifty, advance in a quick pace to the distance of a carbine shot from the enemy, and then, that the fire may be given with the greater certainty, the horses are drawn up, and their pieces discharged; when speedily retiring about a hundred paces, they load and repeat the same mode of annoying the enemy.[20]

While the tactics of the Sikh cavalry were similar to the sixteenth-century European cavalry's caracole tactics (in which successive ranks of horsemen trotted forward, discharged their pistols, wheeled, and retired only to come back again),[21] the Sikh cavalry at the operational level conducted predatory campaigns like the Marathas. Colonel A.L.H. Polier observed in the late eighteenth century: 'the [Sikhs], particularly those on the borders, set off generally after the rains and make excursions in bodies of 10,000 horses or more on their neighbours. They plunder all they can lay their hands on, burn the towns and villages.'[22]

However, long-term sustained campaigning by the Indian armies was impossible because Indian princes rarely paid their soldiers regularly and this in turn caused frequent mutinies. The net result was low military effectiveness. In 1789, the cavalry army of Mahadji Sindia (the Maratha chieftain), had not been paid for three years. So they refused to fight any further unless their arrears were cleared.[23] However, towards the end of the eighteenth century, the restructuring of the Indian militaries did lead to an increase in their military effectiveness.

TRADITION, INNOVATION, AND PARTIAL WESTERNIZATION IN THE INDIAN ARMIES: 1773-1849

The military confrontations with the European powers convinced the Indian princes that a radical transformation of their armies was necessary for survival. However, the Indian chiefs were unwilling to imitate the European military system in its entirety. They attempted a sort of synthesis by trying to graft the imported Western art of warfare onto the indigenous elements of warfare. The Indian rulers' objective was thorough Westernization of a significant portion of their militaries. Instead of imitating all the elements of the Western art of warfare, the Indian rulers selected only some and assimilated these. This process I term the partial Europeanization/Westernization of the Indian armies. In addition to partial Europeanization and retention of certain traditional elements of warfare, Indian rulers also attempted innovation by inducting new elements of warfare, which were totally unrelated to the western way of warfare.

CONTINUITY AND CHANGES IN THE INDIGENOUS MILITARIES: 1773-1849

One innovative feature of the post-Mughal armies of India was the induction of religious warriors in significant numbers. Due to their religious fervour they were willing to die on the battlefield in the hope of gaining *moksha* (salvation). In 1773, during the

Battle of Barsana against the Mughal chieftain Najaf Khan, the Jats hired 5,000 Naga monks armed with muskets. Their leader was Balanand Gosain.[24] In 1784, when Mahadji Sindia was campaigning in north India, his force included a contingent supplied by Gosain Himmat Bahadur. Himmat Bahadur was an ascetic warlord who had previously served with the Awadh *Nawab's* military. Similarly, Ranjit Singh also employed the Akalis, the religious fanatics of Punjab, in his irregular cavalry.[25]

Besides maintaining Westernized contingents that were drilled and disciplined in the Western style and were administered by military bureaucracies, the Indian chiefs also retained the traditional-style infantry and cavalry. Those infantry and cavalry equipped with indigenous weapons, lacking discipline, and raised by *jagirdars* were categorized as irregulars. Unlike the Mughals, the eighteenth-century Indian rulers experimented by recruiting new ethnic elements. Haidar Ali maintained an irregular Abyssinian infantry armed with spears.[26] The Maratha chieftain Jaswant Rao Holkar, in 1801, maintained 20,000 irregular cavalry and 5,000 Rohilla irregular infantry.[27] Raghuji Bhonsle (ruler of Nagpur) recruited Arabs as irregular infantry.[28] Instead of using the irregular Arabs as skirmishers and sharp-shooters, Bhonsle made a tactical mistake in trying to use them as line infantry. During the Battle of Argaum, fought in 1803, Bhonsle deployed 2,000 Arabs. However, the Arabs although brave were indisciplined. Hence, they could not withstand the volley firing and bayonet charge of the British infantry regiments.[29]

The Marathas also retained the *ban*s (traditional Indian rockets). The Marathas borrowed this weapon system from Tipu Sultan. In 1740, the Marathas possessed 300 camels which carried men armed with rockets. In 1779, during the First Maratha War when the British army from Bombay tried to invade Maharashtra through the Western Ghats, the Maratha rocket corps caused much disorder among them.[30] However, the *ban*s were still at an experimental stage and were yet to become a decisive battle-winning weapon.

The *zamburaks* (light guns dragged by camels) that were used by Nadir Shah's Persians were retained by the Sikh army till its end in 1849. *Zamburaks* were the Indian response to the European horse artillery. However, the *zamburaks* were less mobile, hence less manoeuvrable than the horse artillery. During the Sikh Wars (1846-7 and 1848-9), the EIC's horse artillery came within 300 yards of the heavy artillery within the Sikhs' entrenched camps and retired quickly after destroying them. The rapidity of the horse artillery's movement prevented the *zamburaks* from catching up with them.[31]

The irregular Sikh cavalry and infantry used the ancient Hindu weapon known as the *chakra*. When thrown from a distance of 50 yards at the enemy, it skimmed through the air and inflicted dangerous cuts. The horses of the enemy became confused by seeing such flying weapons.[32] *Chakras* were the Indian near equivalent of European bayonets.

PARTIAL WESTERNIZATION OF THE INDIGENOUS MILITARIES AND THE TUSSLE WITH THE EIC: 1780-1849

The end of the eighteenth century witnessed the partial Western-ization of the Indian military machines. This process occurred in halting stages, but not because of any cultural lag on the part of the Indian rulers, as C.R. Boxer argues. Boxer asserts that Asian rulers had a strong cultural antipathy against using artillery effectively on the battlefield. Rather, they used artillery for increasing their status by ceremonial firing during rituals like coronation ceremonies, etc.[33] However, the historical evidence refutes Boxer's argument, since the Sikhs and the Marathas were eager to decimate the EIC's soldiers with field artillery supported by disciplined infantry. However, the exigencies of *realpolitik* hampered the Indian rulers' programme of partial European-ization.

First, the lack of adequate numbers of European instructors was one of the principal reasons that prevented the thorough Westernization of those contingents of the indigenous militaries set aside for Europeanization. Western military skill could be imparted to the Indian armies only through European military officers. European officers gravitated towards the Indian king-doms attracted by the prospect of high pay. Hence, the British took all possible measures to thwart the influx of European military specialists into the Indian kingdoms. In the treaty that was signed in 1765 between Clive and the *Nawabs* of Bengal and Awadh, after the EIC's victory at the Battle of Buxar in 1764, the British included the clause that the *Nawabs* would never entertain Sombre (a German mercenary officer) or any of the European deserters. Moreover, the *Nawabs* were bound to deliver up to the British in future any Europeans who may desert from the EIC and come into their domains.[34] This reflects the EIC's fear of the combat effectiveness of Sombre's trained battalions that had fought alongside the army of Mir Qasim against the British at Buxar. By inserting the above clause, the EIC prevented the partial Europeanization of the armies of Awadh and Bengal.

The Gurkha Kingdom of Nepal copied the infantry system of the EIC. The infantry were drilled and organized in battalions. Deserters from the EIC's army taught the Gurkhas Western-style military drill and discipline.[35] To stall the partial Westernization of the Gurkha army in Nepal, the EIC forced a treaty on the Raja of Nepal after the conclusion of the Nepal War in 1815. One of the principal clauses of the treaty was that the Raja of Nepal would never take or retain in his service any European subject without the consent of the British Government.[36]

The only way out of this impasse for the Indian regimes was to establish educational institutions and officer academies where Western professional knowledge could be imparted. The Ottomans and the Russians set up such educational institutions which enabled them to organize indigenous officer corps.[37] But the Marathas, the Sikhs, and the Mysore kingdom never realized the importance of secular modern learning for conducting warfare.

Again, those Asian rulers who attempted assimilation of the Western techniques of warfare met serious obstacles from their nobility who happened to be leaders of the traditional-style military contingents. The latter were jealous of the high perquisites and influence enjoyed by the foreign mercenary commanders in the courts of the Asian rulers. When Sultan Selim III tried to Westernize the Ottoman army in response to the Russian military threat, he faced tough opposition from the traditional Ottoman warriors, the *Janissaries*.[38] Similarly, Mahadji Sindia faced tough opposition from his *sardars* (Maratha *jagirdars*) while implementing the programme of partial Europeanization in response to the military threat posed by the EIC. Due to the *sardars'* hostility, between 1788-90, Sindia failed to increase the number of Western-style infantry battalions from two to ten.[39]

Again, the English and the Portuguese officers were hated by their Indian subordinates. In 1809, the Maratha soldiers turned out the *topiwalahs* (men with hats, i.e. their European commanders) from Sindia's infantry battalions.[40]

In the 1830s, the Sikh *sardars'* hostility towards the European commanders in the Sikh army increased. One way of showing hostility was to withhold the pay of the European commanders. Unlike the irregular Sikh cavalry, the Western-trained soldiers in the Sikh army were paid in cash on a monthly basis in imitation of the EIC. In 1834, the pay of many European commanders and their soldiers remained in arrears for two months.[41] In the long run, this resulted in divided loyalties on the part of the latter. How far were the major Indian powers successful in implementing and adopting the programme of partial Europeanization?

1. Mysore (1780-1799)

In the 1720s, cavalry and elephants constituted the core of the army. In addition, matchlock-armed infantry soldiers were recruited on a short-term basis. They were marginal peasants who joined the army to tide over unfavourable harvests, and after they were demobilized they returned to the land.[42]

The two tigers of Mysore, Haidar Ali and Tipu Sultan, Europeanized part of the Mysore force. Haidar Ali got the idea of Westernizing the force from his brother Mir Ismail, who was a general in the Mysore army. Mir Ismail, in 1751, purchased 2,000 muskets with bayonets and six cannons from the British in Bombay. He enrolled 30 European sailors from the Malabar coast for training his gunners. Thus, Mir Ismail created a corps of infantry armed with firelocks and bayonets and supported by field artillery. Haidar Ali imitated Mir Ismail's experiment on a bigger scale.[43] In 1767, Haidar Ali's field army was composed of 11,000 irregular cavalry and 12,000 infantry. About 8,000 of the infantry were armed with muskets and the remaining 4,000 with matchlocks. Some officers of the regular infantry were Eurasians from Pondicherry. These men had acquired military training under the French. Under Tipu the proportion of infantry vis-á-vis cavalry increased in the Mysore army. In the late 1780s, there were 23,000 infantry and only 3,500 irregular cavalry.[44]

This transition in the force structure resulted in a doctrinal shift as regards the conduct of warfare. While Haidar Ali ravaged

British-occupied Karnataka by conducting manoeuvre warfare with the aid of his light cavalry during 1767-8, Tipu Sultan after his father's death in 1781 reverted to positional warfare. This was because under Tipu the Mysore army became less mobile due to the dominance of the infantry-artillery system. Tipu with the help of French military engineers constructed a fort in his capital at Seringapatam. He equipped this fort with 929 stationary guns and concentrated 22,000 of his 48,000 infantry here. Seringapatam became the *schwerpunkt* of the British military operation in 1798.[45]

In response, the EIC's force became firepower heavy. The Company's army breached the walls of Seringapatam with round shots from forty 18-pdrs. and 24-pdrs. In addition, seven 8- and 5.5-inch howitzers were used for plunging fire inside the fort. There were also fifty-seven 6-pdrs. to provide fire support to the besieging British army against Tipu's infantry.[46] After Tipu's defeat, the Marathas remained the foremost challenge to British power in the Deccan.

2. The Marathas (1790-1818)

The chief strength of the Marathas is horse, the chief strength of Haidar infantry, cannon and small arms. From the one we have nothing to apprehend but ravages, plundering and loss revenues for a while, from the other extirpation.

CLIVE, 17 October 1766[47]

The Marathas probably realized the significance of Clive's statement, and attempted partial Europeanization to strengthen their forces. The various Marathas chiefs did not present as an united front in the game of the subcontinent's power politics. The four hereditary chief tains (Peshwa, Sindia, Holkar, and Bhonsle) represented the Maratha power. The Peshwa's first experiment with Westernized infantry occurred in 1760, when 10,000 infantry organized in battalions commanded by Ibrahim Gardi, the Muslim mercenary soldier trained by the French, joined the Marathas. Gardi's battalions fought against the Afghans during the Third Battle of Panipat in 1761.[48]

The Peshwa faced opposition from the Portuguese and the English traders while purchasing cannons and munitions. So he established a cannon-ball factory at Ambegavan in 1765 and another factory at Poona for manufacturing cannons. However, these factories failed to produce state-of-the-art products.[49] A Scottish officer, Major Dirom, noted, in 1793, the low technological level of the Peshwa's army in the following words:

The gun-carriages, in which they trust to the solidity of the timber, and use but little iron in their construction, are clumsy beyond belief; particularly the wheels, which are low, and formed of large solid pieces of wood united. The guns are of all sorts and dimensions ... although in every respect unfit for use. Were the guns even serviceable, the small supply of ammunition with which they are provided has always effectually prevented the Maratha artillery from being formidable to their enemies.[50]

Mahadji Sindia was more successful than the Peshwa in producing artillery, gun carriages, and gunpowder. Sindia's Western-style infantry battalions were equipped with 4-, 8-, and 12-pdrs. field guns.[51] A British officer who had participated in the Second Maratha War (1803-5) expressed his anxiety about Daulat Rao (nephew of Mahadji) Sindia's force in the following words: 'It is in the Art of Artillery and Engineering alone that the Country Powers, have never yet been able to rival us, though of late years they have been making rapid strides towards it.'[52]

Gradually, not only did the level of Westernization within the Maratha forces increase but Sindia's battalions also reached technological parity with the Company's forces. Partial Europeanization among Sindia's troops was more effective than in the case of Tipu's troops. The Duke of Wellington after fighting the Battle of Assaye informed his brother Henry Wellesley about the military capacity of his opponents in the following words: 'Sindia's French [trained] infantry were far better than Tipu's, his artillery excellent, and his ordnance so good, and so well equipped, that it answers for our service. We never could use Tipu's. Our loss is great, but the action, I believe, was the most severe that ever was fought in this country.'[53]

Despite achieving parity in military hardware, the Marathas failed to solve the doctrinal problem which they faced due to the partial Westernization of their force structure. As a result, they had to pay heavily during their struggle against the British. At the beginning of the eighteenth century, when the Maratha army was composed of light cavalry, they conducted long-range

From Hydaspes to Kargil

mobile guerrilla raids. Though Sindia created a Western-style infantry supported by field artillery, he also retained the traditional Maratha light cavalry. The infantry-field artillery combine could not conduct high-speed guerrilla warfare. Hence, from 1790 onwards, there was a partial shift in the Maratha theory of warfare. With the Westernized infantry and field artillery, the Marathas during Second Maratha War (1803-5) decided to conduct pitched battles. But in such encounters the Maratha cavalry had no role to play because they could not create a shock effect on the enemy ranks by charging simultaneously as could be done by the disciplined heavy British cavalry. Table 1 shows that at the Battle of Assaye (23 September 1803), Sindia's

TABLE 1: DECISIVE BATTLES FOUGHT IN THE FIRST HALF OF THE NINETEENTH CENTURY

Name of battle	Date	Number of troops deployed by the Indian power	Number of soldiers deployed by the EIC	Killed and wounded among the soldiers of the Indian powers	Killed and wounded among the EIC's soldiers
Assaye	23 Sept. 1803	10,000 infantry of Daulat Rao Sindia + 100 guns	8,900 infantry + 1,600 cavalry	KIA = 1,200 WIA = 4,800	KIA = 428 WIA = 1,138 40 per cent casualties among the British contingent of the EIC
Mudki	18 Dec. 1845	12,000 Sikh *infantry + 22 guns	12,350 soldiers + 41 guns		KIA = 215 WIA = 657 Total = 872
Ferozeshah	21 Dec. 1845	60,000 Sikh infantry + 73 guns	35,000 soldiers	KIA = 2,000 WIA = 3,000	KIA = 900 WIA = 2,100 This battle was the only one which lasted for two days.
Sobraon	10 Feb. 1846	30,000 Sikh infantry + 70 guns	30,000 soldiers + 99 guns	KIA + WIA = 10,000	KIA = 320 WIA = 2,063

Chillianwala	13 Jan. 1849	20,000 Sikh infantry + 60 guns	12,000 infantry + 3000 cavalry	Total loss = 89 officers + 2,357 men KIA = 5 per cent of the total force WIA = 12 per cent of the total force

Notes: KIA = Killed in Action; WIA = Wounded in Action
Blank spaces denote that reliable figures are not available.
The Indian irregular cavalry did not take any part in these battles.
Hence, their figures have been omitted here.
* 10,000 disciplined, 2,000 indisciplined.

Sources   Charles Gough and Arthur D. Innes, *The Sikhs and the Sikh Wars: The Rise, Conquest and Annexation of the Punjab State*, 1897, rpt, Delhi: Gian Publishing, 1986, pp. 77-8; Reginald Hodder, 'The Sikhs and the Sikh Wars', *Panjab Past and Present*, vol. 4, no. 1, 1970, pp. 96-7, 100; Lieutenant Colonel H.M. Sinclair, 'Second Sikh War: 1848-49', *Journal of the United Service Institution of India* (henceforth *JUSII*), vol. 28, 1899, pp. 233-5; Captain R.G. Burton, 'Battles of the Deccan', *JUSII*, vol. 20, no. 84, 1891, pp. 166-7; Lieutenant Colonel W.D. Bird, 'The Assaye Campaign', *JUSII*, vol. XLI, no. 187, 1912, p. 117; A.S. Bennell, 'The Anglo-Maratha War of 1803-05', *Journal of the Society for Army Historical Research*, (Autumn 1985), p. 154; The Marquess of Anglesey (ed.), *Sergeant Pearman's Memoirs ... in India from 1845-53*, London: Jonathan Cape, 1968, pp. 32, 51, 90-3; Colonel Lewis, 'Campaign on the Sutlej: 1845-46' *Journal of the Corps of Royal Engineers*, vol. XLIX, 1849, pp. 156-8, 163-5; Ganda Singh, 'Colonel Mouton's Account of the First Sikh War: 1845-46', *Panjab Past and Present*, vol. 15, no. 29, 1981, p. 122.

infantry only slightly exceeded Wellington's soldiers. The combined light cavalry of Sindia and Bhonsle amounted to 35,000. But they remained mute spectators in the ensuing encounter.[54]

The officer corps constitutes the brain of an army. The officer corps of Daulat Rao Sindia's infantry battalions disintegrated before the onset of the war with the EIC in 1803. The British officers deserted just before the war. The dismissal of the Eurasian officers on grounds of suspicion further exacerbated the situation. The Marathas lacked officers with requisite staff training to fill up these vacant posts. Hence, unit-level co-ordination was lost in the heat of the battle.[55]

After the collapse of Daulat Rao Sindia's regular infantry-artillery combine at Assaye, Jaswant Rao Holkar reverted to the traditional *ganimi kava*. The British were overconfident that they would be able to easily checkmate the Maratha cavalry raids. This was evident in Wellington's letter to Lieutenant Colonel Thomas Munro, dated 1 October 1803:

I think that ... the possibility of checking, by defensive measures, a predatory war, carried on by horse only. ... The fact is, that a predatory war is not to be carried on now as it was formerly. All the principal villages in the country are fortified. ... a few peons [irregular infantry armed with matchlocks] keep the horse out; and it is consequently necessary that they should have a camp and a *bazar* to resort to for subsistence, in which every thing they get. ..[56]

In response, Holkar's force structure witnessed an innovation. Instead of depending totally on the light Maratha cavalry, Holkar came up with an integrated force of light cavalry supported by about 200 light guns. This provided increased firepower to his cavalry force, which raided British territories. Thus, Holkar was able to destroy Colonel Monsoon's battle group of 4,000 infantry which had integral artillery support.[57] Against Holkar's high-speed cavalry warfare, the slow-moving infantry and artillery of the Company had no answer. Holkar continued to carry fire and sword in west and north India till 1805.[58] Holkar was also able to cut the supply lines of the British General Lord Lake's force which was shadowing him in north India. A British participant observed on 9 October 1804: 'Halt again! I fear grain is scarce and that this causes the delay—these infernal Marathas even cut off all communications.'[59] Thus, even after the Second Maratha War (1803-5), the Marathas were not extinguished. The Third Maratha War decided the issue in 1817-18.

As a reaction to the treachery of the European officers during 1803, the Marathas relied on an amalgam of *ganimi kava* and positional warfare between 1817-18. While the Maratha chiefs with their cavalry marched up and down, their bases remained some hitherto inaccessible forts. For conducting predatory warfare, the Maratha chieftains hired the Pindari light cavalry. The Pindaris were troopers demobilized from those Indian states that were annexed by the EIC. The Pindaris were armed with 12-foot long spears, somewhat similar to the *sarissa* of Alexander's soldiers. They ravaged and desolated central India.[60] The

Marathas mobilized 78,000 cavalry and 27,000 light Pindari cavalry.[61]

In reaction, the EIC mobilized a bigger army than that deployed during the Second Maratha War. While during 1803-5, the British mobilized only 56,000 soldiers,[62] during 1817-18, the EIC mobilized 1,10,400 soldiers. This time the EIC deployed a large contingent of light cavalry to check Maratha depredations and numerous heavy guns to take the forts. The British were able to capture the forts (which functioned as bases of the Maratha cavalry) thanks to two scientific elements imported from West Europe: engineers and sappers plus heavy ordnance. The British took the fort of Hathras by concentrating 44 mortars.[63] In February 1818, a fort near Satara was captured with the aid of two 5.2-inch howitzers. The location of the Seogarh fort on a hill meant that there was no road for dragging the heavy guns near the wall of the fort. The European engineers solved this problem by constructing a road under the covering fire provided by the 8-inch mortars, and then several breaching batteries were set up near the fort's wall. While these siege guns blasted the masonry, the garrison armed with matchlocks inside the fort had no chance to fight back.[64] It marked, the twilight of the Maratha Confederacy.

3. The Sikhs (1821-1846)

After the collapse of the Marathas, the Khalsa kingdom emerged as the chief competitor of the EIC. The Sikh force before the advent of Ranjit Singh was composed of irregular cavalry under the command of various semi-autonomous chiefs.[65] Ranjit Singh was able to transform a part of the predatory levies of the Sikh horsemen into an army composed of Western-style infantry and artillery. The presence of the European-style infantry of the military entrepreneur George Thomas in Haryana and the failure of the Sikh cavalry against him convinced Ranjit Singh that partial Westernization of the army was necessary.[66] Thanks to the free-floating mercenaries available in the military labour market of India, Ranjit Singh was able to Westernize part of his force. Ranjit Singh had about 50 European officers (English, Italian, Eurasian, Spanish, American, etc.) on his payrolls. Court, a French officer, trained his artillery. Ventura, who trained the infantry, was an Italian.[67]

By 1838, Ranjit Singh's Europeanized contingent comprised 38,000 infantry and 4,000 gunners.[68] The qualitative improvement of the Europeanized contingent of the Khalsa army was sufficient enough to cause consternation among the EIC's observers. Ranjit Singh held a review of his Westernized troops in 1838 allegedly in honour of Governor General Auckland's visit to Punjab but in reality this was an act of deterrent diplomacy. On 6 December 1838, Auckland's sister Fanny Eden noted in her journal:

Ranjit had a review of his troops yesterday and all our people are in astonishment at his state of discipline, and the very superior way in which they performed their manoeuvres ... but I have a notion from what I can gather that our review was a remarkable poor piece of business, compared to theirs. William and I rode through a bit of their camp this morning and they were very quiet but I am rather afraid of them.[69]

Thanks to the strenuous attempts of Ranjit Singh, the Company's troops enjoyed no technological edge over the Europeanized contingent of the Khalsa army just before the First Sikh War in 1845. Both the Sikhs and the Company's infantry used Brown Bess muskets, and the quality of Sikh artillery was equal to that of the Company's artillery.[70]

Ranjit Singh was afraid that in case of war with the EIC, his European military advisers would desert him just as Daulat Rao Sindia's European officers had done. Ranjit Singh took certain steps for the Punjabization of his foreign officer corps. During their appointment, the European officers were bound by oath to domesticate themselves by marrying Indians and if required they would have to fight against their own country. After Ranjit Singh's death, due to the hostility of the Sikh chiefs, most of the European officers were forced to leave the Khalsa army. The chiefs themselves lacked staff training to fill up the vacuum, and there was intense rivalry among them. Hence, the European contingent within the Khalsa army had neither trust nor respect for the chieftains. Just before the war with the EIC, the Khalsa army was an organization without a head.[71]

The Sikh infantry fired in three ranks, the front one kneeling when firing (so that the men in the ranks behind them could also fire simultaneously) and then rising to load. However, their firing was poor because the government allowed a very small quantity of practice ammunition. Only ten shots out of a hundred fell upon the target.[72] This proved to be a serious weakness because the EIC introduced target practice with ball ammunition at least twice a week.[73]

The principal tactical deficiency of the Sikh army, like that of the Maratha army, was the absence of an adequate number of Western-style heavy cavalry which could be used for shock effect in pitched battles. Ranjit Singh had hired Jean Francois Allard who as a captain of the *cuirassiers* had fought with Napoleon Bonaparte at Waterloo. However, Ranjit Singh never allowed him to train more than 2,000 dragoons and 1,000 lancers.[74] This was probably due to the opposition of the Sikh irregular cavalrymen who were sons, relatives and retainers of the *sardars*.[75] Ranjit Singh's successors continued to depend upon irregular cavalry. Henry Steinbach, a Prussian officer employed by the Sikhs, observed the following points about the Sikh irregular cavalry in 1846:

The cavalry of the Sikh army is very inferior in every respect to the infantry. While the latter are carefully picked from large bodies of candidates for service, the former are composed of men of all sorts and sizes and ages, who get appointed solely through the interest of the different sirdars. They are mean-looking, ill dressed and, as already stated, wretchedly mounted. Their horse trappings are of leather of the worst quality.[76]

Since the Sikh irregular troopers armed at random with spears and matchlocks and lacking discipline like their Maratha counterparts were unable to stand up in their stirrups to deliver a concentrated blow, they were no match in the cavalry versus cavalry combat on the battlefield. As a result, the EIC's regular cavalry, assisted by the firepower of the mobile horse artillery, was always able to drive away Sikh cavalry and turn the flanks of Sikh infantry during the battles.[77]

THE CHANGING FACE OF BATTLES IN POST-MUGHAL INDIA

How did partial Westernization among the indigenous powers change the architecture of military confrontations? The labour-intensive Indian militaries became capital-intensive. The chief features of the battles fought were the absence of elephants as battering rams and the disappearance of the horse archers. The prominence of a sabre-rattling and lance-wielding cavalry was replaced by that of artillery and a firepower-heavy infantry.

The battles fought in the eighteenth century were in keeping with the Mughal military tradition. On 9 April 1740, the Battle of Giria between the governor of Bihar Ali Vardi Khan and the *Nawab* of Bengal Sarfaraz Khan was mostly a cavalry encounter. Ali Vardi had 8,000 cavalry against the *Nawab's* 4,000 cavalry. Ali Vardi used an elephant as a command vehicle. Again, in March 1776, Zabita Khan, the Rohilla chief, with 30,000 cavalry fought the Mughal chieftain Najaf Khan who brought into the field 2,000 cavalry and a huge number of irregular infantry. In this battle, cavalry functioned as the decisive shock weapon which scattered Najaf Khan's irregular cavalry. Most of the wounds inflicted on the soldiers were due to arrows and sword cuts.[78]

But in the military encounters of the first half of the nineteenth century, most of the combatants were killed and wounded by artillery and small arms fire. This trend was consonant with that in Europe where artillery and small arms emerged as the principal 'killers' on the battlefield.[79] Back in post-1800 India, elephants were no longer used as a command platform. The battles also revealed the impotence of irregular cavalry against the infantry-artillery combination. In July 1801, at the Battle of Narmada, Jaswant Rao Holkar deployed 10,000 light cavalry. Daulat Rao Sindia's four infantry battalions and 52 guns opposed him. Holkar's repeated cavalry charge failed to make any impact on Sindia's infantry-artillery system. But the shots and shells from Sindia's guns caused much bloodshed and loss among Holkar's cavalry.[80]

The increasing role of infantry and artillery in the battles fought between the Indian powers and the EIC during the first half of the nineteenth century is evident from Table 1. The confrontation between opposing regular infantry supported by field artillery constituted the chief feature of these battles.

What about the experience of battle for the soldiers? A British officer described the fiery charge of the Gurkhas during the Nepal War of 1814-15 in the following words: 'A crowd of men rushing on in disorder like a pack of hounds in full cry, to the harsh sound of huge trumpets.'[81]

Battles were bloody and messy. On 18 December 1845, during

the First Sikh War, about 10,000 Sikh Westernized infantry and irregular cavalry with 22 guns attacked 10,000 of the Company's infantry at Mudki. The Sikh cannonade was very effective. Trooper N.W. Bancroft of the Bengal Horse Artillery remembered: 'Round shot from the enemy's artillery began rolling and plunging among the horses' legs like so many cricket balls, but were not quite so harmless as they look, for they broke several of our horses' legs.'[82]

Sergeant Pearman of the EIC was also fully aware of the dangerous impact created by the Sikh artillery. About the Battle of Sobraon that was fought on 10 February 1846 Pearman wrote:

They [Sikhs] soon returned the fire from the numerous batteries in their entrenchments. After a few shots to try the range, their practice became really admirable. ... We must have been at the time from 1000 to 1200 yards from the enemy. ... But a very short time had elapsed when their round shot shells and shrapnel came as fast as possible to our own batteries. ... Such a cannonade and noise as was now taking place, no thunder was ever equal to.[83]

MILITARY SYNTHESIS IN THE COMPANY'S ARMY: 1750-1849

Certain European military techniques gave the Western powers an edge over their Afro-Asian opponents but these were inadequate for gaining total military superiority in the extra-European world.[84] The absorption and accommodation of certain Indian military elements within the gamut of the Western-oriented military machine not only allowed the EIC to destroy Mysore, the Maratha Confederacy, and the Sikh kingdom but this step also enabled the Company to project military power outside South Asia.

Most of the EIC's British infantry and gunners were urban recruits unlike the European-style infantry of the indigenous powers. Hence, the Company's British regulars were more adaptive to technological changes than the peasant soldiers of India.[85] But white infantry soldiers were available only in very small numbers. Further, they became easy victims to India's hot and humid climate. Death from fever, apoplexy, and cholera further ravaged the limited white military manpower. Hence, the recruitment of brown manpower into the regiments (a unit of about 1,000 infantry soldiers) was a necessity for the British. The biggest British achievement was in importing the European infantry system into India, and then training the Indians into sepoys. Though the French had started this practice, the British were more successful in extending this sepoy system. In June 1757, before the Battle of Plassey, Clive organized the sepoys into regular regiments with some European officers. Each unit had about 820 sepoys.[86]

Officers constitute the directing body of an army. Unlike the Marathas and the Sikhs, the EIC was able to create a professional officer corps. In contrast to the indigenous rulers, the Company's officials were able to transform the motley group of military adventurers into a self-conscious officer corps with its own corporate ethos.[87] There existed a considerable cultural and linguistic gap between the white officers and the brown sepoys. So the EIC trained Indians as non-commissioned officers who functioned as a bridge between the white officers and the sepoys.[88]

Military imperatives made it necessary for the EIC to recruit irregular infantry, and in this regard the Company followed the footsteps of the Indian rulers. The Company's infantry operating in line formation and practicing volley firing did not prove to be suitable in hilly terrain covered with forests. During the Nepal War (1814-15), the EIC made use of 4,000 irregular Rohilla infantry. Recruitment of the Rohillas was a continuation of Maratha military policy. However, the EIC, unlike Raghuji Bhonsle, did not make wrong tactical use of them. Instead of using them in pitched encounters, the British used irregular infantry as skirmishers and sharpshooters. They were encouraged to use their initiative to take aimed shots at the enemy soldiers.[89] Ranjit Singh recruited the Gurkhas because they were excellent light infantry. They took advantage of the terrain to ambush the Company's infantry in rigid formation. Hence, after 1815, the EIC started recruiting the Gurkhas as light infantry.[90]

Disciplined British heavy cavalry (partially armoured trooper riding on bigger horses) played a crucial role by repeatedly turning the flanks of the Indian armies in battles. Nevertheless, due to the huge extent of the Indian theatre of operations, the military forces were stretched to the limit. This in turn required the maintenance of a large number of light cavalry for reconnaissance, foraging, and intelligence gathering activities by every contending power. This point is relevant for the Russian theatre of operations also. An inadequate number of light cavalry hampered both British and Czarist military operations in the subcontinent and in Central Asia. The absence of such a cavalry force created difficulties for the Company's infantry-artillery-oriented military machine during the First Maratha War and in the campaigns against Haidar Ali.[91] The Maratha and Mysore cavalry fought like the Crimean Tatars. In the seventeenth century, the Czarist army, like the EIC's force, was composed of infantry and artillery and found it difficult to come to grips with them. Hence, Czarist Russia attempted a sort of military synthesis by employing the Kalmyk Mongol light cavalry to checkmate the Tatars.[92]

Similarly, in 1792, to check the depredations of Tipù's light cavalry, the EIC hired the Marathas who provided 32,000 cavalry. By plundering Tipu's domain, not only did they create logistical difficulties for the Mysore troops but they also provided these supplies to the Company's army.[93] But in the long run it was dangerous to depend on the Marathas because of the probability of war with them. During the First Maratha War (1774-83), the British Indian army, which advanced from Bombay, did not achieve much due to Maratha superiority in light cavalry. The Marathas were able to impede the march of the EIC's force by ravaging and burning the countryside in order to deny supplies and attacked the British supply convoys.[94] One reason for the destruction of Colonel Monsoon's force during the Second Maratha War in 1804 was Jaswant Rao Holkar's superiority in light cavalry.[95] So the EIC, like the Indian powers, started maintaining irregular cavalry for dispersed outpost duties like scouting, foraging, etc. This was because the big British horses were not suited for such duties and the British troopers found such duties in India's hot climate very tiresome. Moreover, the British found the irregular cavalry much cheaper to maintain. The EIC recruited upper-class Muslims from Awadh for this branch just as the Awadh *Nawabs* had done.[96]

A part of the north Indian light cavalry contingent of Sindia was absorbed within the Company's military machine. The Skinner Irregular Regiment commanded by the Eurasian Captain

James Skinner left Daulat Rao Sindia and joined the Company. Bishop Heber wrote in 1824:

The commander of the party had a long spear with a small yellow pennon, the others had each a long matchlock-gun which they carried on the right shoulder with the match ready lighted. ... They are reckoned, by all the English in this part of the country, the most useful and trusty, as well as the boldest body of men in India, and during the wars both of Lord Lake and Lord Hastings their services and those of their chief were most distinguished.[97]

Technology played a vital role in the conduct of warfare. Deployment of quantitatively and qualitatively superior field artillery was one of the principal reasons behind the continuous British victories. The British officers were aware of this factor. In the battles against the Sikhs, whenever the EIC was unable to deploy superior field artillery, the goddess of victory left them. The Second Sikh War (1848-9) involved several hard-fought battles. At the Battle of Ramnagar, General Hugh Gough deployed 12,500 infantry and 3,500 cavalry against the force commanded by Sher Singh. Due to an inadequate quantity of field artillery, Gough failed to defeat the Sikhs.[98] At the Battle of Gujerat fought on 21 February 1849, Gough deployed 96 guns while Sher Singh lacked field artillery. Gough's tactics was to fix the Sikh army's centre with his infantry. Then the flanks of the Khalsa army were turned by heavy British cavalry acting in conjunction with fire support from horse artillery. Sher Singh's light cavalry armed with lances was overwhelmed by firepower from the artillery.[99]

Systematization of the supply of heavy artillery to the Company's force was secured by establishing a chain of Western-style arsenals and ordnance factories.[100] These factories utilized the raw materials of the subcontinent to produce military stores. To ensure the steady supply of raw materials to these arsenals, Clive, in 1758, imposed a monopoly of the saltpetre (the essential ingredient of gunpowder) trade for the Company. The Company's traders were not to be taxed by the *Nawab's* officials and nor were any Indian traders allowed to buy saltpetre in Bengal, Bihar, and Orissa.[101]

The Company's commissariat system represented the most powerful example of military synthesis. In 1791, due to the failure of supplies, Lord Cornwallis had to retreat from

Bangalore before Tipu's army.[102] Both General Lake in north India and Wellington in the Deccan depended on the cattle taken from Mysore for carrying baggage and on the *banjaras* (grain traders who had supplied the armies in India from the medieval period) for grain.[103] The EIC continued the Mughal tradition of using elephants for dragging the heavy guns in road-less terrain. In 1824, during the First Burma War, the Company used elephants for dragging 6-pdrs. guns through the jungles and hilly tracts of Arakan.[104]

Wellington was known for his expertise in crossing rivers and marching quickly in order to catch up with the Maratha cavalry. After the 1803 campaign, he commented to a fellow officer: 'I think we now begin to beat the Marathas in the celerity of our movements.'[105] One way he accomplished this was by crossing bridgeless rivers in the Deccan. He used basket boats which the Indians used for crossing the streams. These were about 10 feet in diameter and 2 feet and 3 inches high.[106]

After the Sikh defeat at Ferozeshah in 1845, the Company's army quickly crossed the Sutlej and moved into Punjab without giving any respite to the Sikhs to recuperate and reorganize any further defence. The British engineers quickly forded the Sutlej by adopting indigenous techniques. The Sikhs crossed rivers in boats whose bottoms were made of thick cedar planks spiked together with siswoo wood. These boats known as *chuppoos* were tied together to form a bridge. The British used these boats to ferry the infantry across the river,[107] and the Sikh kingdom passed into history.

CONCLUSION

The eighteenth century and the first half of the nineteenth century constituted a crucial interface between the collapse of the Mughal *imperium* and the emergence of the British colonial system. This period represented both continuity and change. If we take a *longue duree* perspective, then it is evident that the two elements that dominated the Indian military scenario from the ninth century, i.e. war elephants and horse archers, withered away. In their place came firearms equipped, drilled, and disciplined infantry, and field artillery. Forts which played a key role in Maratha military strategy became obsolete due to the rapid advance in siege artillery introduced by the British. The *jagirdari* system was replaced by the battalion-cum-regimental system, characterized by the emergence of quasi-centralized military bureaucracies.

The supremacy of Western warfare was not necessarily self-evident in India. Indian rulers did not blindly imitate the Western military system but rather they attempted a creative imitation by a selective assimilation of European elements of warfare. Their aim was to supplement the traditional fighting elements with partial Westernization. So both the Indian kingdoms and the EIC attempted the construction of hybrid military organizations. While the Indian rulers failed in this venture, the EIC succeeded. This was because the Indian princes failed to realize the importance of Western-style cavalry and horse artillery for conducting pitched battles. But the EIC understood the importance of light cavalry and irregular infantry for military operations in India. Besides mortars and howitzers, the induction of Indian light cavalry, manpower, and elephants as commissariat vehicles created a synergy, and this enabled the British to emerge as the chief power broker in South Asia.

NOTES

1. Martin Blumenson, 'The Development of the Modern Military', *Armed Forces and Society*, vol. 6, no. 4, 1980, pp. 670-5.
2. James Michael Hill, 'The Distinctiveness of Gaelic Warfare: 1400-1750', *European History Quarterly*, vol. 22, no. 3, 1992, p. 337; Bert S. Hall and Kelly De Vries, 'Essay Review: The "Military Revolution" Revisited', *Technology and Culture*, vol. 31, no. 3, 1990, p. 502; Knud J.V. Jespersen, 'Social Change and Military Revolution in Early Modern Europe: Some Danish Evidence', *Historical Journal*, vol. 26, no. 1, 1983, pp. 1-2; Michael Howard, *War in European History*, 1976, rpt, Oxford: Oxford University Press, 1977, pp. 61, 78; Hew Strachan, *European Armies and the Conduct of War*, 1983, rpt, London: Routledge, 1993, p. 33; General John Hackett, *The Profession of Arms*, 1983, rpt, London: Sidgwick & Jackson, 1984, pp. 56-64.
3. Jeremy Black, *A Military Revolution?: Military Change and European Society, 1550-1800*, Basingstoke: Macmillan, 1991.

4. Geoffrey Parker, 'The "Military Revolution, 1560-1660"—A Myth?', in Clifford J. Rogers (ed.), *The Military Revolution Debate: Readings on the Military Transformation of Early Modern Europe*, Boulder: Westview, 1995, pp. 37-54.

5. Clifford J. Rogers, 'The Military Revolutions of the Hundred Years War', in idem, *Military Revolution Debate*, pp. 55-93.

6. Lieutenant F.G. Cardew, *A Sketch of the Services of the Bengal Native Army to the Year 1895*, 1903, rpt, New Delhi: Today & Tomorrow's Publishers, 1971, pp. 2-32.

7. D.C. Verma, *Plassey to Buxar: A Military Study*, New Delhi: K.B. Publications, 1976, p. 92.

8. Michael Edwardes, *Clive: The Heaven-Born General*, London: Hart-Davis, 1977, pp. 10-11.

9. Geoffrey Parker, *The Military Revolution: Military Innovation and the Rise of the West, 1500-1800*, Cambridge: Cambridge University Press, 1988, pp. 4-5, 115, 117, 125-36.

10. Pradeep Barua, 'Military Developments in India: 1750-1850', *Journal of Military History*, vol. 58, no. 4, 1994, p. 616; Stewart Gordon, 'The Limited Adoption of European-Style Military Forces by Eighteenth-Century Rulers in India', *Indian Economic and Social History Review* (henceforth *IESHR*), vol. 35, no. 3, 1998, pp. 229-45.

11. Why did the British win against the French? This was because the East India Company, unlike the French, adapted its polity and military in accordance with the demands of South Asian ecology. A proper synthesis in the sphere of the Company's military intelligence was also vital.

12. The focus is on war on land because, India being a continental land-mass, naval supremacy did not yield control over the subcontinent. As Chapters 2 and 3 show, throughout history, only land powers like the Central Asian Turks have been able to dominate India. From the eighteenth century onwards, the British constructed an army for land operations in India. Only then did the East India Company become a serious contender for power politics in the subcontinent.

13. Jagadish Narayan Sarkar, *The Art of War in Medieval India*, New Delhi: Munshiram Manoharlal, 1984, pp. 62, 81-2.

14. Fauja Singh Bajwa, *Military System of the Sikhs during the period 1799-1849*, Delhi: Motilal Banarasidas, 1964, p. 1; Shelford Bidwell, *Swords for Hire: European Mercenaries in Eighteenth-Century India*, London: John Murray, 1971, pp. 2, 4; Jadunath Sarkar, *Fall of the Mughal Empire: 1754-1771*, vol. 2, 1934, rpt, New Delhi: Orient Longman, 1991, p. 174.

15. Jos J.L. Gommans, 'Indian Warfare and Afghan Innovation during the Eighteenth Century', *Studies in History*, new series, vol. 11, no. 2, 1995, pp. 267-8; Steven T. Ross, *From Flintlock to Rifle: Infantry Tactics, 1740-1866*, 1979, rpt, London: Frank Cass, 1996, p. 168.

16. Jos J.L. Gommans, *The Rise of the Indo-Afghan Empire: c. 1710-80*, Leiden: E.J. Brill, 1995, pp. 4-5, 176-7.
17. Ghulam Muhammad (ed.), *The History of Haidar Ali and Tipu Sultan: A Contemporary History*, by MMDLT, General of the Mughal Army, 1855, rpt, Delhi: Cosmo, 1976, p. 33.
18. Yusuf Ali Khan, *The Tarikh-i-Mahabatjangi*, tr. Abdus Subhan, Calcutta: Asiatic Society, 1982, pp. 27-36.
19. Jadunath Sarkar, *Fall of the Mughal Empire: 1780-1803*, vol. 4, 1950, rpt, New Delhi: Orient Longman, 1992, p. 85.
20. George Forster, *A Journey from Bengal to England through the Northern Part of India, Kashmir, Afghanistan, and Persia and into Russia, by the Caspian Sea 1782-84*, vol. 1, 1798, rpt, New Delhi: Munshiram Manoharlal, 1997, pp. 288-9.
21. Frank Tallett, *War and Society in Early Modern Europe: 1495-1715*, 1992, rpt, London: Routledge, 1997, p. 31.
22. Ganda Singh, 'Colonel Polier's Account of the Sikhs', *Panjab Past and Present*, vol. 4, 1970, pp. 239, 243.
23. Jadunath Sarkar, *Mughal Empire*, vol. 4, p. 1.
24. Jadunath Sarkar, *Fall of the Mughal Empire: 1771-78*, vol. 3, 1938, rpt, New Delhi: Orient Longman, 1991, p. 60.
25. Ibid., p. 180; William R. Pinch, 'Who was Himmat Bahadur?: Gosains, Rajputs and the British in Bundelkhand, ca. 1800', *IESHR*, vol. 35, no. 3, 1998, pp. 293-4; W.L. M'Gregor, *The History of the Sikhs*, vol. 1, 1846, rpt, Allahabad: R.S. Publishing House, 1979, pp. 236-7.
26. Muhammad, *Haidar Ali and Tipu Sultan*, pp. 21, 28.
27. Major Lewis Ferdinand Smith, *A Sketch of the Rise, Progress, and Termination of the Regular Corps ... of the Native Princes of India with the Principal Events and Actions of the Late Maratha War*, Calcutta: J. Greenway and Harkaru Press, 1804, p. 14.
28. Colonel G.B. Malleson, *The Decisive Battles of India: 1746-1849*, 1885, rpt, Jaipur: Aavishkar Publisher, 1986, p. 280.
29. Captain R.G. Burton, 'Argaum', *JUSII*, vol. 28, 1899, pp. 297-8.
30. James Grant Duff, *History of the Marathas*, 3 vols combined, 1863, rpt, Delhi: Low Price Publications, 1990, vol. 1, p. 401, vol. 2, p. 261; Mohammed Moienuddin, 'Role of Tipu Sultan in the Progress of Mysore State', in Anniruddha Ray (ed.), *Tipu Sultan and His Age: A Collection of Seminar Papers*, Kolkata: The Asiatic Society, 2002, p. 33.
31. Colonel Lewis, 'Campaign on the Sutlej: 1845-46', *Journal of the Royal Engineers* (hereafter *JRE*), vol. XLIX, 1849, pp. 161, 164; Reginald Hodder, 'The Sikhs and the Sikh Wars', *Panjab Past and Present*, vol. 4, no. 1, 1970, pp. 103-4.
32. Captain F.R. Lee, 'An Ancient Weapon of India', *JUSII*, vol. XLI, no. 187, 1912, pp. 189-92.

33. C.R. Boxer, 'Asian Potentates and European Artillery in the 16th-18th Centuries: A Footnote to Gibson–Hill', *Journal of the Malaysian Branch of the Royal Asiatic Society*, vol. 38, no. 208, 1966, pp. 156-72.

34. D.C. Ganguly (ed.), *Select Documents of the British Period of Indian History*, Calcutta: The Trustees of the Victoria Memorial, 1958, Treaty between Clive and Shuja-ud-Daulah, 16 August 1765, p. 75.

35. John Pemble, *The Invasion of Nepal: John Company at War*, Oxford: Clarendon Press, 1971, p. 26.

36. Ganguly, *Select Documents*, Treaty between the EIC and Nepal, 2 December 1815, p. 228.

37. David B. Ralston, *Importing the European Army: The Introduction of European Military Techniques and Institutions into the Extra-European World, 1600-1914*, Chicago: University of Chicago Press, 1990, p. 175.

38. Stanford J. Shaw, 'The Origins of Ottoman Military Reform: The Nizam-i-Cedid Army of Sultan Selim III', *Journal of Modern History*, vol. 37, no. 3, 1963, pp. 291-2.

39. Herbert Compton, *A Particular Account of the European Military Adventurers of Hindustan from 1784 to 1803*, 1892, rpt, Karachi: Oxford University Press, 1976, pp. 44-5.

40. T.D. Broughton, *Letters Written in a Maratha Camp during the Year 1809*, 1892, rpt, New Delhi: Asian Educational Services, 1995, p. 218.

41. J.S. Grewal and Indu Banga (eds), *Civil and Military Affairs of Maharaja Ranjit Singh*, Amritsar: Guru Nanak Dev University, 1988, Document no. 122, p. 123.

42. Sanjay Subrahmanyam, 'Warfare and State Finance in Woodeyar Mysore, 1724-25: A Missionary Perspective', *IESHR*, vol. 26, no. 2, 1989, p. 215.

43. Muhammad, *Haidar Ali and Tipu Sultan*, p. 35.

44. N.K. Sinha, *Haidar Ali*, 1941, rpt, Calcutta: A. Mukherjee & Co. Pvt. Ltd., 1969, pp. 259, 262; Jadunath Sarkar, 'Haidar Ali's Invasion of the Eastern Carnatic: 1780', in Irfan Habib (ed.), *Confronting Colonialism: Resistance and Modernization under Haidar Ali and Tipu Sultan*, New Delhi: Tulika, 1999, p. 23.

45. Captain G.R.P. Wheatley, 'The Final Campaign against Tipu', *JUSII*, vol. XLI, no. 185, 1912, p. 254.

46. Ibid., p. 255; Major General B.P. Hughes, 'Siege Artillery in the Nineteenth Century', *Journal of the Society for Army Historical Research (henceforth JSAHR)*, no. 243, Autumn 1982, pp. 129, 145-6.

47. Quoted in A.C. Banerjee, *Peshwa Madhav Rao I*, 1943, rpt, Calcutta: A. Mukherjee & Co. Pvt. Ltd., 1968, pp. 86-7.

48. Lester Hutchinson, *European Freebooters in Moghul India*, Bombay: Asia Publishing House, 1964, p. 12.

49. *History of the Regiment of Artillery, Indian Army*, Published by the Artillery Headquarters, Dehra Dun: Palit & Dutt, 1971, pp. 8-9.

50. Major Dirom, *A Narrative of the Campaign in India which Terminated the War with Tipu Sultan in 1792*, 1793, rpt, New Delhi: Asian Educational Services, 1997, pp. 10-11.

51. Jean-Marie Lafont, *Indika: Essays in Indo-French Relations, 1630-1976*, New Delhi: Manohar, 2000, p. 179.

52. D.D. Khanna (ed.), *The Second Maratha Campaign, 1804-05: Diary of James Young, Officer of Bengal Horse Artillery*, New Delhi: Allied, 1990, 9 September 1804, pp. 7-8.

53. Antony Brett-James (ed.), *Wellington at War: 1794-1815, A Selections of His Wartime Letters*, London: Macmillan, 1961, 3 October 1803, pp. 84-5.

54. Captain R.G. Burton, 'Battles of the Deccan', *JUSII*, vol. 20, no. 84, 1891, pp. 166-7.

55. John Pemble, 'Resources and Techniques in the Second Maratha War', *Historical Journal*, vol. 19, no. 2, 1976, p. 394; Randolf G.S. Cooper, 'Wellington and the Marathas', *International History Review*, vol. 11, no. 1, 1989, p. 38.

56. Brett-James, *Wellington at War*, 1 October 1803, p. 83.

57. Khanna, *Diary of James Young*, p. 7.

58. A.S. Bennell, 'The Anglo-Maratha War of 1803-1805', *JSAHR*, Autumn 1985, pp. 155-9.

59. Khanna, *Diary of James Young*, 9 September 1804, p. 35.

60. M.P. Roy, *Origin, Growth and Suppression of the Pindaris*, New Delhi: Sterling, 1973, pp. 23-6.

61. B.K. Sinha, *The Pindaris: 1798-1818*, Calcutta: Bookland, 1971, pp. 155-6.

62. Lieutenant Colonel W.D. Bird, 'The Assaye Campaign', *JUSII*, vol. XLI, no. 187, 1912, p. 105.

63. Dirk H.A. Kolff, 'End of an *Ancien Regime*: Colonial War in India, 1798-1818', in J.A. De Moor and H.L. Wesseling (eds), *Imperialism and War: Essays on Colonial Wars in Asia and Africa*, Leiden: E.J. Brill, 1989, p. 44.

64. P.C. Gupta, 'John Macleod's Private Journal during the Maratha War, 1817-18', *Bengal Past and Present*, no. 190, 1981, pp. 74-9.

65. Forster, *Journey*, vol. 1, pp. 285-6.

66. Jean-Marie Lafont, 'Military Activities of French Officers of Maharaja Ranjit Singh', *Journal of Sikh Studies*, vol. 9, no. 1, 1982, pp. 32-3.

67. Hugh Cook, *The Sikh Wars: The British Army in Punjab, 1845-49*, New Delhi: Thomson Press, 1975, p. 17; Khushwant Singh, *Ranjit Singh, Maharajah of Punjab: 1780-1839*, London: George Allen & Unwin, 1962, p. 141.

68. N.K. Sinha, *Ranjit Singh*, 1933, rpt, Calcutta: Niva Mukherjee & Co. Pvt. Ltd., 1975, p. 157.

69. Janet Dunbar (ed.), *Tigers, Durbars and Kings: Fanny Eden's Indian Journals, 1837-38*, London: John Murray, 1988, pp. 176-7.

70. Charles Gough and Arthur Innes, *The Sikhs and the Sikh Wars: The Rise, Conquest and Annexation of the Punjab State*, 1897, rpt, Delhi: Gian Publishing, 1986, p. 67.

71. H.L.O. Garrett (ed.), C. Grey, *European Adventurers of Northern India: 1785-1849*, 1929, rpt, New Delhi: Asian Educational Services, 1993, p. 12; Ganda Singh, 'Colonel Mouton's Account of the First Sikh War: 1845-46', *Panjab Past and Present*, vol. 15, no. 29, 1981, pp. 117-27.

72. Henry Steinbach, *The Country of the Sikhs*, 1846, rpt, New Delhi: KLM Book House, 1978, p. 88.

73. Jac Weller, *Wellington in India*, London: Longman, 1972, p. 12.

74. C. Grey, *European Adventurers*, pp. 80, 82.

75. B.S. Nijjar, *Anglo-Sikh Wars: 1845-1849*, New Delhi: K.B. Publications, 1976, p. 106.

76. Steinbach, *Sikhs*, p. 89.

77. Donald Featherstone, *At Them with the Bayonet: The First Sikh War*, London: Jarrolds, 1968, p. 3; N.K. Sinha, *Rise of the Sikh Power*, 1936, rpt, Calcutta: University of Calcutta, 1946, p. 151.

78. Yusuf Ali Khan, *Tarikh*, pp. 13-6; Antoine Louis Henry Polier, *Shah Alam II and His Court*, edited with an Introduction, Notes and Appendices by P.C. Gupta, Calcutta: S.C. Sarkar & Sons Ltd., 1947, p. 43.

79. Christopher Duffy, *The Military Experience in the Age of Reason*, London: Routledge & Kegan Paul, 1987, p. 245.

80. Smith, *Maratha War*, pp. 13-14.

81. The quotation is from Colonel W.G. Hamilton, 'Ochterlony's Campaign in the Simla Hills—Some Further Notes On', *JUSII*, vol. XLI, no. 189, 1912, p. 456.

82. George Bruce, *Six Battles for India: The Anglo-Sikh Wars, 1845-46, 1848-49*, Calcutta: Rupa, 1969, pp. 109-10.

83. The Marquess of Anglesey (ed.), *Sergeant Pearman's Memoirs ... in India from 1845-53*, London: Jonathan Cape, 1968, pp. 52-3.

84. For the African case, see John K. Thornton, 'The Art of War in Angola: 1575-1680', *Comparative Studies in Society and History*, vol. 30, 1988, p. 377.

85. V.G. Kiernan, *European Empires from Conquest to Collapse: 1815-1960*, Bungay, Suffolk: Fontana, 1982, p. 15.

86. Lieutenant General S.L. Menezes, *Fidelity and Honour: The Indian Army from the Seventeenth to the Twenty-First Century*, New Delhi: Viking, 1993, p. 10; W.L. M'Gregor, *The History of the Sikhs*, vol. 2, 1846, rpt, Allahabad: R.S. Publishing House, 1979, pp. 78-9.

87. Raymond Callahan, *The East India Company and Army Reform: 1793-98*, Cambridge, Massachusetts: Harvard University Press, 1972, p. xi.

88. Lorenzo M. Crowell, 'Military Professionalism in a Colonial Context, circa 1832', *Modern Asian Studies*, vol. 24, 1990, pp. 259-63.
89. Colonel L.W. Shakespear, 'The War with Nepal: Operations in Sirmoor, 1814-15', *JUSII*, vol. XLII, no. 193, 1913, pp. 376-7.
90. Colonel W.G. Hamilton, 'Ochterlony's Campaign in the Simla Hills: 1814-15', *JUSII*, vol. XLI, no. 187, 1912, pp. 149-54.
91. G.J. Bryant, 'The Cavalry Problem in the Early British Indian Army, 1750-85', *War in History*, vol. 2, no. 1, 1995, pp. 2-3.
92. L.J.D. Collins, 'The Military Organization and Tactics of the Crimean Tatars, 16th-17th Centuries', in V.J. Parry and M.E. Yapp (eds), *War, Technology and Society in the Middle East*, London: Oxford University Press, 1975, p. 275.
93. Dirom, *A Narrative*, pp. 4, 9.
94. M.R. Kantak, *The First Anglo-Maratha War: 1774-1783, A Military Study of the Major Battles*, Bombay: Popular Prakashan, 1993, pp. 222-3.
95. Duff, *Marathas*, vol. 3, pp. 196-7.
96. Seema Alavi, *The Sepoys and the Company: Tradition and Transition in Northern India, 1770-1830*, Delhi: Oxford University Press, 1995, p. 18.
97. M.A. Laird (ed.), *Bishop Heber in Northern India: Selections from Heber's Journal*, Cambridge: Cambridge University Press, 1971, 28 December 1824, p. 224.
98. Lieutenant Colonel H.M. Sinclair, 'Second Sikh War: 1848-49', *JUSII*, vol. 28, 1899, pp. 229-31.
99. Ibid., and 'Discussion', *JUSII*, vol. 28, 1899, pp. 238-41.
100. Military Department, Proceedings of the Board of Ordnance, Letter from Captain Grant commanding at Buxar, to Ensign John Murray, Secy. to the Board of Ordnance, November 1775, p. 460, National Archives of India, New Delhi.
101. James P. Lawford, *Clive, Proconsul of India: A Biography*, London: George Allen, 1976, p. 277; Ganguly, *Select Documents*, p. 62.
102. E.W. Thompson, *The Last Siege of Seringapatam*, 1923, rpt, New Delhi: Asian Educational Services, 1990, p. 10.
103. Major H. Helsham Jones, 'The Campaigns of Lord Lake against the Marathas: 1804-6', *JRE*, vol. 8, 1882, pp. 69-70.
104. George Bruce, *The Burma Wars: 1824-1886*, London: Hart-Davis, 1973, p. 39.
105. Brett-James, *Wellington at War*, 7 February 1804, p. 97.
106. Ibid., 27 March 1803, pp. 74-5.
107. Captain Yule, 'Some Account of the Passage of the Sutlej by the British Army, in February 1846', *JRE*, vol. XLIX, 1849, pp. 177-82.

FIVE

The Pandies *against the Company Bahadur: The Military Dimensions of the 1857 Mutiny*

Mankind belongs to God,
and the land to the Government,
and power to the powerful sahibs.

A Hindustani proverb of nineteenth-century India[1]

Sunday, 10 May 1857 was the date. The day was quite hot. Towards the end of the afternoon, the Bengal army's sepoys (British-trained Indian infantry) and sowars (British-trained Indian cavalry) stationed at the cantonment of Meerut turned their loaded muskets gleefully against their erstwhile white masters. It was the beginning of the general mutiny, the most dangerous of its kind, among the Bengal army scattered from Punjab in the west up to Bihar in the east. The 1857 uprising which resulted in blood, death, and disaster for both Indians and the British in the subcontinent had all the ingredients and grandeur of a 'Wagnerian drama'. As the sun set over the north Indian sky on that fateful Sunday, it represented, ironically, the temporary decline of the sahibs' power in South Asia. However, this demise of British authority in north India only lasted for about a good part of the year.

Most of the modern historians of the 1857 uprising try to accommodate the 'event' within an agrarian paradigm. The supporters of the agrarian paradigm like Eric Stokes view 1857 as the consequence of the agrarian policy of the British Raj towards north Indian rural society.[2] In recent times the 'Subaltern historians' have emphasized, somewhat forcibly, the popular character of the agrarian upsurge.[3] These scholars assert that the 'common Indian masses' led an agrarian uprising against the alien British.

Actually, 1857 was the biggest military challenge which the Company faced after the collapse of the Indian powers like the Marathas and the Sikhs. The rebellious sepoys were more dangerous than either the Maratha army or the Khalsa army because the British trained the former in the Western art of war. And it was chiefly with the help of the sepoys that the British had created their Indian Empire. Why did the British win against the rebels?

The British writers of the colonial period tried to grapple with the military aspect of the 1857 uprising. Colonial British army officers believed that the rebels were defeated because of the moral superiority and cold steel of the European infantry. Field Marshal Lord Roberts writes in his memoirs 'The sepoys were no match for the British bayonets.'[4] He continues 'That their strongest positions were inadequate against British pluck and determination.'[5] Lieutenant General George MacMunn asserts 'The Rebels made determined attacks ... at times to the very point of the defenders' bayonets, repelled again and again by the ... 60th Rifles.'[6]

This sort of racial interpretation of military affairs is inadequate. This chapter shows that the British won because they were able to synthesize certain elements of the Indian military tradition (chiefly manpower, then social groups associated with manning the military's logistical apparatus, intelligence, and procurement techniques) with aspects of the Western tradition of warfare (technology and command apparatus). On the other hand, the military ineffectiveness of the rebels was due to their failure to accommodate Western military hardware within the framework of traditional Indian warfare.

MILITARY LEADERSHIP OF THE REBELS AND
THE COMPANY: A COMPARATIVE ANALYSIS

REBEL COMMAND APPARATUS *VERSUS* BRITISH C3I

Sahib, ham log larai mein bahut tez hain magar jang ka bandobast nahin jante.

An old rebel Indian officer to Field Marshal
Lord Roberts after the British victory at Delhi in 1857 [7]

One constituent part of the nineteenth-century Western-style warfare which the British conducted with certain modifications and which the rebels tried to ape was the construction of an effective command apparatus. And this always had been a chink in the armour for the traditional Indian armies. The managerial limitations of the rebels were exemplified in their C3I (Command, Control, Communications, and Intelligence) arrangements. The rebels failed to fuse the traditional elements of ·Indian leadership with the professional command requirements of nineteenth-century warfare. Leadership was concerned with inspiration and motivation. And for this reason, the rebel soldiers allowed Nana Sahib, the representative of the Maratha power at Kanpur, and the powerless Padshah Bahadur Shah, symbol of the House of Timur at Delhi, to fill the positions of political leadership. However, command signified managerial functions: direction, coordination, and effective battlefield use of military assets. Besides commanding and controlling the military force, the commander was also responsible for the assessment and dissemination of battlefield information. And all these tasks could only be done by professional soldiers. So the rebel troops maintained a firm grasp over the C3I network.[8] The rebels held military personnel with technical professional training in great importance. So Muhammad Bakht Khan, Subedar of the Artillery Regiment of Bareilly, was appointed as the general commanding the rebel army at Delhi.[9]

However, there was gross tension within the rebel leadership, especially at Delhi. For the rebels, this increased the 'friction of war'. The soldiers regarded Mirza Moghul, Bahadur Shah's son, as more dedicated to the rebels' cause than the old *Padshah*. But Bahadur Shah's favourite queen, Zinaat Mahal, was against the appointment of the princes to the command of the troops.[10] She was for the appointment of former Mughal officials like the *thanadars* and the *kotwals* over the soldiers. However, they were inexperienced in the arts of war. Then jealousy developed between Bakht Khan and Mirza Moghul. Further, the mutinous soldiery established a court (somewhat similar to the Revolutionary Soldiers' Committee in the French style which the Soviet soldiers would emulate in 1917), where all policy matters were deliberated upon before being accepted.[11] Thus, a clear hierarchical command structure for taking quick decisions on crucial issues was lacking at Delhi, the most important theatre of war.

Beside the defective regional command structure, at the grand strategic level, the rebel leadership lacked a pan-Indian unity. Worse, there was almost no coordination between the various regional commanders like the Begum of Awadh for the Lucknow theatre, with Tantia Tope for central India, and Bakht Khan at the Delhi theatre. However, the Company possessed an ideal military command structure that was like a chain. At the top link of the chain was the Commander-in-Chief (Lord Clyde or Colin Campbell, a veteran of the Peninsular Campaign against Napoleon's *Grande Armee* and the Crimean War), who commanded all the Company's forces spread over the subcontinent. He had below him a well-defined hierarchy of subordinates, one for each theatre.[12] For example, General Henry Havelock was at Kanpur, Brigadier General James Neill at Benaras, Chief Commissioner John Lawrence at Punjab, etc.[13]

Hence, as regards the higher leadership, the prospect for the rebels was indeed problematic. The situation was not much better at the regimental level. After the rebellion, the sepoy regiments elected commanders from among themselves. Quick promotions awarded to some of the rebel soldiers who were favourites of their political superiors did not help matters. Nana Sahib promoted a resaldar (a junior cavalry officer) named Jawala Prashad to the rank of brigadier.[14] Since they had no training in staff duties, they were ignorant of operational matters and lacked the experience to lead brigade-size formations (a brigade was composed of several regiments, while the strength of a regiment was about 1,000 personnel). Most of the Indian officers in the Sepoy army before the rebellion had commanded companies (about 100 men each) under the supervision of British officers. Further, most of the Indian officers were very old and thus physically and mentally inert. Due to the system of promotion in the Bengal army on the basis of seniority, after about 20 years of service some soldiers became non-commissioned officers. Some of the oldest serving sowars and sepoys reached the starry ranks of subedar major and resaldar major between the age of 55 to 60.[15] For managing war (map reading, gun laying, and staff duties), technical education was necessary. Most of them were illiterate villagers while 60 per cent of the Company's white soldiers and the reinforcements who arrived from Britain were literate. A large proportion of the Company's European recruits was artisans, clerks, surveyors, and draughtsmen recruited from the urban centres. Again, the reinforcements from Britain had 18 months' training behind them.[16] The rebels had neither the time nor the institutions like the Military Academy of Addiscombe, etc., for training new officers in staff duties and for inculcating military theory among them.

One could not expect any initiative from such persons who staffed the officer cadre of the rebel army. In addition, for remaining in power, they had to follow populist policies. In other words, they lacked the coercive authority supported by the military code and the court martial apparatus for maintaining discipline among the rank and file. On the other hand, discipline remained very strict in the British army. Lashing, branding, and several hours of parade ground drill remained in vogue among the Tommies. Thus, gradually the rebel sepoys' corporate military identity evaporated and they were downgraded to a sort of militia. As their corporate coherence dissolved, their military effectiveness against the Company's regulars also declined.[17] The resulting disintegration in the disciplinary apparatus raised the incidence of desertion. At Bareilly, after the uprising, almost every day about 25 rebel troops deserted after plundering the rich men of the city.[18]

TECHNOLOGY AND COMMAND:
INFORMATION WARFARE IN 1857

Thus it is said that one who knows the enemy and knows himself will not be endangered in a hundred engagements. One who does not know the enemy but knows himself will sometimes be victorious, sometimes meet with defeat. One who knows neither the enemy nor himself will invariably be defeated in every engagement.

SUN TZU[19]

By the word 'information' we denote all the knowledge which we have of the enemy and his country; therefore, in fact, the foundation of all our plans and actions. ... This difficulty of seeing things correctly, which is one of the greatest sources of friction in war, makes things appear quite different from what was expected.

CARL VON CLAUSEWITZ[20]

Information is also military power. Knowledge more than physical labour and raw materials remains the crucial factor in conducting war. The importance of transmission of information from political and military commanders to the battlefield units and vice versa so that the high command may be able to respond rapidly to the changing dynamics of battle, i.e. information warfare, is not merely a hallmark of the information age of the late twentieth century, as some American theorists seem to argue.[21] Both the ancient Chinese warrior sage in 2400 BC and the hardboiled Prussian military philosopher of the nineteenth century theorizing about war realized this. Information warfare played an important role in 1857 India, and in this field also the managerial limitations of the rebel leadership were further hampered by low technology inputs.

The rebels brought out newspapers from Delhi for the dissemination of information among their followers 'and the general populace[22] as regards the current situation, which in turn was necessary for maintaining their morale. The tradition of bringing out Urdu and Persian newspapers could be traced to Akbar's policy of appointing *akhbar nawis* (newswriters). These persons collected and transmitted specific items of information. Later, the Mughals also brought out *akhbarat* for the Mughal soldiers.[23] On 12 July 1857, in the *Delhi Urdu News*, Bakht Khan made the following declaration:

Let it be generally known to the persons living in the city and the country, such as chiefs of freeholds, pensioners, landholders of rent free estates, etc., that if, from anxiety for their incomes, they have hitherto continued on the side of the English, and have in any way colluded with them by conveying intelligence or furnishing them with supplies, their having done so will not be considered inexcusable.[24]

The British imitated the Mughal practice of maintaining a horse *dak* between Aligarh and Agra for the rapid transmission of orders. Another Indian technique, the *cassids* (runners) supplemented the British military information system. The *Nawab* of Fatehgarh, an ally of the rebels, responded by ordering his troopers to capture and execute the *cassids*. Since the rebels enjoyed numerical superiority as regards cavalry the imperial communications were occasionally cut.[25]

However, thanks to new technology, the British were saved. Command stands for effective communication within the various units of the armed forces. In case of mobile campaigns, when the military units are scattered over a wide area, command becomes extremely difficult. Innovative technological inputs like the telegraph helped the Company to deploy a superior command structure that in turn functioned as a force multiplier.[26] The electrical telegraph comprised 4,000 miles of telegraphic wire and connected Calcutta with Peshawar, Agra with Bombay, and Bombay with Madras.[27] The quick flow of information due to the telegraph enabled the British to get inside the enemy's decision-making time cycle (also known as the OODA loop) to generate new ventures at a faster tempo. The OODA loop means: Observe, Orient, Decide, and Act. The British military command was able to perform these four acts faster than the rebel military leadership because the Company had the telegraph at its disposal. This made the British command agile and flexible. The telegraph enabled the British to gain real time intelligence. This meant that the British procured information before the rebels acquired it. This reduced the reaction time of the British military response. Hence, the British could react before the rebels had even understood what was happening, making the latter's detailed planning useless.[28]

Robert Montgomery, the Commissioner of Lahore, knew about the Mutiny in north India through the telegraph, and he then immediately disarmed the 6,000 *Purbiyas* (Rajput and Brahmin soldiers from Bihar and Awadh) of the Bengal army before the latter could learn about the Mutiny of their brothers and rise against the British.[29] The telegraph wire followed Lord Clyde's campaigns. Thus, he could contact the Governor General at Calcutta, about 1,000 miles from his base of operations, both during breakfast and dinner. Calcutta and Bombay, about 1,409 miles distant, are within a few minutes' speaking distance by telegraph, and daily discussions for joint strategic planning were conducted regularly. And this in turn reduced the 'fog of war'. A mutineer pointing out to the telegraph wire before execution rightly declared: 'It is that accursed string that strangles us.'[30]

TRANSPORT AND COMMAND

The Company had at its disposal a well-connected transport net which enabled the British high command to swiftly rush troops to the threatened points. The Ganga and its tributaries were navigable and the British had access to steamboats. These boats came from Calcutta up to Kanpur. Moreover, Calcutta and Raniganj were linked by railroad (a distance for about 120 miles). The 84th Infantry Regiment moved up from Calcutta to Allahabad during late 1857, first by railroad up to Raniganj and then by steamers. Havelock at Kanpur received continuous reinforcements of manpower and food from Benares through the steamers.[31] This steady stream of supplies was one of the factors that prevented Nana Sahib's troops from overpowering the Company's contingent at Kanpur.

In 1857, there was a shortage of horses in Awadh. Even with money one could not procure them.[32] Before the Mutiny, the government bought horses from north India (for equipping the Indian cavalry of the Bengal army that ultimately rebelled) at Rs. 700 for each animal.[33] Mudud Ali, a soldier who was discharged from the Bengal army before 1857 and who later became a horse dealer, supplied some horses to Nana Sahib.[34] The rebels could not procure horses from Central Asia because Punjab remained loyal to the British. Thanks to British control over the high seas, the Company was able to import large numbers of horses from Persia and the Cape,[35] and this restored mobility to the British forces.

FEEDING MARS

The Company's immediate task was to maintain their existing Westernized military bureaucracy and the next step was to sustain and expand it with India's manpower. The rebels faced a much more daunting challenge. With an *ad hoc* ragtag leadership, the rebels had to structure a military formation, a hard task in peacetime and almost impossible in times of chaos. The tasks which faced the rebels were procurement of manpower to fill the ranks and the generation of financial resources to feed and clothe the armed personnel for deploying them in the theatres of war at the right moment.

MANPOWER

India's massive manpower resources were adequate for filling the ranks of the armies of both the Company and the rebels. The population of British India in 1857 was 38 million.[36] Just before the Mutiny, the British Indian army had 2,26,352 sepoys, sowars (including Indian officers), and white soldiers. Of them, there were about 30,000 sowars and 1,49,832 sepoys. The Company deployed about 6,170 European officers and 39,352 white troops.[37] About 1,00,000 Indian troops supported the upsurge. Of them, 70,000 took direct part in the rebellion and the rest were fence sitters. The latter group was disarmed by the British and played no military role.[38]

Both the British and the rebels recruited mostly from the countryside. The rebels recruited their force mainly from present-day Bihar and Uttar Pradesh, the two provinces under their control. The Company had the advantage of recruiting from a wider area like Punjab, west India, and south India since these regions were untouched by the Mutiny. Lord Dalhousie was suspicious of the *Purbiyas*. They were called *Pandies* by the British due to the presence of a large number of Pandey Brahmins, who dominated the rebellious Bengal army's infantry. Dalhousie tried to overcome this difficulty by enlisting larger numbers of Gurkhas, Sikhs, and Punjabi Muslims.[39] To reduce the dominance of the *Purbiyas*, the government in 1856 ordered the Bengal army to enlist 200 Sikhs in each infantry regiment.[40] Subedar Sitaram (a *Purbiya*) of the Bengal army while penning his memoirs in 1873 wrote:

Two regiments of old Sikh soldiers were enlisted for the Sarkar and young Sikhs were taken into the native regiments. This annoyed the sepoys exceedingly, for the Sikhs were disliked by the Hindustanis who considered them to be unclean and were not permitted to associate with them. Their position was uncomfortable for a long time. ... these men always keep to themselves and were regarded as interlopers by the older sepoys.[41]

These Sikhs proved to be a salvation for the British during the stormy days of 1857. The British continued to procure the Gurkhas through the recruiting depot at Gorakhpur.[42] When the news of the Mutiny reached Punjab, it was John Nicholson who first mooted the idea of enlisting Pathans from Multan. John Lawrence and Herbert Edwardes procured Afridi tribesmen through their Khans and landowners.[43]

The heavy British horses were ill suited for reconnaissance and skirmishing. So the Company raised a light cavalry from among the Indians. The Indian cavalry proved excellent for

outpost duties, escorting convoys, etc. Before 1857, the cavalry
of the Bengal army was recruited from among the Pathans of
Rohilkhand and the Rajput Muslims of Haryana. Mostly upper-
class Muslims like the Shaikhs, Sayids, and descendants of the
Mughals, joined along with their retainers. Since they had
rebelled, the Company now turned to the Punjabi Muslims.[44]
Mounted police for internal security duties were raised from
among the Baluchis of Sind and Punjab.[45]

In a way, the 1857 insurrection was also a caste war; a trial of
strength between the British plus the low castes against the north
Indian high castes. Contrary to the assertions of the Subaltern
historians regarding the role of common people in the uprising,
the low castes and the tribals sided with the British. This is seen
especially in Awadh where, according to both Marxist[46] and
Subaltern historians,[47] popular agitation was intense; here the
low castes remained loyal to the British. As the high caste soldiers
from Awadh, i.e. the *Purbiyas* started deserting, the British
recruited the low castes, and they remained loyal. Lieutenant
Colonel H. Bruce filled the Awadh Police with the low castes.
The *Pasees* (a low caste of Awadh) were enlisted in the Sapper
Corps as their hereditary occupation was mining. The rebels
lacked sappers and the Pasees would have been of great help to
them.[48]

These marginal groups also played a very important role in
supporting the Company by serving as second-line troops in the
secondary theatres. The Gujarat Police Corps was recruited from
the Bheels of Gujarat and the 1st Khandesh Bheel Corps enlisted
the Bheels of Malwa. The former unit maintained order in Gujarat
and the latter unit guarded the Company's lines of communication in central India.[49] The 44th Merwara Infantry Regiment
composed of the Mhair tribe of Rajasthan remained loyal to the
British despite the provocation of the *Purbiyas* to rebel against
the Raj. The 44th Regiment held the treasury and the arsenal at
Ajmer against the rebellious 15th Bengal Infantry Regiment
during mid-1857 and thus prevented the spread of the rebellion
in Rajasthan. At that critical juncture there were no British troops
in Rajasthan.[50] The Secretary of State for India, Charles Wood
himself acknowledged the vital role played by the marginal
groups in the Company's war machine during 1857.[51]

By 1858, about 18 per cent of the Indian army, i.e. about

17,309 personnel were of low castes and tribals.[52] The low castes and the untouchables sided with the British probably because in the Hindu hierarchy they occupied a peripheral position and also because in the princely armies of pre-British India they had no place. Again, military service with the British provided them economic security and a channel for upward mobility.

The rebels made no significant attempt to enlist the low castes in north India, the region under their firm control, probably because the Indian officers of the Bengal army's infantry regiments that had rebelled were mostly Brahmins and Rajputs.[53] The point to be noted is that before 1857, when the Company tried to recruit some marginal groups, the *Purbiyas* who constituted more than 65 per cent of the Bengal army petitioned their British officers that due to their caste bias, they would not serve with the low castes.[54]

What was the social and regional composition of the 'loyal' Indian army that the British raised to fight the mutineers? The British Indian army was actually an agglomeration of four regional armies: Bengal army, Punjab Frontier Force, Bombay army and the Madras army. The Madras army deployed 2,600 cavalry recruited from the Muslims of Karnataka and Hyderabad. This army possessed about 43,000 infantry enlisted from among the Muslims, Telingas, and Tamils from Karnataka, Mysore, and Tanjore respectively. The Bengal army's organization was in ribbons. Still, about 7,900 men remained loyal to the British. Besides them about 1,400 Sikhs and 1,200 Gurkhas of the Bengal infantry also remained loyal to the British.[55] The Punjab Irregular Force which bore the brunt of the struggle against the rebels was composed of 14,692 Sikhs from central Punjab, 30,188 Punjabi Muslims from west Punjab, and 7,566 middle caste Hindus (Ahirs, Gujars, etc.) from eastern Punjab.[56]

MONEY, MONEY, AND YET MORE MONEY:
THE SINEWS OF MILITARY POWER

Both the Company and the rebels tried to control the countryside for extracting food and revenue for maintaining the armed forces. The British were successful because they were able to keep a large army permanently in the field without bankrupting themselves. The construction of a redistributive machinery for supplying the soldiers with money and cash required the assistance of the *baniyas* and the *mahajans*. The British Raj was able to establish a workable relationship with these two indigenous groups, and a Westernized civil bureaucracy further supported this alliance.[57] But these two groups refused to cooperate with the rebels as the rebel regime was unstable and lacked credibility. Then the rebels were forced to loot and hold to ransom the moneyed class. This could not ensure a steady supply of stores and money, resulting in the dissolution of the rebel army.

In Nana Sahib's domain, Lala Shankar Das, a banker of Kanpur, was arrested by Nana's subordinate Nunee Nawab and was released after paying the rebels Rs. 30. Then the Commissariat *Gomastah* of Kanpur, Lala Badri Nath (who was a British employee), was arrested after the rebellion by Tikka Singh (subadar of the rebel 2nd Light Cavalry), who demanded Rs. 3,000 from him. Badri Nath was released only when his friend, a Khatri trader, paid the troopers Rs. 300 on 16 June 1857.[58] Such unsystematic measures prevented Nana Sahib from building up a stable financial apparatus that could sustain a combat effective force. The ineffectiveness of Nana's force was proved when the Company's soldiers defeated them in late 1857.

When the troops mutinied at Bareilly, they elected Bakht Khan as their leader. His second in command was Muhammad Safi, the resaldar major of the 8th Irregular Cavalry. Bakht Khan's plan was to collect the revenues from Moradabad, Shahjahanpur, and Pilibhit which would raise his fund to about Rs. 30,00,000. But due to lack of an adequate revenue-collecting apparatus, by 31 May 1857 Bakht Khan was able to amass only Rs. 10,00,000. About 10,000 soldiers had to be fed every day. For this purpose, *ghee* (clarified butter), flour, and gram had to be bought. An account of the arms and ammunition ought to have been kept. The troops in the rebel camp, unlike the trained British revenue officials, were not experts in managing finance and in procuring supplies. Whenever money was required to buy provisions or when food had to be distributed, there was chaos. For keeping an account of the daily expenditure, Bakht Khan requested Durgadas Bandopadhyay, the chief clerk of the 8th Irregular Cavalry that had rebelled, to take up the job of treasurer. But Bandopadhyay refused. Muhammad Safi tried to win him over by making tall promises. Safi said that the rebel government would give him a higher salary than what the sahibs provided him. A salary of Rs. 1,000 per month for Bandopadhyay was fixed, and Safi promised that after reaching Delhi, Bakht Khan would make him a minister with a salary of Rs. 2,000 per month. In addition, he would be given the honorary command of 100 cavalry. Still Bandopadhyay refused. This was because he had no faith in the unstable regime established by the rebels and also due to his sense of honour. He could not bring himself to doing *namakharami* (the concept of loyalty to the salt giver was very strong among the people of pre-industrial India) with the sahibs. Bakht Khan responded by putting him under house arrest.[59]

In Bareilly, before 1857, Indian soldiers, British officers, and the *baniyas* took loans from the banker Hiranand Seth. From his residence at Bhimani near Delhi, Hiranand Seth controlled his business ventures whose tentacles were spread over a large part of the subcontinent. At Bareilly the soldiers under British command had taken a loan of Rs. 2,00,000 from Hiranand Seth. The Bareilly branch of his business was looked after by Hiranand's son Jahurimal Seth. Immediately after the insurrection, about 25 sepoys at Bakht Khan's order raided Jahurimal's residence, put him under house arrest, and took away Rs. 40,000. Bakht Khan's order was that he could be released provided he agreed to go to Delhi as a banker for the rebels and advance a loan of Rs. 50,00,000. Jahurimal refused and like Bandopadhyay remained under arrest.[60]

Due to lack of regular supplies and the consequent break-down of discipline, many rebel soldiers resorted to looting the houses of *mahajans*. Though Muhammad Safi tried to curb this unauthorized looting by creating a mounted police force of about 100 sowars, the situation went out of control. The traders responded by closing their shops. Then the *baniyas* failed to buy provisions for the rebel troops from the *bazar*. Due to the heavy incidence of looting, the supply of *ghee* and flour from the countryside to the city had also ceased. Hence, the rebels suffered from logistical difficulties at Bareilly. When in the first week of June 1857, Bakht Khan ordered the *baniyas* to amass food that would supply the troops for at least 15 days, the *baniyas* were able to provide stores for only seven days.[61]

All these commissariat difficulties delayed Bakht Khan's plan of marching to Delhi quickly, and this ruined the rebels' prospect of a quick victory over the Company's emaciated Delhi Field Force that was besieging the rose-coloured Red Fort of Delhi. The Bareilly Brigade composed of 2,300 combatants (much reduced by continuous desertions) and 1,000 carts containing baggage and plunder was able to move into Delhi only on 1 July 1857. By this time, the Field Force at the Delhi Ridge had also received 2,000 reinforcements from Punjab.[62] Instead of a *Blitzkrieg* victory, Bakht Khan faced the prospect of an attritional warfare. Delhi remained under siege from the British force.

TECHNOLOGY AND WAR

Military Hardware and the Conduct of Warfare

Once the armies were organized they had to be given proper weapons. The mid-nineteenth century witnessed the beginning of industrial age war since warfare was dominated by firepower generated by rifles and artillery. Large quantities of rifles and steel artillery could only be manufactured by the industrial nations. In the Crimean War (1853-6), rifles and heavy cannons dominated the battlefields.[63] The Company enjoyed a techno-logical edge over the rebels both in small arms and artillery. The rebels' cavalry had no carbines and most of the militias which the rebels had raised were armed with matchlocks, which could not be fired during rainfall.[64] At times the hardware of the militias was much worse. When, in June 1857, Nawab Khan Bahadur Khan, an ally of the rebels at Bareilly, raised a levy, the men were armed with swords and spears.[65] In Awadh, about 40,000 Muslims who belonged to the disbanded *Nawabi* army joined the rebels but were without any firearms.[66] While the rebels' regular infantry was armed with the Brown Bess, the Company's European infantry was armed with Enfield rifles (a muzzle loader with a long three-grooved rifled barrel designed to impart spin to the .577-inch diameter bullet for greater accuracy) whose bullets had greater velocity, and hence increased penetrative power.[67]

An efficient administrative network sustained the superior military hardware of the British. The cartridges were manu-factured at the regimental magazines by the regimental *khalasies*

(Indian artisans).[68] The Military Department under the Military Member of the Governor General's Council supervised the supporting services of the army. Under him came the Director General of Ordnance who controlled all the ordnance factories that were geared to produce siege and field artillery along with small arms.[69] The Cossipore ordnance factory near Calcutta supplied field guns to the Company's army, which gave it an edge as regards firepower against the rebels.[70]

The imperialists were always nervous about associating the Indians in the artillery arm. The Court of Directors was against recruiting Indians into the artillery arm or their employment in the arsenals and ordnance factories. However, the rapid expansion of the British Indian army in the first half of the nineteenth century forced the British government in India to recruit more and more Indians as gunners.[71] Nevertheless, the number of Indian gunners in the Sepoy army was very low compared with the number of sepoys and sowars. Thus, the proportions of Europeans and Indians in the artillery branch were low compared to the other two branches. In the artillery, the proportion of Europeans and Indians was 1.5:1. But in the cavalry and the infantry the proportion of Europeans and Indians was 1:8.[72] In total, from 4,300 Indian gunners of the Bengal army about 500 joined the rebels while the Company possessed about 7,700 British gunners.[73] Since the gunners and artillery officers required specialized technical training along with knowledge of mathematics,[74] the rebels could not recruit them from the countryside.

Those Indian gunners who rebelled fired well [75] but lacked advanced ordnance pieces and adequate supplies of munitions. The rebels did not possess any ordnance depots. They maintained themselves with the stores acquired from the ordnance depots captured by them. They were able to capture the magazine at Kanpur. The guns and ammunition from this depot equipped Nana Sahib's force.[76] But this provided only a short-time relief. Hence, Nana made desperate efforts to cast guns. He floated a proposal announcing that anybody who could cast a gun would be given a high reward. One craftsman who made a gun was given a lump sum of Rs. 100 by Nana.[77] However, such efforts were few and far between and could not sustain a steady supply of munitions and arms to the rebels. This

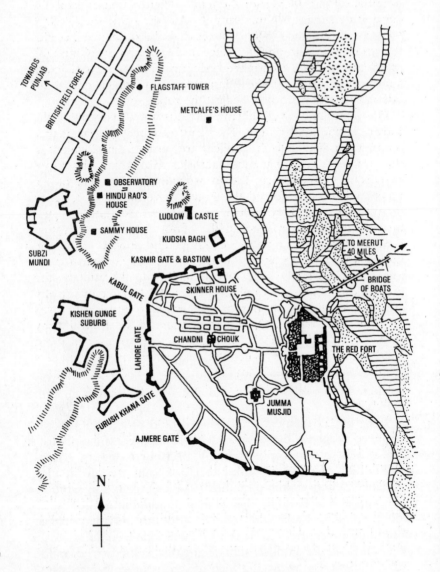

Source: James Leasor, *The Red Fort: An Account of the Siege of Delhi in 1857*
(London: Werner Laurie, 1956). Modified suitably

Map 5: Delhi in 1857

was because the Indians in general lacked the technical know-how and the rebels lacked the infrastructure for the mass production of guns. Hence, at Lucknow the rebels were mostly armed with obsolete brass guns[78] (used mainly for ceremonial purposes) which belonged to the Awadh *Nawab.*

As a result of the above-mentioned deficiencies, the rebels lost all the set-piece battles against the Company's force. Then the rebel strategy was to occupy the cities and transform them into fortresses. Two such cases were Delhi and Lucknow. However, even in siege warfare the Company won due to superior technology and better management of firepower. Heavy ordnance, engineering techniques, and superior logistical know-how gave victory to the British.

SIEGE WARFARE IN SOUTH ASIA

1. Delhi under Siege: June-September 1857

With about 30,000 rebels cooped up inside *festung* (fortress) Delhi, how could just 12,588 troops (loyal Indians plus the British) of the Company[79] blast their way through? This was possible due to the Company's superiority in siege artillery. The task of siege artillery was to breach the walls of the forts with the aid of round shots fired from heavy guns like the 18- and 24-pdrs. Delhi was surrounded by a stone wall 16 feet high, 11 feet thick at the top, and about 15 feet thick at the bottom. The wall had bastions which were provided with parapets about 12 feet thick and these were equipped with static guns fired by the rebel gunners. Outside the wall was a ditch which was about 25 feet wide and 20 feet deep. To destroy this obstacle, the Delhi Field Force deployed five batteries. The Sami House Battery with guns and howitzers engaged the defenders of the Mori Bastion manned by the rebels. The task of the Number 1 Siege Battery armed with five 18-pdrs. guns and one 8-inch howitzer was to blast the Mori Bastion. The Number 2 Breaching Battery with nine 24-pdrs. guns and two 18-pdrs. guns along with seven 8-inch howitzers destroyed the Kashmir Bastion and breached the wall near the Kashmir Gate. The Number 3 Breaching Battery at a distance of only 200 yards from the wall and equipped with six 18-pdrs. guns and twelve 5.5-inch mortars was designed to breach the wall near the Water Bastion. Finally, the Reserve

Battery with four 10-inch and six 8-inch mortars fired plunging shots over the walls to harass the rebels, thus obstructing their flow of reinforcements to those points of the wall that had been breached.[80]

The Company's trump card was the availability of personnel trained in scientific branches of warfare, i.e. military engineers and sappers. The British had about 110 engineers in front of Delhi, and Lieutenant Colonel Baird Smith commanded them.[81] An engineer, Arthur Moffatt Lang, was in charge of the Punjabi sappers and pioneers. Their job was to construct and repair the parapets, revetments, and embrasures of the batteries (gun emplacements). The embrasures were openings in epaulments (battery fortifications) made of fascines (brushwood) and gabions (wicker baskets filled with earth). The sappers under the direction of the engineers also trained the assault infantry on escalading (placing ladders for climbing over the walls during the attack).[82]

In the narrow streets of Delhi, the numerically superior rebel infantry used their muskets with deadly effect, taking advantage of the cover provided by the rubble and the houses. The fierce fighting inside the city was somewhat similar to the twentieth century Battle of Stalingrad. The rebel infantry, like the Red Army infantry, followed 'hugging tactics' by attempting to come close to the enemy for hand-to-hand fighting. However, the Company's troops armed with artillery killed them from a distance. The Company further responded by adopting superior tactics made possible due to the availability of the sappers. The engineers blew up the walls of the houses; the sappers then advanced with sandbags with which a parapet was constructed. From behind the parapet, fire support by both infantry and field artillery was given to the engineers for blowing up the next house. And this step-by-step approach continued till the rebels were driven from the city to the banks of the Jamuna. In many ways, this tactic was similar to Generalfeldmarschall Von Paulas' attempt to drive the Soviet infantry away from festung Stalingrad during late 1992 to the banks of the Volga.[83]

During the long siege of Delhi, the staying power of the rebels was further sapped by a logistical logjam. Initially, in Delhi the troops demanded a daily allowance for food from the *Padshah*. But Bahadur Shah declared that he had no money. Mahbub Ali

Khan, an official of the *Padshah*, was ordered to raise a loan from the merchants and bankers of Delhi for paying wages to the soldiers.[84] Mahbub Ali Khan agreed to pay four annas to a sepoy and one rupee to a sowar per day. Lala Mukand Lal was ordered to raise another loan from the merchants for paying the troops. But he refused. To tide over the desperate financial situation, the rebel government tried to fleece the *seths* (Hindu financiers).[85] But this was no long-term solution. The resulting financial mismanagement and the lack of discipline resulted in pillage and plunder by the troops. On 13 May 1857, the 38th, 54th and 74th infantry regiments plundered the shops of the cloth merchants of Chota Dureeba Street in Delhi. On 16 May 1857, the sepoys looted *mahajan* Narain Das' house. The merchants responded by closing the *bazars,* which further exacerbated the situation.[86]

When the coercive apparatus of the state rebelled, the state structure collapsed. Then powerful landed magnates along with their followers engaged in plundering and looting. What was the response of the rebel government and the Company towards them? The rebel officials demanded that *parwanahs* should be issued to all the rajas and chiefs. This was because the rural landscape could be controlled only through such landed inter-mediaries. Not only would they supply Delhi with money and food but in addition they would also raise new troops.[87] The rebel government tried to enlist their support through a carrot-and-stick policy by appointing them in the new fledgling anti-British state bureaucracy and by a simultaneous show of force.

Moulvi Mohammed Ali, whom the rebel government ap-pointed as the police officer of Najafgarh, wrote to the *Padshah* that the zamindars were ordered to plunder the countryside. After keeping their own prescribed share, they were supposed to forward the surplus to the royal treasury. Shah Mul, a Jat zamindar of Bijroal, plundered the *banjaras* and then burnt the tehsil of Burout. The rebel government of Delhi appointed him the *subadar* of Burout parganah. He was ordered to supply grain for the rebel force at Delhi. The Rao of Dadree (a small town near Delhi) was ordered by the rebel government at Delhi to plunder Meerut so that no supplies could reach the British. None the less, these village officials would only forward supplies to Delhi if the rebel government with infantry regiments demonstrated in their territories.[88] Due to British military pressure, the rebels were forced to concentrate all their available military formations in Delhi. As the rebels failed to detach troops to overawe the zamindars, no supply was forthcoming. Inside the burning hell that was Delhi, amidst the acrid smoke of gunpowder and the stench of rotting human and animal flesh, the rebel troops had to go hungry. All these factors hastened their military collapse.

The British also tried to retain control over the countryside for a steady supply of revenue and food grains. The British were more successful in controlling the hinterland of Delhi due to the superiority of the field army and also due to the support of a large number of indigenous allies. When the Mutiny broke out at Meerut, the government treasury had about Rs. 5,00,000. But expenditure due to military supplies and payments resulted in continuous financial drain. Encouraged by the breakdown of law and order, the Gujars attacked the rich Jat villages. Without the projection of military power, no revenue could be collected. While the British field army engaged the mutineers' regular force, European gentlemen like civilian bureaucrats, and judges, and the Sikh stragglers from the Bengal infantry regiments were organized into the Meerut Volunteer Horse for revenue collection. The Meerut Volunteer Force was engaged in coercing the *lambardars* (headmen of the villages) of Meerut parganah for providing sheep and grain to the Company's force besieging Delhi.[89]

In addition, the rajas of Punjab provided vital service to the British in supplying food and garrisoning the rear bases of the Company's military. The troops of the Raja of Jhind garrisoned Rhai, an outpost in the rear area of the British Field Force at Delhi. This post functioned as a base depot, as the Company's troops could fall back for rest and recuperation.[90]

2. Siege Warfare at Lucknow: April 1857-March 1858

The sad condition of the rebels inside Delhi should be contrasted with a case study of the superior British logistical venture which enabled the British garrison at Lucknow Residency to hold out against overwhelming odds. Unlike the rebels, the British could fall back on the trained civilian bureaucrats, who were experts in bookkeeping and in paperwork. The construction of a superior commissariat system in Lucknow was absent in General Wheeler's entrenchment at Kanpur which easily fell to Nana Sahib's troops in 1857.

From 24 October 1856 onwards, the Deputy Commissioner of Lucknow with the aid of civilian officials started buying up grain from the local sources. A far-sighted policy, indeed. The European grain traders cooperated with the British bureaucracy. The Chief Commissioner was assigned the task of preparing an inventory of all the supplies, including rum, port, and fodder for the baggage animals. Further, he was ordered to prepare an average of the daily expenditure. The daily expenditure of grain was calculated to about 8,000 lb. The total strength of the garrison under siege was 3,420 soldiers. The scale of the daily rations was fixed. Each British combatant received 1 lb. of meat and 1 lb. of flour with some salt. Along with the soldiers, many civilians were also cooped up within the Residency. There were about 700 European civilians, including women and children.A child received about 8 oz. of meat. Every day, a white woman was served 6 oz. meat, 12 oz. *atta*, 1.5 oz. rice, 1 lb. grain, and .5 oz. salt. The dead gun bullocks were used for meat. The siege of the Lucknow Residency lasted from April 1857 till 17 November 1857. When the garrison marched out, it still had 1,60,000 lb. of grain.[91]

When a British relief force reached the Lucknow Residency, the rebels who had laid siege to the Residency were themselves besieged. Concentrated firepower enabled the British to overcome the rebels. In 1858, when Colin Campbell advanced towards Lucknow, his force deployed 54 field guns, 64 siege guns, and of the latter, six were super-heavy 68-pdrs. which were manned by British sailors. To construct batteries for all these giants, the Company fell back on 1,000 Indian sappers.[92] Since none on the rebel side was well versed in sapping techniques, during the siege of the Lucknow Residency the British had an edge in mining and counter-mining operations.[93]

In engagement after engagement, despite possessing numerical superiority, the rebels were defeated due to their inferior technology. On 22 December 1857, at Guilee, near Alambagh in Lucknow, Brigadier Stisted with 1,227 infantry defeated a rebel force composed of 2,000 infantry. This was possible because while the rebels had four guns with inadequate ammunition, Stisted was able to deploy six guns with ample munitions.[94]

On 11 January 1858, the rebels attacked Jallalabad. Though the rebels outnumbered Major General James Outram's force by about ten times, combined artillery and rifle fire from about 1,600 infantry posted inside the Alambagh and the Jallalabad picket crushed the rebel infantry assault. The horse artillery guns were smoothbore muzzle-loading 6-pdr. These guns were a source of mobile firepower in fluid battle situations. The four horse artillery guns opened up at a range of about 500 yards. And the 9-pdr. field guns drawn by bullocks supplemented the firepower from the horse artillery. During the next attack, which was launched on 16 January, the rebels tried a new infantry tactic. They sent out skirmishers instead of coming in dense masses. They were allowed to come within 800 yards and then three field guns under Major Gordon discharged grapes. Shells from an 8-inch mortar supplemented the grapes. When the rebels launched their cavalry to threaten the rear of the Jallalabad picket, Major Olpherts' four horse battery guns turned them away.[95]

Again, the British were able to evolve specialized artillery tactics because they possessed various types of guns and shells. While one battery of six 8-inch mortars under Captain Maude was engaged in counter-battery work, another battery composed of four 18-pdr. iron guns provided fire support to the assault infantry that captured the rebels' guns. The four 9-pdr. field guns along with two 24-pounder howitzers were engaged in anti-personnel bombardment. They used grape shots and shrapnel shells and caused heavy casualties among the rebel infantry.[96]

COULD THE REBELS HAVE WON IN 1857?

Was the defeat of the rebels inevitable? The answer is probably no. The Sepoy Rebellion began at the time, which for the British constituted the worst possible scenario. The mid-nineteenth century was a violent period in the Asian landmass. Along with the mutineers in South Asia, 'Satan' was let loose in China in the form of the Taiping warriors. In the end, both in China and in India, the Taipings and the rebels were defeated by European-led Asian troops who enjoyed technological, tactical, and organizational superiority.[97] Still there were some opportunities for the rebels to emerge victorious.

The Second Opium War, which broke out in the Heavenly

Kingdom during 1856, not only tied down a considerable number of white troops in China but also hampered the supply of reinforcements into the Indian subcontinent.[98] The troop ships took about four months to reach India from Britain.[99] The reinforcements from England reached India in substantial numbers only in November 1857.[100] So the rebels had five precious months in which to destroy the British presence in India. What possible military alternatives were available to them?

In the arena of strategy and tactics, there was much space for the rebels to experiment. As regards strategy, the rebels ought to have followed what B.H. Liddell Hart calls 'indirect strategy'. This involved both geographical and psychological indirectness to upset the opponent's balance. In other words, it meant attacking where the enemy is not expecting it and thus overturn his decision-making structure. Even a small mass by undertaking such indirect attacks could achieve the element of surprise and raise the tempo of operations, making the enemy's detailed planning irrelevant.[101] The rebels could have derived inspiration from the history of mobile guerrilla tactics because the Marathas under Shivaji and during the First Anglo-Maratha War were pastmasters in the use of this indirect strategy. Along with the Marathas, even guerrilla warfare conducted by light Sikh cavalry against the Mughals and the Afghans during the first half of the eighteenth century could have provided a model for the rebels.[102]

The rebels could have achieved decisive battlefield success by following this superior strategy. Simultaneous attacks launched at the enemy's weak points, like depots and hospitals, which the rebels could have done easily given their superiority in cavalry, would have generated a synergy and this would have de-stabilized the British position. The Company would have been forced to dissipate its troops in manning and guarding its ever-lengthy supply lines to provision the far-flung detachments, as was the case with the Americans in Vietnam during the 1960s. And this could have weakened their main field army, thus setting the stage for the decisive phase. Such a stage might have been reached when, due to continuous dissipation, the Company's field army would have been too weak to meet the rebel's field army. However, the rebels only resorted to mobile guerrilla warfare from June 1858, when the military balance had already swung against them. The point to be noted is that even against the numerically and technologically superior forces of the Company, Tantia Tope, the General of Nana Sahib, continued to run wild till April 1859.[103]

At the operational level, instead of following 'positional warfare', by flocking to Delhi and Lucknow, the rebels should have resorted to 'manoeuvre warfare' by attacking Calcutta, the principal node of British power in the eastern rim of the British Indian Empire. If the rebels had manoeuvred around Calcutta and its hinterland, then the Sikhs and the Pathans in the Company's pay would have been unwilling to march in the uncongenial climate towards the humid and swampy terrain of Bengal.[104] Moreover, the longer distance would have further worsened the already acute logistical problems of the movable column (reinforcements sent from Punjab). Dust, distance, and malnutrition could have taken a higher toll, especially among the white soldiers. Sunstroke, agreed the contemporary British combatants, was also a lethal enemy.[105] Like 'General Winter' in the case of the Russians, 'General Summer' was the biggest friend of the Indians against any foreign invaders. The rebellion broke out in summer, the worst possible campaigning season for the British. In twelve months, about 1,000 British died from sunstroke in the force under the direct control of Colin Campbell in north India.[106] If the rebels had adopted a mobile guerrilla strategy over a wider theatre of war, then the number of sunstroke cases for the British in the ensuing attritional campaign would have gone up drastically.

Another reason why the mutineers should have attacked Calcutta and Bombay was that the British control over both the high seas and the coastal waters enabled them to shuffle troops not only from the other presidencies to Calcutta but also to receive vital reinforcements from Britain and her extra Indian territories through these two ports.[107] And water transport at that time was quicker than land transport. On 24 May 1857, the Madras Fusiliers arrived in Calcutta for their journey to north India. The 37th Company of the Royal Artillery came from Ceylon and the 37th Foot from Moulmein. The 64th and 78th infantry regiments came from Persia.[108] Then 5,000 troops destined for China landed at Calcutta and proceeded to north India.[109] The net result was that due to continuous reinforcements, despite the losses suffered due to the rebellion, the strength of the white troops and engineers in mid-1858 increased to about 63,000 and 434 respectively.[110] Raids on Calcutta and Bombay would have choked the British supply of vital reinforcements.

The rebels in the western part of north India, instead of flocking to Delhi, should have attacked the weakly held British ordnance depot at Ferozepore and destroyed the heavy guns and the animal transport along with their carriages held there before the advent of the movable column from Punjab. This would have made the British reinforcements pouring in from Punjab firepower deficient and immobile, thus giving vital time to the mutineers to consolidate their hold over the battlespace along the Ganga–Jamuna doab. The point to be noted is that in the end Delhi fell to the Company's troops because the walls and bastions of the city were breached by the siege train which the British assembled along with elephants, camels, and 700 carts at Ferozepore towards the end of July 1857.[111]

The rebels of central India, especially Tantia Tope with troops from Gwalior, instead of moving into the boiling cauldron of Kanpur should have moved towards the Bombay Presidency. Since the social and regional composition of most of the Bombay army's infantry and cavalry was similar to the rebellious units of the Bengal army, there was a high chance of the Bombay army personnel sympathizing with their brethren in the Bengal army. The Bombay army was largely composed of *Purbiyas* (as in the case of the rebellious Bengal army) and the Marathas. The Bombay army had 1,500 cavalry recruited from among the north Indian Muslims, Rajputs, and Brahmins. About 11,000 infantry of the Bombay army were *Purbiyas*.[112] Any advance of the rebels towards the Bombay army would have encouraged these north Indian soldiers to throw off the British yoke. The Maratha segment of the Bombay army, i.e. 10,000 infantry recruited from the Marathas of the Konkan region would probably have also rebelled if they had heard that Nana Sahib was trying to restore the Peshwaship. Unlike the Bengál army, in the Bombay army, young Indian soldiers were promoted as Viceroy's com-misssioned officers on the basis of their military performance and not on the basis of seniority.[113] So if the Bombay army had rebelled, then the rebels would have acquired an excellent crop of young Indian officers full of determination and capable of seizing the initiative even under adverse conditions.

At the tactical level, instead of blundering into set-piece battles with the Company's firepower-heavy regulars managed by staff officers, the rebels should have followed mobile hit-and-run operations.[114] Attempting to eliminate the Company's force in encounter battles was an impossible task because the rebel military leadership lacked staff college training and failed to coordinate the actions of various battle groups in the heat of action. At the Battle of Nawabganj fought in June 1858, the four groups into which the rebel army was divided failed to co-ordinate their actions against the numerically inferior 'thin red line'. The British troops advanced in the form of a mixed battle group. In it the cavalry, the horse artillery, and the infantry were integrated into a cohesive component and provided comple-mentary support to each other. As a result, after three hours of fighting, the rebel force disintegrated, leaving 600 dead on the field of battle. And the road to Lucknow was opened for the British.[115] Instead, the rebels should have focused on cutting the telegraph lines, since this tactic would have had a strategic effect by paralyzing the Company's C3I network. At times, the mutineers made sporadic efforts to cut the telegraph wires just as they did on the eve of the uprising in Meerut. This positively aided the rebels by preventing the white reinforcements from reaching Meerut when the sepoys and sowars decided to throw off the foreign yoke.[116]

The rebel superiority in light cavalry then could have been used with devastating effect for harassing British columns and their lines of communications. The rebels should have launched mobile guerrilla forces along the Grand Trunk Road, the principal artery for communication between Calcutta and the British military stations in north India. Such rebel attacks would have been quite successful because the Company's troops were transported in small penny packets by bullocks and steamers.[117] The very existence of such a threat would have tied down so many troops of the Company along the Grand Trunk Road that the forces that could have been deployed on the battlefields of north India would have to be drastically reduced. This would have resulted in an attritional campaign and the fate of 1857 India might been turned out like Vietnam in the 1970s.

CONCLUSION

However, speculation can never bypass reality. The British succeeded in absorbing and assimilating particular traditions of the Indian way of warfare (like India's middle castes, low castes, and the moneyed class plus the traditional mechanism of gathering military intelligence) within the format of their industrial-age army. But the rebels failed to synthesize the traditional Indian tradition of mobile guerrilla warfare with their cavalry-heavy army. And this sounded their death knell. Given the social composition of the rebellious Bengal regiments, the rebels were in no position to enlist the support of the low castes. Nor could the rebels do anything to disrupt the British sea lines of communications. The best chance that the rebels had was to conduct what the Prussian General Staff had termed the 'timetable war' before mobilization of the superior resources by the British turned the military balance against them in a *Materialschlacht* (Battle of Materials).

On 31 May 1857, a fleeting window of opportunity appeared before the rebels. The fate of India was hanging in the balance. The situation was one of touch and go. The tactics of cutting telegraph wires and capturing ordnance depots guarded by weak garrisons would have paralyzed the British lion. Instead of following a Fabian strategy of avoiding the enemy's army and conducting a scorched-earth policy, the rebels went for the Clausewitzian strategy of annihilating the Company army in a single and decisive stroke. This was because of the cognitive failure of the rebels to conduct *Kleinkrieg* (dispersed low-intensity warfare) since they were taught in the Sepoy army the tactic of conducting pitched battles. As a result, the gallant but under-armed rebel sepoys and sowars who were led by 'donkeys' tried to measure strength with the Company's field army equipped with state-of-the-art technology and managerial experts. After being defeated in various battles, the rebels shut themselves inside cities like Delhi and Lucknow, only waiting to be blasted into oblivion by British heavy ordnance. By July 1857, for the British the worst was over. The 'goddess of fortune' had abandoned the rebels and they had lost the one and only chance to alter the course of Indian history. *Gotterdammerung* for the rebels was beginning.

NOTES

1. Lieutenant General George MacMunn, *Vignettes from Indian War*, 1901, rpt, Delhi: Low Price Publications, 1993, p. 172.
2. Eric Stokes, 'Rural Revolt in the Great Rebellion of 1857 in India: A Study of the Saharanpur and Muzaffarnagar Districts', *Historical Journal*, vol. 12, no. 4, 1969, pp. 606-27.
3. Rudrangshu Mukherjee, *Awadh in Revolt: 1857-1858, A Study of Popular Resistance*, New Delhi: Oxford University Press, 1984; Tapti Roy, *The Politics of a Popular Uprising: Bundelkhand in 1857*, New Delhi: Oxford University Press, 1994.
4. Field Marshal Lord Roberts, *Forty-One Years in India: From Subaltern to Commander-in-Chief*, vol. 1, London: Richard Bentley & Sons, 1897, p. 156.
5. Ibid., p. 335.
6. Lieutenant General George MacMunn, *The Indian Mutiny in Perspective*, 1931, rpt, Delhi: Sunita Publications, 1985, p. 156.
7. Roberts, *Forty-One Years*, p. 329.
8. For a conceptual discussion on the C3I concept, see G.D. Sheffield, 'Introduction: Command, Leadership and the Anglo-American Experience', in idem (ed.), *Leadership and Command: The Anglo-American Military Experience Since 1861*, London: Brassey's, 1997, p. 1. Pratul Chandra Gupta, *Nana Sahib and the Rising at Kanpur*, Oxford: Clarendon Press, 1963, pp. 44-5, 68-9.
9. Moti Ram (ed.), *Two Historic Trials in Red Fort*, New Delhi: Roxy Printing Press, n.d., p. 388.
10. S. Moinul Haq (ed.), *Memoirs of Hakim Ahsanullah Khan*, Karachi: Pakistan Historical Society, 1958, pp. 3-4.
11. Ram, *Historic Trials*, pp. 390-1, 404; Colonel John R. Elting, *Swords around a Throne: Napoleon's Grande Armee*, 1988, rpt, New York: Da Capo, 1997, p. 30; Edgar O'Ballance, *The Red Army*, London: Faber & Faber, 1964, p. 28.
12. For an understanding of command hierarchy, see Sheffield, 'Command, Leadership', in idem, *Leadership and Command*, p. 8
13. Gupta, *Nana Sahib*, pp. 121-63.
14. G.W. Forrest (ed.), *The Indian Mutiny: 1857-58, Selections from the Letters, Despatches and Other State Papers Preserved in the Military Department of the Government of India*, vol. 3, 1902, rpt, Delhi: D.K. Publishers, 2000, Appendix, no. 16, Deposition of Kanai Prashad, p. cxxxv.
15. David Blomfield (ed.), *Lahore to Lucknow: The Indian Mutiny Journal of Arthur Moffatt Lang*, London: Leo Cooper, 1992, p. 67; *Minutes of Evidence taken before the Commissioners appointed to inquire into the*

Organization of the Indian Army, Parliamentary Papers, Cd 2515, 1859 (hereafter *Peel Committee*), pp. 15, 51.

16. Peter Stanley, *White Mutiny: British Military Culture in India, 1825-1875*, London: Hurst & Company, 1998, pp. 43, 111; idem, '"Dear Comrades": Barrack Room Culture and the "White Mutiny" of 1859-60', *Indo-British Review*, vol. 21, no. 2, 1996, pp. 165-6.

17. S.P. Mackenzie, *Revolutionary Armies in the Modern Era: A Revisionist Approach*, London: Routledge, 1997, pp. 113 4; Bruce Watson, *The Great Indian Mutiny: Colin Campbell and the Campaign at Lucknow*, New York: Praeger, 1991, p. 33.

18. Durgadas Bandopadhyay, *Amar Jivancharit*, in Bengali, 1925, rpt, Calcutta: Ananya Prakashan, n.d., p. 97.

19. Ralph D. Sawyer, *The Seven Military Classics of Ancient China*, Boulder: Westview, 1993, p. 162.

20. Carl Von Clausewitz, *On War*, in Caleb Carr (ed.), *The Book of War*, New York: Modern Library, 1993, pp. 319-20.

21. Such theorists are Lieutenant Colonel Douglas M. Macgregor and the Tofflers. See Macgregor, *Breaking the Phalanx: A New Design for Landpower in the 21st Century*, Westport, CT: Praeger, 1997, p. 101; Alvin and Heidi Toffler, *War and Anti-War: Survival at the Dawn of the 21st Century*, 1993, rpt, London: Warner Books, 1994, pp. 2-4.

22. Ram, *Historic Trials*, p. 397.

23. Michael H. Fisher, 'The Office of Akhbar Nawis: The Transition from Mughal to British Forms', *Modern Asian Studies*, vol. 27, no. 1, 1993, pp. 45-50.

24. Ram, *Historic Trials*, p. 405.

25. Field Marshal Lord Roberts, *Letters Written during the Indian Mutiny*, 1923, rpt, New Delhi: Lal Publishers, 1979, pp. 85, 99.

26. For a discussion on the concept of command, see Martin Van Creveld, *Command in War*, Cambridge, MA: Harvard University Press, 1985, pp. 1-2, 4.

27. Arthur Mills, *India in 1858*, 1858, rpt, Delhi: Gian Publishing House, 1986, p. 171.

28. Sheffield, 'Command, Leadership', in idem, *Leadership and Command*, p. 3.

29. Charles Allen, *Soldier Sahibs: The Men Who Made the North-West Frontier*, London: John Murray, 2000, p. 270.

30. William Wilson Hunter, *The Marquess of Dalhousie and the Final Development of the Company's Rule*, Oxford: Clarendon Press, MDCCCXCV, p. 199.

31. MacMunn, *Indian Mutiny*, pp. 92, 100, 104-5, 110-11.

32. Roberts, *Letters*, p. 93.

33. *Papers Connected with the Reorganization of the Army in India,*

Supplementary to the Report of the Army Commission, Parliamentary Papers, Cd 2541 (henceforth *Supplementary Report*), p. 274.

34. Forrest, *Indian Mutiny*, Deposition of Kanai Prashad, p. cxxiii.
35. MacMunn, *Indian Mutiny*, p. 198.
36. Hunter, *Dalhousie*, p. 178.
37. *Peel Committee*, Appendix no. 17.
38. Stephen P. Cohen, *The Indian Army: Its Contribution to the Development of a Nation*, 1971, rpt, New Delhi: Oxford University Press, 1991, p. 35.
39. *Peel Committee*, p. 13; Hunter, *Dalhousie*, p. 214.
40. *Peel Committee*, Appendix no. 58, Lord Clyde's replies, para 1.
41. James Lunt (ed.), *From Sepoy to Subedar being the Life and Adventures of Subedar Sita Ram*, 1970, rpt, London: Macmillan, 1988, p. 159.
42. *Supplementary Report*, p. 162.
43. Allen, *Soldier Sahibs*, pp. 266, 276-7.
44. Military Despatches from the Secretary of State to the Governor General, India Office, London (hereafter Military Despatches), nos. 59, 77, 14, and 24 February 1860, National Archives of India (henceforth NAI), New Delhi; *Supplementary Report*, pp. 274-5, 308; *Peel Committee*, p. 5.
45. *Supplementary Report*, p. 47.
46. P.C. Joshi, '1857 in Our History', in idem (ed.), *Rebellion 1857: A Symposium*, 1957, rpt, Calcutta: K.P. Bagchi, 1986, pp. 119-24.
47. Mukherjee, *Awadh in Revolt*, pp. 170-1.
48. Captain E. Hall, to Major, commanding at Saugor, Lieutenant Colonel H. Bruce, Chief of Awadh Police, to the Adjutant General, Lucknow, Progs. nos 7 and 549, 9 January and 6 February 1860, Military Department Proceedings (hereafter MDP), NAI.
49. *Supplementary Report*, p. 46.
50. Digest of Services of the 44th Merwara Infantry: 1818-1916, Origin of the Merwara Battalion, NAI. (This manuscript is without pagination and the information is organized under various headings.)
51. Charles Wood to the Governor General, no. 73, 8 February 1861, Military Despatches.
52. *Peel Committee*, Appendix no. 22.
53. A. Bopegamage, 'Caste, Class and the Indian Military: A Study of the Social Origins of Indian Army Personnel', in Jacques van Doorn (ed.), *Military Profession and Military Regimes: Commitments and Conflicts*, The Hague/Paris: The Mouton, 1969, pp. 142-3.
54. *Report of Major General H. Hancock of the Bombay Army* (hereafter *Hancock's Report*), Cd 2516, *Parliamentary Papers*, 1859, pp. 27-8.
55. *Peel Committee*, Appendix no. 22.
56. *Supplementary Report*, pp. 4, 14.
57. Douglas M. Peers, 'Introduction', in idem (ed.), *Warfare and Empires: Contact and Conflict between European and Non-European Military*

and Maritime Forces and Cultures, Aldershot: Variorum, 1997, p. xxx.

58. Forrest, *Indian Mutiny*, Appendix nos 18 and 21, pp. cxxxiii, cxlvi.
59. Bandopadhyay, *Jivancharit*, pp. 81-7, 108.
60. Ibid., pp. 87-9.
61. Ibid., pp. 97-8.
62. C.A. Bayly (ed.), Eric Stokes, *The Peasant Armed: The Indian Revolt of 1857*, Oxford: Oxford University Press, 1986, pp. 22-3.
63. Winfred Baumgart, *The Crimean War: 1853-1856*, London: Arnold, 1999, pp. 79, 131-7; Major General J.F.C. Fuller, *The Conduct of War: 1789-1961*, 1961, rpt, London: Methuen, 1971, pp. 77-94.
64. Robert Henry Wallace Dunlop, *Service and Adventure with the Khakee Ressalah or Meerut Volunteer Horse during the Mutinies of 1857-58*, 1858, rpt, Allahabad: Legend Publications, 1974, pp. 74-5.
65. Bandopadhyay, *Jivancharit*, p. 111.
66. Roberts, *Letters*, p. 95.
67. Lieutenant Colonel Rufus Simon, *History of the Corps of Electrical and Mechanical Engineers*, vol. 1, New Delhi: Vikas, 1977, p. 31; Alexander Llewellyn, *The Siege of Delhi*, London: Macdonald & Jane's, 1977, p. 7.
68. Ram, *Historic Trials*, p. 394.
69. Simon, *Their Formative Years*, p. 13.
70. From Lieutenant Colonel E.W.S. Scott, Inspector General of Ordnance and Magazines to the Secretary to the Government of India, Fort William, 20 June 1860, Progs. no. 4, MDP, August 1860.
71. Simon, *Their Formative Years*, p. 436.
72. Brigadier R.C. Butalia, *The Evolution of Artillery in India: From the Battle of Plassey to the Revolt of 1857*, New Delhi: Allied, 1998, pp. 320-3.
73. *Peel Committee*, Appendix no. 17; *Hancock's Report*, p. 24.
74. Elting, *Swords around a Throne*, p. 17.
75. *Peel Committee*, p. 17.
76. MacMunn, *Indian Mutiny*, pp. 97, 100.
77. Forrest, *Indian Mutiny*, Appendix no. 18, p. cxxxii.
78. Roberts, *Letters*, pp. 81, 98.
79. General Orders by the Commander-in-Chief, 23 November 1857, NAI.
80. Roberts, *Forty-One Years*, p. 162; Major General B.P. Hughes, 'Siege Artillery in the Nineteenth Century', *Journal of the Society for Army Historical Research* (henceforth *JSAHR*), vol. LX, no. 243, 1982, pp.129-30, 146-7.
81. *Peel Committee*, Appendix no. 17; Blomfield, *Lahore to Lucknow*, p. 55.
82. Blomfield, *Lahore to Lucknow*, pp. 59, 67-9, 78.
83. Llewellyn, *Siege*, p. 132; Antony Beevor, *Stalingrad: The Fateful Siege, 1942-1943*, 1998, rpt, Harmondsworth, Middlesex: Penguin, 1999, pp. 123-235.
84. Haq, *Ahsanullah Khan*, p. 5.

85. Ibid., pp. 7, 10, 12.

86. Haq (ed.), Appendix, *Copy of a Journal kept by Kedarnath, late Clerk in the Delhi Gazette Press*, pp. 37-8.

87. Haq, *Ahsanullah Khan*, p. 5.

88. Ibid., p. 9; Dunlop, *Khakee Ressalah*, pp. 45-6, 94; Ram, *Historic Trials*, pp. 402-3.

89. Dunlop, *Khakee Ressalah*, pp. 54-7, 64-5, 69, 96, 99.

90. Roberts, *Forty-One Years*, p. 182.

91. Brigadier Humphrey Bullock, *History of the Army Service Corps: 1760-1857*, vol. 1, New Delhi: Sterling Publishers, 1976, pp. 222, 225, 238-9, 243-46, Appendix I, 249.

92. Roberts, *Letters*, pp. 132-3.

93. John Fraser, 'Captain Clifford Henry James', *JSAHR*, no. 243, Autumn 1982, pp. 172-3.

94. Forrest, *Indian Mutiny*, pp. 422-3.

95. Ibid., pp. 425-9; T.A. Heathcote, *The Indian Army: The Garrison of British Imperial India, 1822-1922*, Newton Abbot: David & Charles, 1974, p. 46.

96. Forrest, *Indian Mutiny*, pp. 435, 437, 439, 441.

97. MacKenzie, *Revolutionary Armies*, pp. 80-106.

98. Yu Sheng-Wu and Chang Chen-Kun, 'China and India in the Mid-19th Century', in Joshi, *Rebellion 1857*, pp. 338, 340-1.

99. *Hancock's Report*, p. 9.

100. Bayly (ed.), Stokes, *Peasant Armed*, p. 19.

101. J.J.A. Wallace, 'Maneuver Theory in Operations Other Than War', *Journal of Strategic Studies*, vol. 19, no. 4, 1996, pp. 207-23; Captain B.H. Liddell Hart, *Strategy*, New York: Frederick A. Praeger, 1954.

102. For an account of Maratha *ganimi kava* (guerrilla warfare), see M.R. Kantak, *The First Anglo-Maratha War: 1774-1783, A Military Study of Major Battles*, Bombay: Popular Prakashan, 1993, pp. 5-23; Arjan Das Malik, *An Indian Guerrilla War: The Sikh Peoples War, 1699-1768*, New Delhi: Wiley, 1975.

103. Rajni Kant Gupta, *Military Traits of Tatya Tope*, New Delhi: Sultan Chand, 1987, p. 133.

104. V.G. Kiernan, *European Armies from Conquest to Collapse: 1815-1960*, Suffolk: Fontana, 1982, pp. 47, 50.

105. Roberts, *Forty-One Years*, p. 173.

106. MacMunn, *Indian Mutiny*, p. 217.

107. Hunter, *Dalhousie*, p. 183.

108. MacMunn, *Indian Mutiny*, pp. 104-5.

109. Bayly (ed.), Stokes, *Peasant Armed*, p. 28.

110. Mills, *India in 1858*, p. 66.

111. Blomfield, *Lahore to Lucknow*, p. 56.

112. *Supplementary Report*, p. 45; *Peel Committee*, Appendix no. 22.

113. *Peel Committee*, p. 15.
114. Kiernan, *European Armies*, pp. 48-9.
115. P.J.O. Taylor (general editor), *A Companion to the 'Indian Mutiny' of 1857*, Delhi: Oxford University Press, 1996, pp. 351-2.
116. Bayly (ed.), Stokes, *Peasant Armed*, p. 17.
117. Ibid., pp. 25, 27.

SIX

Past Imperfect, Future Uncertain: Kargil, the Indian Military, and the New Millennium

The Combat is the real warlike activity, everything else is only its auxiliary; let us therefore take an attentive look at its nature. Combat means fighting, and in this the destruction or conquest of the enemy is the object, and the enemy, in the particular combat, is the armed forces which stands opposed to us. This is the simple idea ... our wars are made up of a number of great and small simultaneous and consecutive combats,

CARL VON CLAUSEWITZ, *Vom Kriege*, 1832[1]

26 May 1999. A batch of MIG-21s flying in sub-Arctic conditions along the ice-capped Himalayan peaks in north Kashmir unleashed surface-to-air missiles. For the first time in the history of independent India, fighters and fighter-bombers along with attack helicopters were used to flush out the insurgents. The peaks reverberated with the sound of artillery. *Jawans* shouted '*Bharat mata ki Jai*' while trying to advance towards the enemy-held peaks but were scattered. The enemy machine guns mowed down the assault columns of the Indian infantry. It was a living hell on earth. In Kargil, the battle, 'real warlike activity' in Clausewitz's words, had begun.

1999 is indeed a turning point in the evolution of warfare in South Asia. For the first time in the annals of Afro-Asian warfare, the two states India and Pakistan, despite possessing nuclear weapons conducted a air-land war against each other. What are the implications of this conflict for the military policy of India in the context of the ongoing so-called military revolution? In the first section, the attempt is to analyse the dynamics of the Kargil conflict. The next section tries to place the recent conflict within the broader context of the 'revolution in military affairs' (RMA) that is occurring at the international strategic scenario. The last section discusses preparation by India's armed forces for the twenty-first century. And we will see that the process of military synthesis remains crucial in all these developments.

DISINTEGRATION OF CONVENTIONAL
DETERRENCE AND KARGIL

THE INDO-PAK MILITARY BALANCE

How come despite possessing numerical superiority vis-á-vis Pakistan, New Delhi failed to deter Islamabad from resorting to a 'quasi-conventional war' on land? By this term, I mean a sort of conflict that is more intense than the low-intensity conflict (small wars conducted by stateless actors) but that does not escalate into a full-scale conventional conflict. Let us look at the military balance as it existed in 1997-8. The India-Pakistan border is 3,000-km. long. In 1996, Pakistan's defence expenditure was $3.7 billion and that of India's was $10.4 billion. While the size of the Pakistan army was 5,20,000, the strength of the Indian army was 9,80,000. Against the 2,120 tanks and 1,590 towed artillery of the Pakistan army, the Indian army could put into the field 3,314 tanks and 4,175 towed guns. Against 310 combat aircraft of the Pakistan Air Force (PAF), the Indian Air Force (IAF) possessed about 745 warplanes.[2]

India's operational doctrine was to conduct high-speed mobile armoured warfare with armoured brigades and mechanized infantry under an air umbrella as was attempted along the Indo-Pak border in Punjab in 1965 and in 1971. Deep armoured thrusts along multiple axes were planned. Assaults on a wide front were to be carried out by composite combat formations, which included self-propelled artillery and infantry travelling in the armoured personnel carriers.[3]

However, India could not neglect the bigger threat: China. After 1962, India always had to deploy about 12 mountain divisions along its long northern frontier.[4] Hence, India's theoretical superiority was never translated into actual superiority against Pakistan. This enabled Pakistan to plan military adventures against India. Except India, Pakistan had no other aggressive neighbours with whom it had to contend. After the withdrawal of the Soviet forces, and the establishment of the Taliban regime, Afghanistan had become friendly with Pakistan. Relation with Iran became cordial following cooperation in defence matter from 1993 onwards.[5]

After suffering humiliating defeat in Bangladesh during the 1971 war, Pakistan was unwilling to engage India in a full-scale conventional conflict. By amalgamating the teachings of the Koran with the historical tradition of insurgency warfare of the Pathans, the Pakistan army's officer corps had synthesized a concept of 'quasi-limited war' against the 'infidels'. In the nineteenth and early twentieth century, the Pathan tribesmen faced with the technologically and numerically superior British Indian army refused to engage in a conventional conflict. The Pathan and Afghan *lashkars* (tribals organized for military campaigns) crossed the frontiers stealthily and then engaged in hit-and-run expeditions, marauding and killing the Hindu civilians along the frontier districts. By the time the British Raj concentrated its military assets, the *lashkars* vanished among the hills and ravines of the Indus. The absorption of the above-mentioned military traditions were expressed in Islamabad's strategy dating from the 1980s to encourage a low-intensity war in Kashmir and thus to keep the maximum number of units of the Indian army engaged in counter-insurgency activities.[6] This further reduced India's numerical superiority in conventional weapons along the Line of Control (LoC).

Recent measures initiated by Pakistan also blunted the advantages that India had traditionally enjoyed in the sea. To prevent a repeat of the 1971 maritime war, when India carried out missile attacks against the West Pakistani ports and used the aircraft carrier to blockade East Pakistan, Pakistan invested heavily in submarines and torpedo boats to increase the 'sea-denial' capacity of her navy. Pakistan had 5 submarines. These were equipped with Harpoon anti-ship missiles. One aspect of the modernization of the Pakistan Navy was the procurement of 8 missile boats from China, which were equipped with missiles.[7] The anti-ship capability of the Pakistan Navy further rose when, in 1997, China sold Sardine missiles to Pakistan.[8]

In early 1999, India possessed 2 aircraft carriers, 6 frigates, 19 corvettes, 7 patrol ships, 3 first attack crafts, 18 minesweepers, and]3 destroyers against Pakistan's 4 frigates, 3 first attack crafts, 3 minesweepers, and 2 destroyers. Despite possessing numerical superiority, the Indian Navy was unwilling to risk its surface ships against Pakistan's anti-shipping capabilities. So the Indian Navy remained inactive in the Arabian Sea when the Pakistan army crossed the LoC in Kashmir.[9]

THE BATTLE FOR KARGIL: DEFEAT IN DISGUISE

1. Strategy, Tactics, and Equipment of the Opposing Sides

Pakistan's strategy was to grab the heights in an attempt to redefine the LoC and to focus international attention on the 'plight of the Kashmiri Muslims' by further encouraging militancy in Kashmir. Pakistan perhaps hoped that any tension along the LoC would force India to remove troops from Kashmir engaged in counter-insurgency operations towards the border and this would give a fillip to the militants. It was a joint Inter Service Intelligence-Pakistan army operation. Normally, except in Siachen (a 685 sq. km. piece of glacier), both India and Pakistan used to withdraw their troops to lower altitudes in winter and reoccupy the heights during summer. Pakistan broke this pattern by retaining troops in Kargil. Thus, a stretch of about 110 km. of the LoC in Kashmir was threatened. The intruders (mostly *mujahideen* guerrillas and Pakistani regulars)[10] were on the point of cutting the 510 km.-long Srinagar-Leh road. Had it been cut, then the only road link between the Indian troops in Srinagar and Leh in Ladakh would have been severed. This would have left the Indian contingent in Siachen without any ground connection with the principal bases in the Kashmir Valley.[11]

India responded by bringing in the 6th Mountain Division from Jozila. While it functioned as an operational reserve, the 8th Mountain Division attacked in the Drass Sector. To prevent any further intrusion, all the five Indian corps along the Punjab, Rajasthan, and Gujarat Indo-Pak border were alerted. All leaves were cancelled. The artillery brigades were moved into forward positions. Special trains were used to transport tanks and munitions to the forward depots. As part of the civil defence programme, sirens and blackout drills were practiced in the border areas. Meanwhile, Pakistan responded by concentrating its troops in western Punjab, the most effective area to launch an offensive in case a full-scale war did break out.[12]

About 600 guerrillas, who had initially infiltrated into the Kargil-Drass Sector, and later supported by 1,700 Pakistani troops, built concrete bunkers.[13] These were further reinforced with iron girders and corrugated sheets. The intruders were perched on barren peaks whose height varied between 10,000 to 16,000 feet. The temperature hovered between −5 to −11°C. The intruders had AK-47 rifles, hand-held heat-seeking Stinger missiles, and light anti-aircraft guns. These troops had supplies (rice, wheat, and pulses) for about six months. From the other side of the border, the intruders were given long-range fire support by heavy artillery and 122 mm. multi-barrel rocket launchers of the Pakistan army.[14]

The Indian attack started on 14 May with the 18th Grenadier Battalion. The Pakistani tactics were to interrupt the radio messages of the Indian troops with sophisticated electronic jammers and to pin the Indians down with artillery and machine gun fire. The tactics of the Indian army were aimed at making infantry assaults on the peaks both from the front and the rear with the aid of artillery support. This style of attack was somewhat similar to that practiced by the Allied troops against the peak of Monte Cassino in Italy held by German infantry in early 1944. At the ground level, it was the company commanders' battle, as in Vietnam. The normal Indian assault team was composed of 30 men led by a commissioned officer.[15] Every Indian *jawan* had to climb carrying about 25 kg. of equipment and rations. Hand-to-hand fighting on top of the peaks was common. While attacking, the *jawans* were motivated by Hindi songs played on their walkmans and radios and by pictures of the beautiful Indian film actress Sonali Bendre, which they carried in their hip pockets.[16] Since the infiltrators had occupied the heights, it was an uphill task for the Indian soldiers.[17] The outcome was very heavy casualties. By June 24, India had lost 175 soldiers and 550 were injured.[18] By 26 July 1999, the total casualties suffered by the Indian armed forces were 479 killed and 1,109 wounded.[19]

After continuous request by the army and under pressure from the hawks, which included the Defence Minister George Fernandes and the Home Minister L.K. Advani, the Indian Prime Minister ordered air strikes. For the first time since 1971, the IAF used jets in action against the insurgents.[20] The use of air power to flush out insurgents from the frontier area was nothing new in the context of international military history. The Royal Air Force first started the technique of bombing insurgents along the borders of the far-flung British Empire during the 1920s and 1930s.[21] The adoption of this technique by the far more advanced aircraft of the IAF may be categorized as a process of military synthesis.

The problems that the IAF faced were many. In the history of airwar, no air force has had to conduct ground attacks on snow-clad mountain peaks of about 16,000 feet in height. Amidst icy winds howling across the terrain with near-zero visibility due to almost continuous snowstorms, the IAF pilots were near the threshold of the danger zone. The terrain resembled the lunar landscape and was uncharted for the IAF. It had not conducted any exercises for ground support in that region previously. On 25 May 1999, with MIG-21s (fighters), 23s and 27s (fighter-bombers), and MI-17s (big helicopters armed with machine guns), the Western Air Command began its operation named *Safed Sagar* (White Sea). The MI-17s attempted low-altitude attacks on the intruders. On 27 May, a MIG-27 crashed on Pakistan's side of the LoC due to engine trouble. When a MIG-21 was looking for it on the same day, it fell a victim to the shoulder-fired Stinger missiles, which also bought down a MI-17 on May 28. Previously, on 21 May, a Stinger missile damaged a Canberra aircraft while it was carrying out an aerial survey of the Kargil sector. After the loss of two aircraft and one MI-17, the IAF reviewed its tactics. From 7 June onwards, Mirages were used for precision attacks with 1,000 lb. bombs, each of which was fitted with a laser kit. Jaguars and the MIG-25s were used for reconnaissance. The IAF flew at heights above 30,000 feet since Stinger missiles could not reach beyond 28,000 feet. At an average about 10 strike sorties by the IAF occurred every day. The logistical support given to the army personnel by the helicopters should not be underrated. The air force lifted 6,500 tons of ammunition, food, and water, and 30,000 men were transported in the form of casualties and reinforcements. The other side of the LoC was guarded by Pakistan's F-16s. On two occasions, these fighter-bombers. flew only 15 km. away from the IAF's planes.[22]

2. *Indian Military Effectiveness in Kargil:*
   An Assessment

Towards the end of July, the Indian government claimed that Operation Vijay which was launched to eliminate the Pakistan-backed infiltrators from the Kargil-Drass Sector was a complete success. But there was a caveat. How was it the IAF and the best units of the Indian army supported by heavy artillery took so much time to drive back the lightly armed guerrillas who were supported by intermittent indirect artillery fire from Pakistan? The reality was that even after two months of gruelling combat, the Indian armed forces were unable to annihilate the enemy units as the latter were allowed to pull back safely. It is difficult to swallow this bitter pill because the same Indian military had been instrumental in the capitulation of one-fourth of the Pakistan army in Bangladesh in 1971.

The Chief of Army Staff (COAS) General V.P. Malik, even when the war was going on, publicly admitted that the IAF strikes were not very effective.[23] This was because of defective military synthesis on the part of the Indian military. Technological and tactical limitations hampered the IAF and the Indian army. The IAF also failed to absorb historical experiences. The IAF failed to work out an effective military synthesis by synthesizing the experience of the Soviet Air Force within the gamut of its operational doctrine and force structure. The scenario which the IAF faced in Kashmir was somewhat similar to that faced by Soviet air power in Afghanistan in the 1980s. The flying machines used by both the Soviets and the Indians in Afghanistan and Kargil respectively were more or less similar. The Soviets and the IAF made massive use of the MIG-21s, 23s, and 29s. The physical environment in which both the air forces operated was also similar. Both areas are mountainous and the peaks are barren, covered with snow. Interestingly, both the air forces faced the same opponents: *mujahideen* guerrillas and their patrons, the Pakistani regulars. To cap it all, both the air forces were defeated by the same weapon-Stinger missiles. The Soviet Air Force and the IAF were incapable of operating in the night, while the guerrillas moved mostly after daylight. The Soviets found out that bombings by high-speed fixed-wing aircraft were inaccurate, a factor which the IAF neglected to take into consideration. Again, to hit the scattered bands of the elusive guerrillas in Afghanistan, the Soviet MIGs flew low and used cluster bombs to cover a wide area. This tactic was never thought of by the IAF. However, from 1986, the tables were turned against the Soviet Air Force with the supply of American Stinger missiles to the guerrillas through Pakistan. Interestingly, the intruders in Kashmir were also supplied from Pakistan. The Stingers forced the planes to fly at higher altitude and this resulted in inaccurate bombing. By the end of 1986, the Soviets had lost about 500 aircraft to this lethal weapon. This hastened the Soviet decision to withdraw from Afghanistan just as the ineffectiveness of the IAF and heavy losses among the infantry forced the Indian Premier to offer a 'free exit' to the intruders in July 1999.[24]

Besides the inability to learn valuable lessons from history, the IAF used outdated technology and tactics. The IAF used iron bombs and unguided rockets from MIG-21s, 23s, 27s, and MI-17s on the militants who occupied the peaks. The Army Air Corps (AAC) helicopters flew during daytime when they were fired upon by the intruders. The IAF and the AAC could have gained the initiative by acquiring night-fighting capabilities. The helicopter pilots should have been trained with night-vision equipment. Again, the MI-17 and MI-26 helicopters could have been used to transport troops behind the intruders during the night so that the latter could be attacked with the advantage of surprise. But this would have required the use of heliborne infrared sensors for acquiring detailed knowledge of the terrain.[25] The *Cheetah* (reconnaissance) helicopters of the AAC could have carried thermal imaging sets for surveys in the night. Night-vision glasses for the pilots and the gunners equipped with third-generation image intensifiers/starlight scopes would have provided the IAF, and the AAC night-fighting capability. Again, the heat-seeking Stinger missiles might have been avoided if the aircraft equipped with missile warning systems had dropped flares. India lacked an adequate amount of laser-guided bombs of 100-250 kg. that have been available in the international arms *bazar* for the last 20 years.[26]

The problems in hardware for the Indian ground forces were

lack of snowmobiles and inadequate spares for the Bofors gun. About 10 per cent (40) of the Bofors were unusable due to lack of spares that resulted in cannibalization. This was a serious problem because, in a way, Kargil was also a gunners' war. The Indian infantry took the aid of heavy artillery firestorms before making assaults, just as the British infantry had asked for the support of heavy artillery before advancing frontally in the bloody and muddy terrain of Somme during the First World War. In the Drass, Batalik, and Kaksar sectors, the army deployed 90 Bofors guns. On an average, each day, the gunners' fired 5,000-6,500 shells from the Bofors and the 105 mm. field guns. However, most of the shelling was inaccurate, just like the ineffective Allied shelling of Monte Cassino. This was because the peaks were occupied by the enemy and the Indian gun observer teams, like those of the Allied gunners, had no access to these areas. The artillery continued shelling even in the night without proper equipment. Binoculars fitted with man-portable laser range-finders for the artillery observers would have enabled the artillery to fire effectively at the intruders during the night.[27]

In general, Pakistan had better knowledge of the terrain because from September 1998 onwards the Pakistan army had used remotely piloted vehicles (RPVs) for reconnaissance and for taking photos of the Indian army installations, military outposts, and the mountains. India did not possess any un-manned aerial vehicles (UAVs) for thorough reconnaissance of the terrain.[28] Hence, the Indian army had to fight like a blind man in a ground chosen by the Pakistan army.

Again, India lacked a unified command at the top for con-ducting operations against Pakistan. While the battle in the Kargil Sector was controlled by the Northern Command from Udhampur, the rest of the LoC was supervised by the Western Command situated at Chandigarh. On the Indian side, the divisional commanders planned the battle and fought it with the corps commanders overseeing it. Malik, the COAS, deliberately con-structed a decentralized command system, which was indeed a positive trend for the Indian army. Another plus point for the Indian army was that, unlike the American army officers in Vietnam, the Indian officers' led from the front. This is evident from the very high officer casualties.[29] For this India has to thank the army's regimental organization. However, the Pakistan army's regimental organization is also very impressive since both the armies inherited the regimental fabric of the British Indian army.[30] Now the question is: how far could these two South Asian armed forces cope with the mind-boggling changes that are occurring in the international military scene, and what effects would this have on the contours of South Asia's strategic environment?

THE 'REVOLUTION IN MILITARY AFFAIRS' AND SECURITY IMPLICATIONS FOR THE INDIAN MILITARY

Is the West Experiencing a Revolution in Military Affairs (RMA)?

In the last two decades, the armed forces of both the British and the United States have moved away from the concept of a protracted conventional war, and adopted a new concept of non-nuclear war. This shift is called RMA or the rise of the information age warfare. Actually the 'RMA' is the integration of classical manoeuvre war and *Blitzkrieg* theory with recent advances in software. Besides technological advances, this form of war has an original element: the inability of the Western public to accept a high level of military casualties. So it would be more correct to categorize the 'RMA' as a synthesis in military affairs (SMA). This becomes clear when we analyse the technological, doctrinal, and organizational aspects of the so-called RMA.

The imperative behind 'RMA' is also quite traditional. The initial impetus behind the 'RMA' was to win quickly before the Warsaw Pact could mobilize its numerically superior armoured forces.[31] After the collapse of the USSR, the need for 'RMA' is due to the required Western interventions in 'small wars' along the peripheries of Eurasia for gaining politico-military advantages.[32] The imperative behind rejecting attritional war as the one which the Allies conducted in Normandy in 1944 in favour of manoeuvre war is the fact that the media and the public would not tolerate a huge loss of manpower that would result in a protracted campaign. The new form of local war, which the West is now planning to conduct, is somewhat similar to the nineteenth-century cheap and quick British colonial wars against the Afro-Asian polities. The aim of the West is not annexation of enemy states but limited gains as expressed as 'salami slicing' and redrawing of the borders. Hence, such wars may also be compared with Louis XIV's limited wars of the seventeenth century.[33]

Instead of a highly structured form of battle which depends on detailed orders and deliberate preparations, the aim is to resurrect manoeuvre warfare under high-tech conditions; the aim is to get inside the enemy's decision cycle or the OODA loop to operate more quickly than the enemy. The key elements of the classical manoeuvre war as practiced by the Huns and the Mongols are surprise, speed, mobility, and risk taking. The aim of the theorists of the RMA is to upset the enemy both physically and psychologically. The British theorists derive their concept of manoeuvre war from Captain Basil Liddell Hart's concept of the indirect approach, where Liddell Hart advocates against frontal attacks and criticizes the conduct of positional warfare against the enemy. Liddell Hart argues in favour for flank attacks against the enemy, especially at the peripheries. Along with his geographical indirectness, the later-day theorists of the RMA added the dimension of psychologically upsetting the enemy by outmanoeuvring and outflanking its forces and thinking quickly than the enemy.[34]

Future battlefields witnessing mobile actions instead of static warfare would be fluid and chaotic, and in order to win, writes the British theorist Major General John Kiszely, one needs to maintain a high tempo. This could be maintained if the traditional pyramidal command apparatus with its many intermediate layers is flattened. This in turn would result in the quick flow of information from the 'men on the spot' to the higher-level commander and vice versa, and it would also cut down the time required in decisions being taken and implemented.[35]

Besides the requirements of a mobile battle, the latest technology is another imperative behind the construction of a decentralized command mechanism. The introduction of new lethal technologies like smart bombs and precision-guided missiles, argue the supporters of the RMA, will force the post Cold War armies (termed the information age armies) towards greater dispersion, unlike the industrial age armies which were geared for concentration in order to deliver massive firepower. Thus, the new armies have to generate flexible command frameworks. One key aspect of ensuring it is to give greater scope to the junior commanders. Quick reactions for dispersion in order to survive in the lethal 'killing field' require a dispersed and agile command system in place of a rigid, centralized, and hierarchical command style. In place of *Befehlstaktik* (top down command), the need of the hour is to introduce *Auftragstaktik* (mission-oriented command which gives lot of space to the subordinates and allows full play of their initiatives). The aim is to encourage, educate, and allow the junior officers to take high-level decisions for quick responses in fast-moving battles conducted with the state-of-the-art technology.[36] *Auftragstaktik* would also enable the lower-level commanders to exploit the Clausewitzian fog and friction which will be inherent at the operational level in future battlefields.[37]

The British theorists want to adopt a modified version of the German mission command system. But the American theorist Douglas A. Macgregor wants to emulate successful American business houses which have survived cut-throat business competition by reducing the number of intermediate-level executives and increasing the power of junior-level executives for quick decision making.[38]

Thus, the conceptual basis of the RMA may be traced to the indirect strategy proposed by Liddell Hart and the *Blitzkrieg* theorists of Germany. The key elements of *Blitzkrieg*, like that of the classical manoeuvre war conducted by the cavalry armies, were speed, surprise, and mobility as practiced by the *Wehrmacht*, and the aim was to hit the C3I (Command, Control, Communications, and Intelligence) of the enemy. All these are accommodated within manoeuvre warfare as preached by the advocates of the RMA. Similarly, *Auftragstaktik*, a key element of the information age forces, was first introduced by Generalfeldmarschall Von Moltke in the latter half of the nineteenth century.[39] So the RMA is not a complete break with the past but is an amalgam and modification of traditional manoeuvre war, British indirect strategy, Germany's *Blitzkrieg* theory combined with the rapid advances that are occurring in the field of software technology and electronics.

The emphasis of this new form of manoeuvre war is on electronic gadgets for jamming the enemy's command system. Digitization of the battlefield, which means all the elements would be bound together by an electronic web, will permit the rapid transfer of data to the commanders. This in turn would enable them to take decisions quickly in order to gain 'real time' intelligence, and to issue orders to the weapons platform for timely and precise fire. The command-and-control systems will be highly dependent on information technologies. Thus, the German system of *Auftragstaktik* will be made more effective with the aid of modern software techniques. Hence, C3I becomes C4I (Command, Control, Communications, Computers, and Intelligence). The intelligence, surveillance, target acquisition and rec onnaissance systems of the enemy would become the prime targets of destruction at best and of neutralization at worst. To paralyse the electronic nervous system of the information age forces, the civilian and military computers will be attacked. It is argued that computer hackers will be the new soldiers of revolutionary post Cold War armies.[40]

The very emphasis on information technology has encouraged some theorists like Alvin and Heidi Toffler to categorize the new form of war as the information age war.[41] The point to be noted is that both Clausewitz and Sun Tzu had also emphasized the crucial role of information in war. Thus, the concept of information as a crucial factor in warfare is traditional;[42] only the system for procuring information, i.e. computers is new.

Due to the rise of public consciousness in democratic societies, building a rapport with the public to gain support from the home front is an aspect of the new warfare. During the Gulf War, credit goes to the US military for successfully managing the media. General H. Norman Schwarzkofp projected himself as a fighting man.[43] This is in direct contrast to the mismanagement of the press by the American armed forces during the Korean and the Vietnam Wars. This corroded the morale and willingness of the soldiers to offer their lives in local limited wars that did not directly threaten their homelands.[44]

CHINA: A RISING MINI-SUPERPOWER

1. Force Posture and Chinese Military Doctrine

The RMA or even better the recent SMA is also influencing Asian military thinking. A paradigm shift is occurring in China's strategic thought and force structure. The Chinese military realize that the SMA should be interpreted within the format of the traditional Chinese philosophy of warfare. Sun Bin and Sun Tzu, two Chinese military philosophers who lived around 2000 BC, were advocates of deception, surprise, and ambush instead of bloody frontal assaults involving set-piece battles. Unlike Clausewitz, both were against the total destruction of the enemy forces resulting in complete victory. For these two Chinese military theorists, a bloody victory serves no useful purpose. Sun Bin writes: 'Those who win ten out of ten battles have skilled commanders, yet give rise to calamity.' Rather than total victory, coercive diplomacy backed by military power was recommended by Sun Bin and Sun Tzu.[45] This form of warfare seems similar to the recent Western conceptualization of limited local war, the hallmark of the SMA.

In recent times, some other Chinese military theoreticians have elaborated on this strand of thought. Major General Yu Qifen asserts that the danger of a Third World War has vanished with the collapse of the USSR. In the emerging multi-polar world, numerous limited local wars would occur, and there is the danger of Western intervention to control the pace of limited conflicts in Asia. For this, the Unites States is focusing on rapid reaction forces to contain the instability that will be created by the off-stage medium powers.[46] Colonel Yao Youzhi and Colonel Liu Hongsong argue that China must prepare to conduct limited local war along the Asia-Pacific rim under a nuclear umbrella. They argue that the very presence of nuclear warheads will prevent these limited skirmishes from transforming themselves into major wars. For fighting such wars, China needs to develop her maritime forces and also needs to modernize the logistical apparatus of the armed forces. General Fu Quanyou asserts that an essential prerequisite for winning limited local wars is a managerial revolution for absorbing and integrating the revolutionary technologies.[47]

Deng Xiaoping was the chief actor who initiated the SMA in China. He advocated a shift away from Marxian class warfare. Deng demanded that the army's size should be reduced and that the forces should be prepared for qualitative improvement. He aimed to reduce the size of the armed forces by about a million men. He also focused increasingly on technology, and education and concentrated on increasing the scope of research and development in the military sphere.[48]

At present and in the near future, China might pursue an aggressive strategy. This is because the political regime is under threat due to the ongoing political and economic reforms. The ruling class is on shaky ground because its ideological foundations have been loosened with the failure of classical socialism and pursuance of Deng Xiaoping's policy of 'get rich quick'. Any enhancement of the nation's military prestige will give time to the Communist Party to consolidate its hold on power after the tragedy at the Tiananmen Square. Similarly, any diminution of military status would at best result in domestic chaos and at worst disintegration of the 'Middle Kingdom'. Hence, China's overreaction in the case of Taiwan.[49] Another imperative behind the increasing professionalization of China's armed forces is the war in Kosovo which raises the possibility of Western interventions in disputes involving China and her neighbours.[50]

What about China's military capacity vis-á-vis a medium Asian power like India? We need to take stock of recent acquisition of weapon systems by the Chinese military and its operational level of warfare. The Chinese military is preparing for limited local wars at its peripheries with state-of-the-art technologies. For this China is structuring elite units with special training and equipment which could conduct manoeuvre war on a limited scale. This kind of thinking is a complete break with the Maoist strategy of a protracted Peoples' War involving mass mobilization. This shift in the operational style started from the 1980s. Instead of luring the adversary inside the country and taking advantage of depth, the enemy is to be defeated at the borders in the initial battles.[51] For this combined arms operation is the new focus. China is also attempting to extend the reach of air operations in support of amphibious assaults and naval operations.[52]

The Chinese coastal navy is in the process of becoming a force that could operate along the Asia-Pacific rim. The shrinkage of the Russian naval presence and the slow reduction of the American war-fighting assets in the Asia-Pacific region has given the Peoples Liberation Army's Navy (PLAN) space and opportunity to flex its muscles. Till the 1980s, the PLAN was a brown water navy as it was structured as a coastal defence force. Then it was composed of torpedo submarines and torpedo speed boats.[53] At present, the PLAN could conduct offensive action in the distant seas like a green water navy but not oceanic offensive like a blue water navy. This it can probably conduct by 2010 when Beijing will acquire an aircraft carrier.[54] In 1995, the PLAN introduced the doctrine of conducting maritime local war in the littoral regions with advanced technologies. At present it is undergoing electronization, automation, and nuclearization. The navy is in the process of introducing automated command systems for raising speed, efficiency, and accuracy of transmission of information. The aim is to increase the speed of radar transmission at least fifteen fold.[55] As regards the weapon platforms, China is purchasing two Russian guided missile destroyers and an Israeli-made long-range airborne radar system. This will increase the operational range of the PLAN. With more than a hundred conventional powered submarines and several nuclear submarines, China's submarine corps is the second largest in the world. What is worrying from India's perspective in the long run is that China's South Sea Fleet, destined for operating in the Indian Ocean, is getting priority in terms of men and materials compared to the Eastern Sea and the Northern Sea Fleets which are supposed to operate in the Pacific Ocean.[56]

At present, the Peoples Liberation Army Air Force (PLAAF) is the third largest air force in the world, with 3,740 combat aircraft in its inventory. And the Dragon's Dragonfly is getting stronger. In the near future, the SU-27s will constitute the backbone of the Chinese air force. By 2005, the PLAAF will possess about 300 Su-27, which will be more than a match for 100 Indian MIG-29, Mirage-2000, and Su-30. What is more worrisome is the fact that, the PLAAF has three airborne divisions under its command, while India has none.[57] The PLAAF is showing interest in acquiring weapons for electronic warfare. The Chinese plan is to acquire four Airborne Early Warning aircraft system from Russia and Israel. Along with the long-range radar, these A-50s will carry electronic intelligence systems and advanced communications systems.[58]

One aspect of the rising professionalism of the Chinese military is the retreat from its lucrative business empire which it started acquiring from the 1980s. In July 1998, President Jiang Zemin ordered the Peoples Liberation Army (PLA) to give up its commercial enterprises and the latter obeyed.[59] Another aspect of professionalism among the officer corps is their rising educational levels.[60] Any increase of the military effectiveness of the PLA automatically heightens the gap between the Chinese and the Indian armies.

2. Emergence of the Beijing-Yangoon-Islamabad-Isfahan Axis

It seems that China is encircling India with its client states. In the east, China's collaboration with the military *junta* in Myanmar started from 1988 onwards. In return for economic-cum-diplomatic support and supply of military hardware, Beijing is allowed enormous leverage within the country. Since 1992, China has been pushing the *junta* to accept the Dragon's demand of building a port on Hainggyi Island on the mouth of Bassein river which flows into the Bay of Bengal. In the near future, this base would be capable of handling the kilo class submarines, which China has procured from Russia. This would be the culmination of China's quest for an outlet into the Indian Ocean and threaten the Indian Eastern Naval Command. Worse, China is probably building a naval base in the Great Coco Islands, and these installations will be able to oversee the Indian naval base in the Andamans Islands and also the Indian missile base at Chandipur in Orissa. Since the *junta* is in no position to pay for the military equipment supplied, Myanmar cannot afford to obstruct China's demand. In addition, Pakistan, the other traditional enemy of India and a semi-satellite of China is also supplying hardware to the *junta*.[61]

What is of more concern for India is the active partnership between China, Pakistan, and Iran. China is continuing to assist their missile programme. China is assisting Pakistan in the construction of two M-11 missile plants, and one of the factories is located at Fatehgunj, about 40 km. west of Islamabad. The M-11 missiles transferred to Iran and Pakistan are capable of carrying nuclear warheads. Worse, Pakistan, in accordance with the demand of the SMA, is going ahead with the construction of a C4I2 (Command, Control, Communications, Computers, Intelligence, and Information) for its nuclear arsenal.[62] The Chinese are providing Iran and Pakistan with guidance systems, gyroscopes, and accelerometers. With these instruments, both Pakistan and Iran tend to upgrade their Intermediate Range Ballistic Missiles (IRBMs) and attempting to construct Intercontinental Ballistic Missiles (ICBMs).[63]

THE PEACOCK RESPONDS: FORCE STRUCTURE,
DOCTRINE, AND ARSENAL

In the near future, the strategic calculus will be further loaded against India. There might be many more lethal Kargil-type conflicts conducted by the stateless marginal groups backed by both the Pakistani and Chinese regulars equipped with the latest hardware along the western and northern borders of India. A Western analyst has termed these quasi-conventional wars conducted by insurgents armed with latest state-of-the-art technologies as post-modern warfare. This sort of warfare has made useless the conventional armed forces geared for attritional industrial warfare [64] like the present Indian army. The two-front war for India is a possibility, but this belongs in the realm of the worst possible scenario. In addition, a long-term maritime threat from China is emerging which might result in diplomatic humiliations at best and the loss of the outlying island chains at worst. What steps are being taken by India to meet these challenges?

FORCE STRUCTURE FOR THE TWENTY-FIRST CENTURY

Before designing a force structure for the new millennium, it is necessary to grasp the basic fundamentals of our existing military force. The present Indian army is more or less based on the British Indian Sepoy army. After the 1857 Mutiny, the British maintained their rule by a sort of military synthesis. The three constituents of this synthesis were the sepoys and the sowars (Indian manpower) who were incorporated within the regimental system (that was imported from Europe) under the guidance of British officers. The first challenge to this British-designed military synthesis came during World War I (1914-18) when the consciousness of Indian soldiers broadened while serving in western Europe. During World War II (1939-45), anti-British consciousness among the sepoys further increased with the collapse of the British position in South-East Asia. Due to heavy officer casualties and the expansion of the army due to wartime requirements, the British were forced to recruit urban middle-class educated Indians into the officer corps. Between 1939 and 1945 the number of commissioned Indian officers rose from 396 to 8,340. The presence of a sizeable chunk of the Indian officer corps and the emergence of an alternate military tradition in the form of *Azad Hind Fauj* destroyed the very basis of the British-designed military synthesis. After 1947, the Congress government maintained the regimental structure of the Sepoy army. Only the brown sahibs replaced the white sahibs. In addition, the Indian army remained seeped in the British army's doctrine of attritional warfare. Now the British army itself is changing[65] and conditions in the twenty-first century will be different from those of the preceding century. What the Indian army is supposed to do now?

The Indian armed forces require to synthesize traditional military doctrines (both foreign and indigenous) with advanced military hardware. A strong conventional force equipped with the latest technology and command apparatus is required to deter or at least dissuade any hostile moves by India's neighbours. India needs to prepare for a repeat of the coercive naval diplomacy of the 1971 style when an American carrier task force structured around the nuclear powered aircraft carrier named Enterprise moved into the Bay of Bengal. In the near future, instead of the USA, China might attempt such an adventure. In 1971, the Indian Navy's attempt to conduct an unopposed amphibious landing in Bangladesh proved to be a fiasco. The navy is yet to learn about an opposed amphibious landing in a shore that will be defended by the enemy air-ground forces. The Indian Navy is still weak in areas of electronic warfare, early warning systems, and sonar and subsurface missiles,[66] and is fast becoming a rusting brown water navy.

For rapid response to any crisis scenario like Kargil, the need of the hour is to possess air-assault and air-mobile brigades. This means availability of more transport planes. By their very mobility, these sorts of troops can alter the 'speed of battle' and upset the enemy's timetable. Moreover, such units could easily overcome physical obstacles in the mountainous terrain and bypass the enemy's strong points. The heliborne and the paratroop operations would cut the enemy's lines of communication and prevent his consolidation till the ground forces come up to deliver the knockout blow. By attacking the enemy's C3 nodes (a technique of *Blitzkrieg*) in advance of our land forces, they would spread chaos and alter the design of battle in our favour. But India lacks a trained staff structure for conducting air assault and airborne operations. The advanced light helicopter (ALH) is still waiting to go into serial production. Indian helicopters need to evolve electronic surveillance systems so that they could function as 'directed telescopes' of the commanders. A greater integration between the Indian Army and the IAF as regards joint tactical doctrine and maintenance of hardware regarding the helicopters is yet to be established.[67]

The Indian army's command apparatus needs to be democratized by allowing junior officers more autonomy. In the Indian Army, some of the senior commanders believe that the best way to command the junior officers is to frighten them into obedience. This stifles initiative among the subordinate junior officers and transforms them into semi-automatons. These sorts of officers are unsuited for fighting an information age war.[68] A portrayal of our top-down command system is the fictional incident that occurred along the Indo-Pak border in Rajasthan during the 1971 war in the film *Border* directed by J.P. Dutt. When the local commander, a major (actor Sunny Deol) asked for autonomy as regards troop disposition along the probable enemy attack routes, he was overruled by the military bureaucrats at the distant army head-quarters. In the end, the major's view about the enemy axis of attack turned out to be the right one. General V.P. Malik's attempt to decentralize the command by maintaining a loose supervision over the subordinates during the Kargil operation ought to be followed further down the line.

New Delhi needs to possess at best nuclear superiority or at the least nuclear parity vis-á-vis her neighbours for conducting aggressive conventional counter-strikes in case of border violations. Pakistan views its nuclear arsenal as a corollary to its conventional force and thus refuses to accept India's offer of a 'no first use treaty'.[69] India's nuclear programme is ambiguous and still unoperational. A consensus is yet to emerge about the number of warheads New Delhi requires. The upper tier is fixed by an analyst, Bharat Karnad, to be 400 warheads and the lowest limit as propounded by ex-COAS General K. Sundarji is to be merely 20 bombs. The dominant opinion among the civilian-military elite is that nuclear weapons are meant for strategic use. India is unwilling to go for tactical battlefield nuclear warheads because they are costly and require sophisticated command systems.[70] A credible nuclear deterrence is also impossible because India does not have the apparatus for commanding and controlling the warheads.[71]

The draft of nuclear doctrine as prepared by the Atal Behari Vajpayee government states that India should possess air, land, and sea-borne strategic nuclear capacity. The indigenous nuclear submarine ought to be operational by 2005. However, there is a missile gap between Pakistan and India. The former possesses more advanced missiles. This is because Indian missiles are made indigenously, while Pakistan imports missiles from China and North Korea. The American attempt to curb the transfer of missile technology from China to Pakistan has failed. Pakistan's Haft 2 and Haft 3 are nothing but the Chinese M-11 and M-9 missiles. As far as India is concerned, the Agni 2 due to its solid fuel system which is non-corrosive and easy to handle is suitable for carrying nuclear warheads. But due to American pressure, its development has been more or less shelved. They are not yet ready for serial production. Prithvi is not suitable for carrying nuclear warheads, and its liquid propulsion system makes it more cumbersome. Worse, according to recent American intelligence estimates, the size of Pakistan's nuclear arsenal is regarded as bigger than that of India. Against the ICBM-equipped China, India just has no answer.[72]

INDIA'S *AD HOC* DEFENCE ARSENAL:
PROBLEMS AND PERSPECTIVES

Besides nukes, India has problems in maintaining its conventional arms arsenal. Both China and India are moving away from centralized command economies and liberalizing government regulations regarding trade and technology transfer, thus opening up the economy for absorbing new technologies especially in the field of software to meet the demands of the SMA.[73] However, grave problems remain.

There is a continuous tussle between the Defence Research Development Organization (DRDO) and the armed forces. The DRDO's indigenous products are dated, so the three services always demand the import of the latest military hardware and their production under licence in India. For maintaining military effectiveness in the immediate context, the government had to give in to the demands of the military but in the long run India still lacks the capacity to innovate and produce world-class military hardware. For example, if India in the near future inducts the indigenous light combat aircraft (LCA), the effectiveness of the IAF will suffer because the LCA would be unable to match the state-of-the-art interceptors.[74] There seems no way out of this vicious circle and India seems to have been caught in the technology trap.

The import of military hardware not only eats up scarce foreign resources but there are also additional problems. Between 1986 and 1990, India bought 188 engines for MIG-29, and out of them about 133 engines failed. In 1996, India signed an agreement with Russia to buy 50 Sukhoi-30 aircraft. They were not operational even in 2000.[75] The 40 Mirages which India bought from Dassault in the mid-1990s continue to constitute the core of the IAF.[76]

Again, there is no long-term and consistent policy in place to acquire weapons systems. The government buys off the rack whatever is available cheaply and quickly.[77] In the immediate aftermath of Kargil, the Indian government is willing to modernize its armed forces piecemeal. The IAF has been asking for advanced trainer jets (ATJs) for the last two decades. Now the government has finally given the green signal. After experiencing the Kargil conflict, the army is demanding a minimum one battery of Smerch multi-barrel rocket launchers. A technical team visited Russia in September 1999 and recommended its acquisition.[78] India has signed a contract to buy 1,000 Russian laser-guided 155 mm. Krasnopol-M rounds and 10 laser range finders to give its artillery a precision-strike capability. These shells are to be fired from the Bofors guns. The shells have been successfully tested in the Rajasthan desert but have yet to perform properly at the high altitudes of Kashmir's mountainous terrain.[79]

INDIAN MILITARY THEORY FOR THE FUTURE

Warfare is the greatest affair of the state, the basis of life and death, the Way (*Tao*) to survival or extinction. It must be thoroughly pondered and analysed.

SUN TZU[80]

Sun Tzu's warning is all the more relevant in the Indian context because India still lacks a coherent operational doctrine for using its hardware properly. Rear Admiral Raja Menon argues for meshing maritime strategy with the doctrine of continental war.

He visualizes India as a middle-ranking landpower. So he wants India to have a conventional weapons equipped brown water navy primarily comprising amphibious ships and diesel submarines. The navy would conduct a littoral war at the periphery of the enemy country while the Indian army and the IAF would conduct an air-land campaign against the landpower that would threaten India.[81]

To be frank, Menon's perspective is narrow. The Indian Navy with its coastal defence role appears to be marginal in his doctrinal scheme. He fails to recognize the maritime threat that would come from the PLAN in the distant future. Moreover, Menon's doctrine does not provide a blueprint for saving our distant island chains like the Lakshadweep and the Andaman and Nicobar Islands. Nor does he address the problematic of naval nuclear deterrence due to the presence of the nuclear-equipped PLAN submarines in the Indian Ocean.

In reaction to Kargil and the ongoing SMA, there seems to be a renaissance in Indian strategic thinking. Indian analysts like Brigadier Vinod Anand and the retired Air Commodore Jasjit Singh accept that it is the age of 'information warfare'. The focus of future warfare should be on electronic counter counter-measures, sensor technologies, and space-based satellites for reconnaissance. New gadgets for acquiring, processing, and synthesizing information are required. All these need jointness in planning and prosecuting war.[82] Captain A.K. Sachdev writes that CNN brought instant pictures of the Gulf War to American homes. Similarly, Kargil was the first television war for Indians. Naturally, the Indian middle class, like its American counterpart, would not tolerate heavy casualties inherent in an attritional land campaign. Media coverage is also part of the information warfare. Instead of treating the media as an enemy and hiding behind official secrecy, the Ministry of Defence, asserts Sachdev, must learn to use the media as a force multiplier to galvanize the public for winning the war.[83]

Nevertheless, it is unfortunate that the Indian military theoreticians are guided by Western philosophical tools while analysing SMA. For example, Akshay Joshi, an analyst at the IDSA, views the RMA from the perspective of American military theoreticians.[84]

We need not ape Western military theoretical tools in totality. While the Chinese are interpreting SMA with the aid of the analytical tools of ancient Chinese military philosophy, India could also afford to do the same. The concept of *Chakravyuh* was introduced by the ancient Hindu theoreticians[85] long before the concept of *Kesselschlacht*, i.e. double envelopment for out-flanking the enemy, a key component of manoeuvre warfare was invented by Hannibal in the West. Kautilya emphasizes *Kutayuddha* (which is similar to modern misinformation and disinformation campaigns) for limited gains rather than bloody battles aiming at the complete destruction of the enemy. This is similar to Sun Tzu's concept. In *Arthashastra's* concept of *mandalas*, that is surrounding India with a string of client states, India have a grand strategy for theorizing on limited local war and pursuing a hegemonic national security policy,[86] the hallmark of SMA. Kautilya's emphasis on establishing politico-diplomatic ties with our enemy's enemy[87] (Vietnam and Japan for countering China) is India's best possible strategy for the new millennium.

CONCLUSION

To sum up, there is an absence of creativity as regards theorizing warfare and a mismatch between theory and practice of warfare in India. While the Indian military theorists stress the need to get ready for the new form of war in the subcontinent, the armed forces are still continuing their emphasis to acquire as many weapons platforms as possible for conducting an industrial conventional war in the traditional style. There is no attempt by the three service headquarters to focus on the sophisticated communications network. Regardless of the theoreticians' emphasis on jointmanship for streamlining the command apparatus for conducting war, inter-service rivalry remains the bane of the Indian military system. India's arms procurement policy remains at worst *ad hoc* and at best geared to meet short-term crises. The absence of long-term planning for the future remains the characteristic feature of the Indian military estab-lishment.

True, India's defence budget is not elastic. India probably cannot spend more than 2.5 per cent of the GNP on defence,[88] but the government can afford to change the priorities. The armour-heavy dinosaur (Indian war machine) needs to be more agile and mobile. By cutting down the number of infantry divisions and armoured brigades, money could be used for the modernization of weapons system and the automation of the command apparatus. This scheme is bound to face opposition from vested interest groups (regimental colonels) in the army, and to overcome it requires strong political will. India cannot afford to miss the microchip and the managerial revolutions accompanied by absorption of classical strategic thought for the military organization. If we fail to design a proper military synthesis for our armed forces, history will never forgive us.

NOTES

1. Carl von Clausewitz, *On War*, ed. and with an Introduction by Anatol Rapoport, 1968, rpt, London: Penguin, 1982, p. 303.

2. Raj Chengappa, Rohit Saran and Harinder Baweja, 'Kargil War', *India Today*, vol. 24, no. 27, 5 July 1999, p. 22; Tim McGirk, Meenakshi Ganguly and Maseeh Rahman, 'The Kashmir Knot', *Time*, vol. 152, no. 21, 30 November 1998, p. 20.

3. Ross Masood Mirza, 'Threat Perception and Military Planning in Pakistan: The Impact of Technology, Doctrine and Arms Control', in Eric Arnett (ed.), *Military Capacity and the Risk of War: China, India, Pakistan and Iran*, Oxford: Oxford University Press, 1997, pp. 134-5.

4. Brian Cloughley, *A History of the Pakistan Army: Wars and Insurrections*, Karachi: Oxford University Press, 1999, p. 339.

5. Yezid Sayigh, 'Arms Production in Pakistan and Iran: The Limits of Self-Reliance', in Arnett, *Military Capacity*, pp. 162, 181.

6. Stephen P. Cohen, *The Pakistan Army*, 1984, rpt, Karachi: Oxford University Press, 1993, pp. 98-104; Jaswant Singh, *Defending India*, Chennai: Macmillan, 1999, pp. 256-7; Alan Warren, *Waziristan: The Faqir of Ipi and the Indian Army, The Northwest Frontier Revolt of 1936-37*, Karachi: Oxford University Press, 2000; T.R. Moreman, *The Army in India and the Development of Frontier Warfare: 1849-1947*, London: Macmillan, 1998.

7. Eric Grove, 'Maritime Forces and Stability in Southern Asia', in Arnett, *Military Capacity*, pp. 299-300, 303-4; Major General Ashok Kumar Mehta, 'The Silent War', *Sunday*, vol. 26, 1-7 August 1999, p. 27.

8. Eric Arnett, 'Military Research and Development', in *Sipri Yearbook 1998: Armaments, Disarmament and International Security*, Oxford: Oxford University Press, 1998, p. 286.

9. Mehta, 'Silent War', pp. 26-7.

10. Anthony Spaeth, 'Foghorns of War', *Time*, vol. 152, no. 21, 30 November

1998, p. 15; Jason Burke, 'Kargil War', *India Today*, vol. 24, no. 28, 12 July 1999, pp. 22-4.

11. Jasjit Singh, 'Pakistan's Fourth War for Kashmir', *Asian Strategic Review* (henceforth *ASR*), 1998-99, New Delhi: IDSA, 1999, p. 395.

12. Chengappa et al., 'Kargil War', p. 20; Army Chief General V.P. Malik interviewed by Major General Ashok Mehta, *Sunday*, 18-24 July 1999, pp. 50-1; Sunil Narula and Ranjit Bhushan, 'Drawn into Battle', *Outlook*, vol. 5, no. 21, 7 June 1999, pp. 20-1.

13. *From Surprise to Reckoning: The Kargil Review Committee Report*, New Delhi: Sage, 2000, p. 96.

14. Harinder Baweja, 'Long Haul', *India Today*, vol. 24, no. 28, 12 July 1999, pp. 30, 32; Brigadier Vinod Anand, 'India's Military Response to the Kargil Aggression', *Strategic Analysis* (henceforth *SA*), vol. 23, no. 7, 1999, p. 1057.

15. Harinder Baweja and Ramesh Vinayak, 'Peak by Peak', *India Today*, vol. 24, no. 24, 14 June 1999, pp. 29-30, 33; J.F.C. Fuller, *The Second World War: 1939-1945*, 1954, rpt, New York: Da Capo, 1993, pp. 271-4.

16. Sunil Narula and Ranjit Bhushan, 'Drawn into Battle', *Outlook*, vol. 5, no. 21, 7 June 1999, pp. 20-1; Chengappa et al., 'Kargil War', and Ramesh Vinayak, 'Taking Tololing', *India Today*, vol. 24, no. 27, 5 July 1999, pp. 20, 27, 29, 32-3.

17. Rear Admiral Raja Menon, 'The Road Not Taken', *Outlook*, vol. 5, no. 24, 28 June 1999, p. 27.

18. Chengappa et al., 'Kargil War', p. 20.

19. *From Surprise to Reckoning*, p. 232.

20. Narula and Bhushan, 'Drawn into Battle', pp. 20-1.

21. Keith Jeffrey, 'Colonial Warfare: 1900-1939', in Colin McInnes and G.D. Sheffield (eds.), *Warfare in the Twentieth Century: Theory and Practice*, London: Unwin Hyman, 1988, pp. 44-5.

22. Anand, 'India's Military Response', pp. 1054, 1062-3; Pranab Dhal Samanta, 'Top Guns', *Sunday*, vol. 26, 25-31 July 1999, pp. 52-3.

23. Malik interviewed, p. 51.

24. For the use of Soviet air power in Afghanistan, see Philip Towle's, 'Air Power in Afghanistan', in Air Commodore E.S. Williams (ed.), *Soviet Air Power: Prospects for the Future*, London: Tri Service Press, 1990, pp. 184-200. Anand, 'India's Military Response', p. 1064.

25. Raja Menon, 'View to a Clean Kill', *Outlook*, vol. 5, no. 21, 7 June 1999, p. 16.

26. Menon, 'Road Not Taken', pp. 27-9.

27. Ibid., pp. 28-9; Chengappa et al., 'Kargil War', pp. 23-5; Pranab Dhal Samanta, 'The Gunner's War', *Sunday*, vol. 26, 18-24 July 1999, p. 49; A.J.P. Taylor, *The First World War: An Illustrated History*, 1963, rpt, Harmondsworth: Penguin, 1985, pp. 119-20; Brian Holden Reid, 'The

Italian Campaign, 1943-45: A Reappraisal of Allied Generalship', in John Gooch (ed.), *Decisive Campaigns of the Second World War*, London: Frank Cass, 1990, p. 142-3.

28. *From Surprise to Reckoning*, pp. 126-7, 159.

29. Malik interviewed, *Sunday*, 18-24 July, 1999 pp. 50-1; Menon, 'Road Not Taken', p. 27; Richard A. Gabriel and Paul L. Savage, *Crisis in Command: Mismanagement in the Army*, 1978, rpt, New Delhi: Himalayan Books, 1986.

30. John Gaylor, *Sons of John Company: The Indian and Pakistan Armies, 1903-91*, 1992, rpt, New Delhi: Lancer, 1993.

31. Brian Holden Reid, 'Introduction', in idem and Major General J.J.G. Mackenzie (eds.), *The British Army and the Operational Level of War*, New Delhi and London: Lancer in association with Tri Service Press, 1989, pp. 2, 10.

32. Brian Holden Reid, 'Introduction', in idem (ed.), *Military Power: Land Warfare in Theory and Practice*, London: Frank Cass, 1997, pp. 1-2.

33. John A. Lynn, 'A Quest for Glory: The Formation of Strategy under Louis XIV ', in Williamson Murray, MacGregor Knox and Alvin Bernstein (eds.), *The Making of Strategy: Rulers, States and War*, Cambridge: Cambridge University Press, 1994, pp. 187, 196; Colonel C.E. Callwell, *Small Wars: A Tactical Textbooks for Imperial Soldiers*, 1896, rpt, London: Greenhill, 1990; John Keegan, *Six Armies in Normandy: From D-Day to the Liberation of Paris*, 1982, rpt, London: Pimlico, 1992.

34. B.H. Liddell Hart, *Strategy*, New York: Praeger, 1954, pp. 15-26, 333-72; J.J.A. Wallace, 'Manoeuvre Theory in Operations Other Than War', *Journal of Strategic Studies* (hereafter *JSS*), vol. 19, no. 4, 1996, pp. 207-10.

35. John Kiszely, 'The British Army and Approaches to Warfare since 1945', *JSS*, vol. 19, no. 4, 1996, pp. 179-81.

36. Brian Holden Reid, 'Introduction', *JSS*, vol. 19, no. 4, 1996, pp. 6, 8; G.D. Sheffield, 'Introduction: Command, Leadership and the Anglo-American Experience', in idem (ed.), *Leadership and Command: The Anglo-American Military Experience Since 1861*, London: Brassey's, 1997, pp. 3-5.

37. Clayton R. Newell, *The Framework of Operational Warfare*, London: Routledge, 1991, pp. 121-41.

38. Lieutenant Colonel Douglas M. Macgregor, *Breaking the Phalanx: A New Design for Landpower in the 21st Century*, Westport, CT: Praeger, 1997, pp. 1-5, 32-7.

39. Martin van Creveld, *Command in War*, Cambridge, MA: Harvard University Press, 1985, pp. 193-4, 270-1.

40. Major General Alistair Irwin, 'The Buffalo Thorn: The Nature of the Future Battlefield', *JSS*, vol. 19, no. 4, 1996, pp. 227-35.

41. Alvin and Heidi Toffler, *War and Anti-War: Survival at the Dawn of the 21st Century*, 1993, rpt, London: Warner, 1994.

42. Michael I. Handel, *Masters of War: Classical Strategic Thought*, 1992, rpt, London: Frank Cass, 1996, pp. 121, 124, 127, 130, 133.
43. Stephen Badsey, 'Coalition Command in the Gulf War', in Sheffield, *Leadership and Command*, pp. 195, 198, 207.
44. Robert O'Neill, 'US and Allied Leadership and Command in the Korean and Vietnam Wars', in Sheffield, *Leadership and Command*, pp. 185, 193.
45. Sun Tzu II, *The Lost Art of War*, tr. with Commentary by Thomas Cleary, New York: Harper Collins, 1996, pp. 2, 5-6, 14, 21, 33, 143, 147. Sun Tzu, *Art of War*, tr. with a Historical Introduction by Ralph D. Sawyer, Boulder: Westview, 1994, pp. 129-31. The quotation is from p.48 of Sun Tzu.
46. Major General, Yu Qifen, 'The International Military Situation in the 1990s', and Gao Heng, 'Future Military Trends', in Michael Pillsbury (ed.), *Chinese Views of Future Warfare*, 1997, rpt, New Delhi: Lancer, 1998, pp. 70-3, 81-4, 86-90.
47. Colonel Yao Youzhi and Colonel Liu Hongson, 'Future Security Trends in the Asia-Pacific Region', and General Liu Huaqin, 'Defence Modernization in Historical Perspective', and General Fu Quanyou, 'Future Logistics Modernization', in Pillsbury, *Future Warfare*, pp. 95-103, 118, 120-8.
48. Colonel Peng Guangqian, 'Deng Xiaoping's Strategic Thought', and General Zhao Nanqi, 'Deng Xiaoping's Theory of Defence Modernization', and Colonel Hong Baoxiu, 'Deng Xiaoping's Theory of War and Peace', and Colonel Fang Ning, 'Defence Policy in the New Era', in Pillsbury, *Future Warfare*, pp. 8, 14, 20, 25, 49, 51.
49. Di Hùa, 'Threat Perception and Military Planning in China: Domestic Instability and the Importance of Prestige', in Arnett, *Military Capacity*, pp. 25-36.
50. Susan V. Lawrence, 'A Model People's Army', and Chester Dawson, 'Blueprint for Controversy', *Far Eastern Economic Review* (hereafter *FEER*), 13 July 2000, pp. 14, 19-20.
51. Swaran Singh, 'China's Doctrine of Limited Hi-Tech War', *ASR, 1998-99*, pp. 337, 340-2.
52. Wendy Friedman, 'Arms Procurement in China: Poorly Understood Processes and Unclear Results', Arnett, *Military Capacity*, pp. 82-3.
53. Srikanth Kondapalli, 'China's Naval Equipment Acquisition', *SA*, vol. 23, no. 9, 1999, pp. 1513-14, 1519.
54. Swaran Singh, 'Continuity and Change in China's Maritime Strategy', *SA*, vol. 23, no. 9, 1999, pp. 1498, 1502-3.
55. Srikanth Kondapalli, 'China's Naval Training Programme', and idem, 'Chinese Navy's Political Work and Personnel', *SA*, vol. 23, nos. 8 & 10, 2000, pp. 1339, 1341, 1755, 1757.
56. Mark L. Clifford, Stuart Young and Dexter Roberts, 'Taiwan's Tightrope', *Business Week*, 20 March 2000, p. 21; Srikanth Kondapalli, 'China's

Naval Structure and Dynamics', *SA*, vol. 23, no. 7, 1999, pp. 1098-1101.

57. Captain A.K. Sachdev, 'Modernisation of the Chinese Air Force', *SA*, vol. 23, no. 6, 1999, pp. 994, 998, 1000-1.

58. *Strategic Digest* (hereafter *SD*), vol. 29, no. 12, 1999, p. 1857.

59. Lawrence, 'People's Army', pp. 14, 16.

60. Srikanth Kondapalli, *China's Military: The PLA in Transition*, New Delhi: Knowledge World, 1999, pp. 77-109.

61. Rahul Roy-Chaudhuri, 'The Limits to Naval Expansion', in Kanti P. Bajpai and Amitabh Mattoo (eds), *Securing India: Strategic Thought and Practice*, New Delhi: Manohar, 1996, p. 199; Andrew Selth, 'Burma and the Strategic Competition between China and India', *JSS*, vol. 19, no. 2, 1996, pp. 214-23.

62. Ahmed Rashid, 'Islamabad Cool', *FEER*, 13 July 2000, p. 18; Murray Hiebert and Nayan Chanda, 'Dangerous Liaisons', *FEER*, 20 July 2000, p. 16.

63. 'Intelligence', *FEER*, 20 July 2000, p. 10.

64. Martin Van Creveld, 'Technology and War II: Postmodern War?', in Charles Townshend (ed.), *The Oxford Illustrated History of Modern War*, Oxford: Oxford University Press, 1997, pp. 305-14.

65. Correlli Barnett, *Britain and her Army: 1509-1970, A Military, Political and Social Survey*, London: Penguin, 1970, pp. 424-6, 445-94; Lieutenant General Harbakhsh Singh, *In the Line of Duty: A Soldier Remembers*, New Delhi: Lancer, 2000, pp. 171-90; Kaushik Roy, 'Netaji's Military Strategy', *Asian Studies*, vol. 17, no. 2, 1999, pp. 13-21; Lieutenant Colonel Gautam Sharma, *Nationalization of the Indian Army: 1885-1947*, New Delhi: Allied, 1996, pp. 184-5; *Indian Voices of the Great War: Soldiers' Letters, 1914-18*, Selected and Introduced by David Omissi, London: Macmillan, 1999, pp. 8-9.

66. Rahul Roy-Chaudhuri, *Sea Power and Indian Security*, London: Brassey's, 1995, pp. 133, 197; Vice Admiral G.M. Hiranandani, *Transition to Triumph: History of the Indian Navy, 1965-1975*, New Delhi: Lancer, 2000, pp. 170-82.

67. Major General Afsir Karim, 'Airborne Forces: AB Division in its Classic Role', Part II; and Brigadier Vijai K. Nair, 'Employment of Military Helicopters: The Indian Experience and Compulsions', Part II, *Indian Defence Review*, January 1992, pp. 97-109; Barry R. Posen, *The Sources of Military Doctrine: France, Britain and Germany between the World Wars*, Ithaca: Cornell University Press, 1984, pp. 182-219.

68. For an account of tight control through the mechanism of 'fear and punishment' see Major General F.L. Freemantle, *Fred's Foibles*, New Delhi: Lancer, 2000, p. 109.

69. Sanjay Dasgupta, 'Command and Control in the Nuclear Era', in Maroof Raza (ed.), *Generals and Governments in India and Pakistan*, New Delhi: Har-Anand, 2001, p. 123.

70. R. Prasannan, 'Cost of Deterrence', *Week*, 9 July 2000, p. 37.
71. Lieutenant General V.R. Raghavan, 'Beyond Missile Machismo', *Outlook*, vol. 5, no. 15, 26 April 1999, p. 37.
72. Ibid., and R. Prasannan and Riyad Mathew, 'Stealing a March', *Week*, 9 July 2000, pp. 32-7; B.R. Srikanth, Sunil Narula and Sanjay Suri, 'Sparring in Thin Air Seriously', *Outlook*, vol. 5, no. 15, 26 April 1999, p. 40; K.P. Nayar, 'China Arms Sale to Pak Punctures Delhi High', *Telegraph*, 5 July 2000, p. 7.
73. Erik Baark, 'Military Technology and Absorptive Capacity in China and India: Implications for Modernization', Arnett, *Military Capacity*, pp. 87, 99, 102.
74. Raju G.C. Thomas, 'Arms Procurement in India: Military Self-Reliance versus Technological Self-Sufficiency', in Arnett, *Military Capacity*, pp. 113-15, 117, 119-21.
75. Suman Bhattacharya, 'Time to Crash Land', *Outlook*, vol. XL, no. 9, 13 March 2000, pp. 12, 14.
76. R. Prasannan, 'Doubtful Deals', *Week*, 11 June 2000, p. 17.
77. Chris Smith, *India's Ad Hoc Arsenal: Direction or Drift in Defence Policy*, New York: Oxford University Press, 1994, pp. 105-43.
78. Prasannan, 'Deals', pp. 16-17, 20.
79. *SD*, vol. 29, no. 12, p. 1859.
80. Sun Tzu, *Art of War*, p. 167.
81. Rear Admiral Raja Menon, *Maritime Strategy and Continental War*, London: Frank Cass, 1998.
82. Brigadier Vinod Anand, 'Future Battlespace and Need for Jointmanship', *SA*, vol. 23, no. 10, 2000, pp. 1623-5, 1631, 1635; Jasjit Singh, 'Strategic Framework for Defence Planners: Air Power in the 21st Century', *SA*, vol. 22, no. 12, 1999, pp. 1814-16.
83. Captain A.K. Sachdev, 'Media Related Lessons From Kargil', *SA*, vol. 23, no. 10, 2000, pp. 1797-1801, 1807.
84. Akshay Joshi, 'A Holistic View of the Revolution in Military Affairs (RMA)', *SA*, vol. 22, no. 11, 1999, pp. 1752-4.
85. Waheguru Pal Singh Sindhu, 'Of Oral Traditions and Ethnocentric Judgements', in Bajpai and Mattoo, *Securing India*, p. 175.
86. Jagadish Narayan Sarkar, *The Art of War in Medieval India*, New Delhi: Munshiram Manoharlal, 1984, pp. 274, 279; Gerard Chaliand (ed.), *The Art of War in World History: From Antiquity to Nuclear Age*, Berkeley: University of California Press, 1994, pp. 287-327.
87. Kautilya, *The Arthashastra*, ed., tr. Rearranged and Introduction by L.N. Rangarajan, New Delhi: Penguin, 1992, pp. 559-62.
88. Air Vice Marshal Samir K. Sen, *Military Technology and Defence Industrialization: The Indian Experience*, New Delhi: Manas, 2000, p. 13.

SEVEN

Why Generals did not Rule India: Warfare, the Armed Forces, and Politics in South Asia, 300 BC-AD 2001

> The subordination of the political point of view to the military would be contrary to common sense. ... The subordination of the military point of view to the political is, therefore, the only thing which is possible.
>
> CARL VON CLAUSEWITZ[1]

Despite the warning of the Prussian military philosopher and theorist Carl von Clausewitz, the global landscape in recent times has been characterized by frequent military coups against the political establishments of the day. Military coups are more frequent in the Latin American and the Afro-Asian states that emerged in the aftermath of World War II. In most of these countries, the army engineers the coup. This is because the army controls most of the armed manpower compared to its sister branches: the navy and the air force. Moreover, the military hardware of the army is more suitable than the weapons platforms manned by the navy and the air force for dominating the political establishments that are located on land. However, in some countries like Britain, the USA, and the former USSR, the Royal Navy, the Strategic Air Force, and the Strategic Rocket Force enjoy a disproportionate amount of funding and technological superiority over their respective armies.[2] But both India and Pakistan are land powers and are also technologically backward. Thus, the armies of India and Pakistan are dominant within the armed forces, a situation that poses a political threat to the civilian rulers. This chapter attempts to assess the political management of the militaries in the subcontinent by comparing and contrasting the experiences of India and Pakistan.

A transcontinental cross-cultural comparison is also attempted to prevent the notion gaining ground that India's experience is unique. While the key feature of Pakistan's politics is the repeated occurrence of military coups from the late 1950s onwards, in India civilian control has been successful in managing the armed forces. This dissimilarity at first appears striking because the subcontinent constitutes a single geopolitical unit and both the Indian and the Pakistan armies seem to share a common ancestry. After all, both these armies evolved from the British-controlled Sepoy army.[3] However, unlike the Pakistan government, the Indian government has been able to control the military by a judicious mixture of organizational systems imported from the West, such as the civilian bureaucracy, and through strengthening indigenous traits, i.e. Hindu politico-military traditions. This successful military synthesis is possible because, before the British era, the historical experience of the subcontinent had been more diverse. Let us have a quick survey of this history.

MILITARY AND POLITICS IN HISTORY

POLITICAL PHILOSOPHIES, POLITICIANS, AND WARLORDS IN THE ANCIENT WORLD

Many other states that have been disarmed have lost their liberties in less than forty years. No state therefore can support itself without any army. If a state has no soldier of its own, it must be forced to hire foreign troops; this will be much more dangerous because they are more likely to be corrupted and become subservient to the ambition of a powerful citizen who—when he has nobody to deal with but an unarmed and defenceless multitude—may easily avail himself of its assistance to overturn the established government.

NICCOLO MACHIAVELLI[4]

Military intrusions into the political sphere were rare in ancient India. This was because of the influence of Hindu political and religious thought. Between 800 and 400 BC, the Hindu sages wrote the *Upanishads*, which emphasized the concept of otherworldliness and the superiority of the spirit over the material world. The *Chandogya Upanishad* tells us:

In this world they call greatness the possession of cattle and horses, elephants and gold, servants and wives, lands and houses. But I do not call this greatness. ... Atman is above and below, North and South and East and West. Atman is the whole universe. He who sees, knows, and understands this, who finds in Atman, the spirit, his love and his pleasure and his union and his joy, becomes a Master of himself. His freedom then is infinite.[5]

Hinduism, unlike Islam, never gave the call for a people's war. A general levy in the Hindu monarchies, unlike in the Islamic states of the medieval world, was absent. Within the Hindu kingdoms, soldiering became the occupation of a particular group known as the *Kshatriyas*.[6] So the Hindu societies, unlike the Islamic societies, were never militaristic.

The standing of the military organization within ancient India's political structures was very low, both in political theory and in practice. The ancient Indian rulers instead of maintaining permanent standing armies mostly relied on the militias which were raised only during emergencies and demobilized when the crises were over. Kautilya, the political sage of ancient India, who propounded an early version of Machiavelli's theory of *realpolitik*, advised the rulers that 'people fighting among themselves can help the King by their mutual rivalry'. The rulers encouraged caste rivalry within these temporary levies. Unlike the permanent Roman legions, the ancient Indian military forces, being *ad hoc* formations ridden with endemic caste divisions, were never able to generate a corporate ethos and *esprit de corps*. Moreover, Kautilya's *Arthashastra* emphasized the elimination of troublesome ambitious military leaders with the help of assassins. Thus, while the Praetorian Guards could make and unmake emperors in Rome, the Indian military operated at the margins of the political sphere.[7]

Within the Hindu political philosophy as represented by the *Arthashastra*, finance rather than military affairs holds the supreme position. Kautilya asserts: 'It is the army which is dependent on finance.' He continues: 'All state activities depend first on the Treasury. Therefore, a King shall devote his best attention to it.'[8] Even when Kautilya refers to warfare, the emphasis is on *Kutayuddha* (intrigues, diplomacy, and covert operations) rather than on set-piece battles conducted by large armies. His focus is on espionage and counter-espionage warfare which are to be conducted with various types of spies. The rulers are advised to use ascetics and widows as spies for manufacturing discontent among potentially hostile states. The information collected by the roving spies is to be processed and then transmitted by the intelligence officers in code language.[9] Kautilya elaborates:

Miraculous results can be achieved by practicing the methods of subversion. In the enemy's country, those who are easily subverted shall be won over by conciliation and gifts. Those who are not easily subverted shall be tackled by sowing dissension, use of force or by pointing out to them the defects of their own king.[10]

The point to be noted is that the Western military theorists like Xenophon, Tacitus, Vegetius, Machiavelli, and finally Clausewitz have always emphasized the importance of decisive encounter battles to annihilate the enemy. But this trend was absent in ancient Indian political philosophy. For Kautilya, diplomacy, palace intrigues, and counter-intrigues were more important. As a result, India's grand strategy (an amalgam of foreign, domestic, and economic policies) was always passive and concerned with internal affairs.[11] Hence, in the sphere of strategic thought, the role assigned to the army was almost negligible. As the army was never given any space in the process of power projection, its role in regard to policy formulation remained low.

The role of organized violence in national security further declined when a paradigm shift in strategic theory occurred under Emperor Ashoka. He replaced the concept of *digvijaya* (conquest by sword) with *dhammavijaya* (conquest by the spiritual force of non-violence). The core of *dhammavijaya* was *ahimsa*, the doctrine of non-violence. Ashoka transformed *ahimsa* from an act of personal virtue to an act of collective national virtue.[12] This concept was revived and utilized by Gandhi during the freedom struggle between the 1920s and the 1940s.[13] This created an indifference towards the armed forces within the public consciousness and contributed to the strengthening of democracy in India after 1947. Ancient India's notions of political strategy had much in common with pre-Communist Chinese military thought. As taught by Sun Tzu and Sun Pin, ancient Chinese politico-military philosophy focused on deception, disinformation, spying, and psychological warfare. About two hundred years before Kautilya, Sun Tzu advised: 'Warfare is the *Tao* (way) of deception. Thus, although you are capable, display incapability to them. When committed to employing your forces, feign inactivity. When your objective is nearby, make it appear as if distant; when far away, create the illusion of being nearby.'[14] Both Kautilya and Sun Tzu recommended feeding the enemy with wrong information with the help of spies and thus disabling him rather than opting for a brutal, direct, and bloody assault on his military.[15] Instead of relying on organized violence, the Chinese regimes, following the counsel of Sun Tzu, focused on the Confucian virtues in order to accommodate and assimilate the 'barbarians' who threatened the northern frontier of the Middle Kingdom.[16] This is similar to Ashoka's *Dhammavijaya*. Both Sukracharya and Confucius (500 BC) emphasized the spiritual forces (*chi* in Chinese) rather than the material and martial forces.[17] As a result, Chinese generals in the Heavenly Kingdom, like the *senapatis* of the ancient Hindu kingdoms, played second fiddle to politicians and bureaucrats.

THE BARBARIANS RIDE SOUTH

The men on horseback who erupted from Central Asia around AD 800 overwhelmed both the Middle Kingdom and the agrarian bureaucracies in the Indian subcontinent. In India, the raids of the horse-riding nomads took the form of repeated Turko-Muslim expeditions against the Rajput principalities, which finally lead to the founding of the Delhi Sultanate at first and later the Mughal Empire. Both these *imperiums* were influenced by Chingiz Khan and Timur's imperial structures. Unlike the Hindu imperial hierarchy or the Middle Kingdom's imperial fabric, in Timur's empire, the second-in-command to the ruler was the *Amir-ul-Umara*, i.e. the commander-in-chief of the cavalry.[18] So the commander of the army enjoyed much more prestige and power in the Muslim states.

Within the Muslim polities various chieftains were assigned land revenue for raising and maintaining cavalry contingents numbering between 10 to 10,000. They were known as *iqtadars* under the Delhi Sultanate and as *mansabdars* in the Mughal

Empire. Unlike the *senapati* of the Hindu *Chaturanga* armies of the ancient period, they were in charge of both civil and military administration. Actually the Sultans and the *Padshahs* attempted to prevent the emergence of a military cabal by occasionally transferring civilian officers to the military commands and vice versa. The net result was that the civilian administration suffered and the growth of military professionalism among the army officials suffered. A professional military develops only when the warriors can acquire and retain military skills by protracted and continuous training. In the long run this policy of amalgamating civil and military offices backfired. During their transfers to civilian posts, the military officers acquired control over revenue and civilian officials. Hence, it was possible for the *mansabdars* to enthrone themselves frequently as *Padshahs*.[19] Strong rulers like Alauddin Khalji tried to eliminate the successful generals either by transferring them to peripheral provinces like Bengal or by eliminating them with the help of assassins,[20] a policy that Kautilya had advocated for the ancient Indian rulers.

Another feature of the medieval polities was the intermixture of religion, politics, and warfare. To provide the armed personnel with the moral fervour necessary to conduct *jehad* against the infidels and to legitimize the rule of Muslim minorities over the Hindu masses, Muslim theologians played a vital role in the war machine.[21] The Muslim religious preachers continue to play a pivotal role in the Pakistan army and in that country's politics even today. This in turn strengthens the role of army in society.

CIVIL-MILITARY RELATIONS IN THE BRITISH RAJ

By the second half of the eighteenth century, the cavalry armies of the Mughal successor states were wiped out by the infantry-dominated British-led Indian Sepoy army. The genesis of the Sepoy army with its British officer corps could be traced back to the military transformation in early modern Europe which gave birth to the professional militaries. Such professional armies were permanent bureaucratic organizations over which the state maintained supervisory control through a centralized impersonal machinery. The state accepted the duty of feeding, clothing, and equipping the armed forces. Such armed forces were characterized by a strict hierarchy and the introduction of military academies for imparting specialized knowledge to the officer corps. The military academies educated the officers in monastic isolation away from the public political life. They inculcated the belief among the officer corps that politics was not part of a soldier's business. The officer corps acquired its own ethos, code of conduct, and corporate spirit. Promotion was based on merit and not on birth or wealth. Soldiering became a full-time profession for the officers.[22]

However, the professionalism of the British officers under the Raj was not flawless. In 1796, the British officers were on the verge of mutiny because the British government in India tried to reduce their perquisites like double *batta* (extra pay that was given for postings away from Calcutta). In addition, the officers demanded quicker promotions and higher pay. The Governor-General John Shore brought the rebellious white officers under control with the aid of loyal sepoys, and with the help of the military forces of satellite powers like the troops of the *Nawab* of Awadh. The Governor-General also asked for the cooperation of General De Boigne, the commander of Mahadji Sindia's forces in north India.[23] In 1796, the commander-in-chief of the Army in India (British contingent of the East India Company, and the British army units stationed in India plus the Sepoy army), Lord Abercomby, sided with the Governor-General. But between 1904-5 when Lord Kitchener, the commander-in-chief of the Army in India, disobeyed the order of the Viceroy, Lord Curzon, the most serious challenge to civilian supremacy in the history of the British Indian Empire occurred. Kitchener was partly successful when he abolished the post of the Military Member in the Viceroy's Council, since the occupant of this post functioned as the Viceroy's watchdog over the activities of the army commander. But Kitchener's victory was circumscribed by the fact that, till 1947, the army remained under the tight control of the Indian Civil Service officers, especially in regard to the budget.[24]

THEORIES OF CIVIL-MILITARY RELATIONS FOR TWENTIETH-CENTURY SOUTH ASIAN MILITARIES

To assess the political influence of the present-day militaries in South Asia, recourse to contemporary political theories is necessary. Samuel Huntington, the American political theorist, rightly claims that the crux of the civil-military interaction is the attitude of the officer corps (who constitute the brain of the army) towards the state.[25] This brings us to the problematic of professionalism among the officer cadre. Rear Admiral Raja Menon, a strategic theorist of contemporary India, defines professionalism as acquiring tactical skills for managing military assets in the battlefield.[26] This narrow conceptualization of the officers' sense of duty may be categorized as positive professionalism. The traditional view that a professional officer corps is apolitical[27] needs to be revised. The Prussian officer corps was extremely professional as proved by the high military effectiveness of the German Army during the two World Wars. Nevertheless, the Prussian officers interfered in politics. The Prussian officers' professionalism is an example of negative professionalism. Historian William C. Fuller defines negative professionalism as the perception of the officers that they are superior to other groups of civilian society. And this sense of superiority in all walks of life justifies the officers' insubordination to the civilians' orders.[28] The Pakistan army's officer cadre is influenced by negative professionalism.

Negative professionalism generates militarism. Militarism connotes different types of distortion in the relationship between the armed forces and the government of different polities at various points of time. To link militarism with modernization, imperialism, and capitalism smacks of determinism. Militarism could be institutional as well as non-institutional. Pakistan exhibits both types of militarism.

INSTITUTIONAL MILITARISM

Alfred Vagts, an American political scientist, defines institutional militarism as a regime possessing a militaristic army whose primary duty is not to fight wars but to justify its status and vested interests which results in military intrusion into the affairs of civilian society even in peacetime.[29] This sort of militarism leads to the evolution of the 'garrison state'. Such polities are characterized by fiscal-militarism. This means the use of most of the revenue for the armed forces, which in turn enables the military forces to intervene in matters of finance.[30] In the twentieth century, fiscal-militarism in the highly industrialized states resulted in the genesis of the military-industrial complex. The latter term means the emergence of a military-industrial infrastructure that makes possible an arms race and raises the armed forces' status within the internal power structure of the country concerned.

The military-industrial complex is not a unique feature of capitalism because the Communist states also possess such complexes. The PLA runs many factories even in the civilian sector. About 10 per cent of China's industrial output is devoted to the armaments sector which employs six million workers, i.e. 15 per cent of China's labour force.[31] Again, non-intervention in politics by the military is not an exclusive characteristic of the Western democratic polities. Though China is an authoritarian country with a military-industrial complex, still Beijing is able to prevent coups. To control a powerful military, the Communist regimes of China and the former USSR have evolved a symbiotic relationship with their respective militaries. While in the Western democracies, the militaries are subordinated to the government to varying degrees, in the Communist polities, the armed forces are joint partners with the ruling parties. In the totalitarian socialist countries like the former USSR and China, the indoctri-nation of the soldiers in Communist tenets at the military academies and the appointment of the political commissars who perform a 'watchdog' role over the military officers enable the Communist parties to control their respective armed forces. Encouraging officer participation in the party apparatus results in the integration of the military personnel with the party. Thus, a dual system of politico-military command extends from the general staff to the platoon level.[32]

The military-industrial complex as present in the USA, Britain, France, Russia, and China does not exist either in India or Pakistan. Even in 1971 India imported 70 per cent of her military hardware from the USSR. India's attempt to build an indigenous defence industrial base for producing sophisticated hardware is a failure. The DRDO at best could only copy the sophisticated conventional weapons imported from the West and go in for licensed production.[33] India has 40 ordnance factories but they only manufacture small arms and explosives. Further, these factories are under civilian control, and the armed forces have no say in their management and policy making.[34] In Pakistan, even in the 1990s the indigenous contribution was only 20 per cent of the military hardware (especially unsophisticated small arms) required by her armed forces.[35] But one aspect of militarism, i.e. military-fiscalism (the use of most of the revenue for the armed forces) is a feature of present-day Pakistan where half of the government's budget goes to defence. At times like the period between 1959-63, the defence expenditure as a percentage of the total expenditure crossed the 50 per cent mark.[36] This scenario should be contrasted with the situation in India. In British India, the armed forces consumed about 32 per cent of the government's revenue.[37] But after independence Jawaharlal Nehru drastically reduced defence spending. India's defence budget as a percentage of the total government expenditure between 1959-61 fluctuated between 21-22 per cent.[38] Till 1962, India's defence expenditure was below 2 per cent of her GNP. In 1992-3, it marginally rose to 2.7 per cent of her GNP.[39]

NON-INSTITUTIONAL MILITARISM

Theorists of non-institutional militarism expand the scope of their search for militarism beyond the military institutions. One aspect of such militarism is the prevalence of militaristic ideas even in a functioning democracy. Militarism is regarded as the harbinger of war. One author characterizes pre-World War I USA as having been influenced by non-institutional militarism because the American society believed that war was not only inevitable but also desirable.[40] According to the British historian John Keegan, this sort of militarism also signifies the predominance of the notion in society that regards the maintenance of the armed forces as the first priority of the nation, and service in the military as an honourable profession.[41]

In India, the middle class shuns military service to such an extent that the Indian army is currently suffering from a severe shortage of officers. In 1994, the Indian army experienced a shortfall of 12,972 officers and this increased to 13,500 officers by June 1999.[42] In contrast, Pakistan's society believes that the army is the saviour of the nation, hence it has the first call on finance. How can one explain this difference in perception?

India is officially secular but practically a Hindu state.

Hinduism pervades all spheres of life because about 80 per cent of the population is Hindu. Hindu political culture marginalizes organized violence, as discussed before, and this ideology dominates Indian society. Due to the influence of Kautilya's concept of *mandalas*, the Indian strategic posture has always been defensive and inward-looking in nature. This has resulted in the complete absence of the armed forces in the implementation of foreign policy goals.[43] The core of Nehru's foreign policy was the Non-Alignment Movement (NAM).[44] And the theoretical basis of NAM, which rules out the use of the army to realize the goals of coercive diplomacy, is very similar to Ashoka's non-militaristic foreign policy.

Pakistan is officially an Islamic state. Historical continuities do exist between the medieval Muslim states and Pakistan. General Zia-ul-Haq's attempt to indoctrinate the officer corps in Islamic doctrine is the medieval legacy of the notion of *jehad* against the *kafirs*. It would be wrong to argue that the generals are utilizing religion for legitimizing their rule. In fact, the 'modernizing' generals often come under pressure from the religious elements of the society for the further Islamization of both state and society. General Ayub Khan in his memoirs described the pressure exerted by the *ulema* led by Maulana Abul Aala Maudoodi's Jama't-e-Islami party which demanded the rigorous Islamization of Pakistan in the late 1950s and in the 1960s. In early 2000, General Parvez Musharraf, the military dictator of Pakistan, came under pressure from Sami-ul-Haq's followers functioning from Pakistan's North-West Frontier Province.[45] Benazir Bhutto, a former prime minister of Pakistan, claimed some years ago that both the military personnel and the Islamic fundamentalists come from west Punjab and that an alliance between them makes the functioning of parliamentary democracy in the country almost impossible.[46]

Democracy was an exception within the Islamic polities of the twentieth century. This is because in Islamic history the spiritual head (*Caliph*) is also the head of temporal affairs (commander-in-chief). Christianity from the time of Emperor Charlemagne onwards emphasized the difference between the church/religion and the state. Contrary to the popular perception that secularism is a modern Western idea imported into India, the basic distinction between politics and religion may be traced back to

Hindu politico-religious thought. The core message of the *Bhagavad Gita* is the division of labour. So, unlike Hindu India and Christian Europe, Muslim Pakistan's society finds it difficult to maintain the distinction between the army and civil society.[47]

What sorts of social groups dominate the society that generates militarism? Along with industrialists, the other group may be conservative proto-feudal elite. While in late nineteenth-century USA, the industrialists propagated militaristic ideas, in the Kaiser's Germany it was the East Prussian landed aristocracy, the *Junkers*, who dominated the army.[48] The point to be noted is that both Pakistan's civilian bureaucracy and the army are dominated by the landlord class of Punjab. How to explain the army's rise to power vis-á-vis the civilian bureaucracy in Pakistan?

MILITARY BUREAUCRACIES AND POWER POLITICS IN POST-1947 SOUTH ASIA

To understand the role of the militaries in generating militarism, the organizational model is necessary. This approach assumes that the organizational machinery (military bureaucracy) is the key variable. This is not to deny the importance of cultural ethos and social structure which spawn an armed force. They certainly mediate the organizational norms of the military machine. The organizational approach seems viable because the armed forces are complex bureaucratic machines with their own customs, laws, and regulations largely alienated from civil society. However, uncertainty governs the structure of the military organizations. The relations between inputs and results are non-linear because the behaviour of most systems under similar environments happens to be chaotic and unpredictable. The world does not operate in a mechanical, deterministic fashion. Hence, similar organizations with similar inputs could generate dissimilar outputs.[49]

This is evident in the case of both the Pakistan army and the Indian army which retained the British regimental format and started functioning within a democratic setup in 1947 but within ten years went their different ways. Again, both Pakistan and India inherited the same civilian bureaucratic structure which in the last two hundred years had slowly expanded its administrative and financial control over the military.[50] But, while in Pakistan the civilian bureaucracy formed an alliance with the military, in India, the civilian bureaucracy became an instrument in the hands of the politicians for controlling the armed forces. Therefore, extra military organizational variables are also important.

Military organizations more than other organizations are driven by a concern for power and socio-political prestige. For this reason they frequently get into confrontations with other institutions.[51] In India, the government utilizes the confrontations between the military and the non-military institutions as opportunities to extend the scope of civilian control. Several organizational schemes which are Western in character are ushered in by the Indian government to reduce the armed forces' power and to ensure strict civilian supremacy over the military.

ORGANIZATIONAL CONTROL

Just after Independence, in India, Jawaharlal Nehru absorbed and extended the political tradition of the British Raj in establishing bureaucratic control over the armed forces. The commander-in-chief of the armed forces ceased to be the vice president and his seat in the cabinet was abrogated. This position was taken over by a civilian defence minister. The post of the commander-in-chief was abolished and in its place three service chiefs—Chief of the Army Staff (COAS), Chief of the Naval Staff, and the Chief of the Air Staff—came into existence respectively. In India, on 1 April 1955, the position of the military officers in the Warrant of Precedence was lowered vis-á-vis the IAS and the IPS personnel. While several IAS officers become secretaries at the centre simultaneously, only one army personnel, that is the COAS, is given the equivalent status of a central secretary. The lieutenant generals lost their entitlement to gun salutes. As a reaction to the coup in Pakistan and on the recommendations of Lord Ismay and Admiral Louis Mountbatten, Nehru, instead of integrating the three service headquarters, separated them and then subordinated them under the civilian secretariat of the Ministry of Defence (MoD). The three service headquarters even today are not allowed any formal channel for joint strategic planning.[52] This prevents the coordination of military planning by the army, the navy, and the air force but it does ensure the hold of the babus, i.e. civilian bureaucrats, over a hopelessly divided military organization. The Indian government deliberately prevents the construction of the post of a Chairman of the Joint Chiefs of Staff (JCS) also known as the Chief of Defence Staff (CDS). The government apprehends that the creation of such a post might result in a military coup.

Several military and non-military vested interest groups also aid the government. The civilian bureaucrats in the MoD are afraid that the creation of such a post would result in reduced power in their hands. The Indian Air Force and the Indian Navy are also against such a proposal, as they fear that an army personnel would always occupy the post of the JCS. After the 1971 war, Indira Gandhi wanted to appoint the COAS, Sam Manekshaw as the CDS. However, the bureaucrats in tandem with the IAF stalled this move. Even the COAS who came after Manekshaw feared that the creation of a JCS would result in the increased autonomy of the two sister branches.[53]

One of the principal devices that the Indian government utilizes to emasculate the military within the MoD is the appointment of IAS personnel, who dominate policy formulation and implementation.[54] In the policy-making section of the MoD not a single uniformed man is allowed entry, which reduces the status of the 'specialists of violence' within the state.[55]

Unlike the ISI in Pakistan, the military intelligence agency in India is made toothless. For the procurement of strategic information just before the India-China War, Nehru used the Intelligence Bureau (IB) under B.N. Mullick. Mullick in his memoirs claims that he protested because the IB lacked specialized training for undertaking counter-intelligence activities. The IB was already overburdened with collecting information in regard to the internal condition of India and was in no position to assess the Chinese military build-up in Tibet. Still Nehru insisted. The result was one of the greatest disasters for India—the war with China in 1962.[56]

The armed forces in India function under the tight fiscal control of the civilian government. But in Pakistan the civilian-military elite takes the issue of a threat from India very seriously. The Indian view of regional paramountcy is not acceptable to Pakistan. The Pakistani elite believes that the Pakistan army constitutes the last line of defence. The result is the slow encroachment of the Pakistan army into the political economy of the state. In 1952, under the civilian government, the military acquired a 'watchdog' role over defence spending. In 1954, the COAS of Pakistan took over the defence portfolio and in 1958, the first coup occurred.[57]

Exploiting the Pakistani elite's paranoia about national security, in the 1980s the Pakistan military grabbed control over the nuclear establishment. Benazir Bhutto admitted that when she was prime minister of Pakistan, the civilian politicians were denied access to or information about the nuclear establishment by the military.[58]

ETHNIC IMBALANCES IN THE ARMIES AND ORGANIZATIONAL DISINTEGRATION

The Pakistan army's rise to supremacy is further facilitated by the dominance of selected ethnic communities from a narrow region within the military. History has proved time and again that unrepresentative militaries are prone to conduct coups. Long before the American political sociologists pointed to the importance of ethnic politics, many Islamic states of the medieval world had implemented the policy of ethnic diversity in their militaries to ensure the survival of the reigning sultans. The Ghaznavids who ruled north-west India and Afghanistan during the twelfth and thirteenth centuries recruited their army from a wide range of communities. They tried to maintain a balance between the Turks from Central Asia, Khurasanis from Iran, Dailamis from the Caspian region, and Indians from Punjab to prevent any community from becoming very strong and from attempting to dethrone the sultan in favour of their own candidate. To ensure their own survival the sultans encouraged Hindu-Muslim rivalry between the Turks and the Indians.[59] Similarly, the Seljuk sultans who ruled over West Asia between the eleventh and thirteenth centuries maintained an ethnic balance between Armenians, Central Asian Turks, and Greeks in their army.[60]

The narrow socio-geographical base of military recruitment is a serious defect for the armies of both Pakistan and India. Over-dependence on Punjab is the bane of both these militaries. Both the armies inherited this as a colonial legacy. This defect may be traced to the recruitment policy of the Sepoy army. British colonial power depended on an ethnically restrictive military that depended on recruitment from marginal/peripheral groups. The rise of the martial race theory from the 1880s made the pre-1947 Indian army over-dependent on the Sikhs from central Punjab (present-day Indian Punjab) and the Muslims from west Punjab (present-day Pakistan Punjab). During World War I, about 54 per cent of the combatant soldiers came from Punjab. This created a tradition of vested interests which has been difficult to break, even for the post-1947 governments in South Asia.[61]

The point to be noted is that the lack of proper ethnic representation in the colonial armies is not unique to British Indian imperialism. In the former Soviet army, the non-Slavic communities like the Georgians, the Chechens, and the Central Asian Muslims were not encouraged to join because these communities were considered politically unreliable by the regime in Moscow.[62] As a result, the Muslims were alienated and they proved to be a problem during the Soviet invasion of Afghanistan.

The Indian army's ethnic imbalance is reflected in the disproportionate number of Sikh soldiers. In 1981, though Punjab contained only 2.4 per cent of India's population, 15 per cent of the military personnel were from this province. In the 1980s, of the 35,000 officers in the Indian army, about 20 per cent of them were Sikhs. India faced a dangerous situation when 2,000 Sikh military personnel (of them about 1,500 were privates) mutinied and deserted just after Operation Blue Star. In the aftermath of the crackdown on Amritsar's Golden Temple, the recruitment of Sikh commissioned officers had drastically gone down as a result of deliberate government policy.[63]

The government of India does have a back up plan—that is the retention of a mercenary contingent: the Gurkha battalions for balancing the Sikhs. Despite massive unemployment in India, about 10 per cent of the Indian army personnel are from Nepal. They are enlisted for the same reason the British used them in the colonial army. Being foreigners, they would willingly clamp down on popular insurrections in any part of India, if necessary even in Punjab, the principal recruiting zone of the Indian army.[64]

Islamabad has no such policy for balancing the far more ethnically unrepresentative Pakistan army. Punjabi Muslims and

Pathans dominate the army. About 75 per cent of the 4,00,000 men of the Pakistan army hail from three districts of Punjab (Jhelum, Campbellpur, and Rawalpindi) and two districts of the North-West Frontier Province (Kohat and Marolan). These five districts known as the Potwar region contain only 9 per cent of Pakistan Punjab's male population. Any would-be dictator has to gain the loyalty of the Punjabi personnel. Ayub Khan established his hold over the army by showing greater attention to the Punjabi ex-servicemen. He set up a cloth mill in Punjab as part of the post-war rehabilitation scheme. In 1965, there were only 13,000 Bengali Muslims in the Pakistan army and none in the senior posts, though more than half of United Pakistan's population resided in East Pakistan. Because of a lack of ethnic affiliations with the East Pakistanis, the Punjabi and Pathan personnel initiated a reign of terror in that province in 1970. This served to strengthen the movement of Bengali separatism. The Punjabi military personnel prevented General Yahya Khan from reaching any compromise with the elected representatives of East Pakistan. Hence, the army's intervention in politics was an attempt to maintain Punjabi predominance over other ethnic communities like the Sindhis, the Baluchis, and the Bengali Muslims before 1971.[65] Ethnic imbalances are further strengthened by successive military coups, which tend to strengthen the pre-coup ethnic patterns.[66]

The political institutions of Pakistan are eroding due to the failure of the polity to end Punjabi dominance both in the civil and military bureaucracies. The result is a handshake between the civil and the military apparatus against the elected leaders. The civil administrative and military oligarchy is further strengthened due to their acceptance by the USA as a conduit for the flow of military aid to Pakistan[67] for training the Afghan militants in order to check Russian and Chinese ambitions in Central Asia.

To start with, political institutions have always been weak in Pakistan. Hence, in the battle royal between politicians and military officers, the latter—with the backing of a strong and ambitious organization like the army—has been able to move into and occupy the power vacuum. Compared with the Indian National Congress, the Muslim League's grass roots support base was weak. Especially in Punjab, the League had to depend on the landlords and the *pirs* to garner votes. After Mohammad Ali Jinnah and Liaqat Ali Khan, no Pakistani politician had the charisma of Congress leaders like Nehru and Sardar Patel to mobilize mass-based support. Thus, when political agitation erupted in Pakistan, the army was able to move into the political sphere. The absence of paramilitary forces in Pakistan made the civilian bureaucracy dependent on the army. Once martial law was proclaimed, the army was able to justify its hold on power by emphasizing the need for administrative stability and the 'proper' maintenance of law and order. This enabled several generals to legalize the army's intrusion into the political sphere by the 'pull' factor generated due to the collapse of organized politics in Pakistan.[68]

FUTURE PROSPECTS

What is the future of relations between politicians and military officers in Pakistan and India? Sun Tzu, the ancient Chinese sage who lived around 550 BC, although a supporter of civilian supremacy over the military, cautioned against the political micro-management of the armed forces. Sun Tzu advocated limited local autonomy of the military forces, especially in regard to operational matters and internal administration.[69] And this observation also has relevance for India.

The over-cautious approach adopted by Indian civilian leaders against the Indian military in order to prevent coups has resulted in the growth of a rigid civilian command structure. This has made the Indian armed forces very weak vis-á-vis China, a potential threat. In India the absolute civilian control over the armed forces ought to be replaced with a more flexible civilian control, which should give enough space to the military for effective strategic planning in structuring the forces and in preparing the war-fighting doctrine. This is necessary for raising the military effectiveness of the army, especially if we take into account the threat from the PLA which at present is undergoing the 'digital revolution'. The PLA is acquiring electronic counter-countermeasures and laser-warning receivers in order to conduct information age warfare in the near future.[70] Generally, it is seen that tight government control over the armed forces prevents the latter from exploiting innovative ways of utilizing the state-of-the-art technology for raising combat effectiveness. In Iraq, the over-dominance of the *Baathist* Party under Saddam Hussein prevented the army from assimilating the latest technology in the First Gulf War. This explains the low military effectiveness of the much vaunted Iraqi army against the US-led coalition forces.[71] Hence, the Indian Defence Minister Jaswant Singh's green signal in March 2001 for the creation of the post of the JCS is a step in the right direction.[72]

Further, the Indian political elite should realize that civilian supremacy does not necessarily mean IAS supremacy. Instead of IAS officers, the induction of technocrats and scientists at the top echelons of the MoD will aid the management and future planning of the armed forces due to their expert inputs in the decision-making process.

India ought to go in for the occupational military instead of the institutional military that the country possesses. The institutional militaries are characterized by the domination of military values that represent divergence from civilian values. This is due to the presence of long-service volunteers as military personnel. Technologizing and the short-service scheme for the officers would result in the transformation of the institutional militaries into the occupational militaries. Occupational militaries are shaped by market forces: the supply-demand dynamic and civilian values predominate due to the presence of a large number of short-service civilian technicians who are required for manning the capital-intensive weapons and electronic gadgets of the armed forces. Both China and India reduced the power of the infantry generals in the 1990s by depending more on missile technology which gives greater scope to civilian engineers and scientists at the cost of military officers in designing, procuring, and manning such weapons platforms.[73] Further, the short-service scheme in the officer corps results in a rapid turnover of military personnel. This in turn reduces primary group solidarity and weakens the inculcation of militaristic values in the officer corps while allowing increasing civilian interference in matters military. The turnover of manpower is very high in the US army. In the 1970s, the US army was characterized by a 35 per cent quarterly turnover in personnel assigned to the units. Such militaries pose no political threat and become marginal in the society.[74]

Would the Pakistan army change in the near future? The transformation into an occupational military integrated with the missile-based force structure instead of a peasant-based infantry army requires political intervention or external military pressure.[75] In Pakistan, the politicians are hard pressed to struggle for their own survival rather than attempting to transform the military. However, the conservative military bosses of Pakistan are bound to transform their peasant army in the face of external pressure and the logic of technology. The adoption of the missile system by the Indian army will force a change in the Pakistan army. An action-reaction dialectic has set in between India and Pakistan. The deployment of short-range and intermediate-range missiles like the Prithvi and the Agni by India in the 1990s forced Pakistan to go ahead with the Haft and the Ghauri missiles.[76] Again, the 'information revolution' in the field of warfare[77] will accelerate the pace of change in the Pakistan army. Harnessing the information warfare techniques will result in the proliferation of the capital-intensive weapons platforms involving sophisticated software programmes, electronic sensors, surveillance equipment, and advanced digital telecommunications switching equipment, including global positioning system navigation satellites. This would most likely result in an influx of civilian technocrats who would gradually replace the long-service 'heroic' officers emphasizing the ethic of warrior comradeship mostly drawn from the lower middle class devoted to Islamic revivalism and imbued with anti-Western feelings.[78]

CONCLUSION

To sum up, India is lucky due to the widespread influence of the anti-militaristic Hindu tradition in almost all spheres of its national life while Pakistan's bane is the prevalence of militaristic Islam. Credit is due to Nehruvian political vision for subordinating the military through a judicious military synthesis of British-designed bureaucratic systems and statecraft based on the Kautilya-Ashokan format. But there is no room for complacency because the international scenario is changing due to the rise of China, the ongoing microchip revolution, and the increasing need for harnessing technology in the militaries. So the elements that constitute India's hitherto successful military synthesis in the civil-military sphere need to be revamped in accordance with the demands of the shifting global strategic calculus.

At present, both India and Pakistan are treading on uncharted ground. While the military domination of Pakistan might result in the very disintegration of the polity, the over-domination of the military by the generalist babus, i.e. the IAS officers recruited through an obsolete competitive examination seriously emasculates the military effectiveness of the armed forces in India. In the case of a limited war with China, first the Indian military and then the state will probably collapse. Any Indian defeat will generate a further centrifugal force that will engulf the Indian republic.

Both India and Pakistan ought to move in opposite directions. Pakistan needs to strengthen civilian control over its armed forces, and India needs to significantly ease its stultifying bureaucratic control. Otherwise, in the near future the impending implosion in the subcontinent will engulf both the armed forces as well as civil society in India, and the 'Nights of the Generals' will continue in Pakistan.

NOTES

1. Carl Von Clausewitz, *On War*, tr by Colonel J.J. Graham with introduction and notes by Colonel F.N. Maude, vol. 3, London and Boston: Routledge & Kegan Paul, 1968, pp. 124-5.
2. For the Soviet case refer to Harriet Fast Scott and William F. Scott, *The Armed Forces of the USSR*, 1979, rpt, Boulder: Westview Press, 1984, pp. 105-71. In Britain, between 1967-9, while the army absorbed only 26 per cent of the military budget, the share of the RAF and the Royal Navy were about 25 per cent and 30 per cent respectively. Paul Kennedy, *The Rise and Fall of British Naval Mastery*, 1976, rpt, London: Fontana, 1991, p. 390. For the US military, see Paul Kennedy, *The Rise and Fall of the Great Powers: Economic Change and Military Conflict from 1500 to 2000*, 1988, rpt, London: Fontana, 1990, p. 676.
3. See John Gaylor, *Sons of John Company: The Indian and Pakistan Armies, 1903-1901*, 1992, rpt, New Delhi: Lancer International, 1993.
4. Niccolo Machiavelli, *The Art of War*, Introduction by Neal Wood, 1965, rpt, New York: Da Capo, 1990, pp. 30-1.

5. *The Upanishads*, tr. from the Sanskrit with an Introduction by Juan Mascaro, Harmondsworth, Middlesex: Penguin, 1965, pp. 119-20.

6. Bimal Kanti Majumdar, *The Military System in Ancient India*, Calcutta: Firma KLM Pvt. Ltd., 1960, pp. 14-5.

7. Stephen Peter Rosen, *Societies and Military Power: India and its Armies*, New Delhi: Oxford University Press, 1996. Rosen claims that even in the British period, a professional bureaucratic army did not emerge in South Asia. Here, I differ with Rosen's argument. The Sepoy army was indeed a quasi-professional mercenary army. The quotation is from Kautilya, *The Arthashastra*, tr. ed. and Rearranged by L.N. Rangarajan, New Delhi: Penguin, 1987, p. 132.

8. Kautilya, *Arthashastra*, pp. 125, 253.

9. Ibid., pp. 158, 505.

10. Ibid., p. 519.

11. P.C. Chakravarty, *The Art of War in Ancient India*, 1941, rpt, New Delhi: Low Price Publications, 1989, pp. vii, 1; Azar Gat, *The Origins of Military Thought: From the Enlightenment to Clausewitz*, Oxford: Clarendon Press, 1989.

12. Indra, *Ideologies of War and Peace in Ancient India*, Hoshiarpur: Vishveshvaranand Institute Publications, 1957, pp. 101-2.

13. Bipan Chandra et al., *India's Struggle for Independence*, 1988, rpt, New Delhi: Penguin, 1990, pp. 505-28.

14. Sun Tzu, *Art of War*, tr. with a Historical Introduction by Ralph D. Sawyer, Boulder, Colorado: Westview, 1994, p. 168.

15. Michael I. Handel, *Masters of War: Classical Strategic Thought*, 1992, rpt, London: Frank Cass, 1996, p. 124; Kautilya, *Arthashastra*, pp. 576-7.

16. *The Seven Military Classics of Ancient China*, tr. Ralph D. Sawyer, Colorado, Boulder: Westview Press, 1993, pp. 2, 145-86, 398-9, 404.

17. Jagadish Narayan Sarkar, *The Art of War in Medieval India*, New Delhi: Munshiram Manoharlal, 1984, p. 24.

18. Abdul Aziz, *The Mansabdari System and the Mughal Army*, Delhi: Idarah-i Adabiyat, 1972, pp. 14, 20; Beatrice Forbes Manz, *The Rise and Rule of Tamerlane*, 1989, rpt, cambridge: Canto, 1999, pp. 120-1.

19. S. Inayat A. Zaidi, 'Rozindar Troopers under Sawai Jai Singh of Jaipur (A.D. 1700-1743)', *Indian Historical Review*, vol. 10, 1983-84, pp. 45-65; Ali Athar, 'Military Hierarchy and Designations under the Sultans of Delhi (13th-14th Centuries)', *Journal of Asiatic Society*, vol. XLII, nos 1-2, 2000, pp. 1, 3; Stanislav Andreski, *Military Organization and Society*, 1954, rpt, Berkeley: University of California Press, 1968, p. 34.

20. *The Tabaqat-i-Akbari* of Khwajah Nizamuddin Ahmad, vol. 1, tr B. De 1911, rpt, Calcutta: The Asiatic Society, 1973, p. 159, footnote 1.

21. Iqbal Husain, *The Ruhela Chieftaincies: The Rise and Fall of Ruhela*

Power in India in the Eighteenth Century, New Delhi: Oxford University Press, 1994, p. 191.

22. Martin Blumenson, 'The Development of the Modern Military', *Armed Forces and Society*, vol. 6, no. 4, 1980, pp. 672, 674-5; Frank Tallett, *War and Society in Early Modern Europe*, 1992, rpt, London and New York: Routledge, 1997, p. 80; Clifford J. Rogers (ed.), *The Military Revolution Debate: Readings on the Military Transformation of Early Modern Europe*, Boulder: Westview Press, 1995; John Keegan, *The Mask of Command*, 1987, rpt, Harmondsworth, Middlesex: Penguin, 1988, p. 5.

23. Raymond Callahan, *The East India Company and Army Reform, 1783-1798*, Cambridge, MA: Harvard University Press, 1972, pp. 150-80.

24. Stephen P. Cohen, *The Indian Army: Its Contribution to the Development of a Nation*, 1971, rpt, Delhi: Oxford University Press, 1991, pp. 22-8.

25. Samuel Huntington, *The Soldier and the State*, Cambridge, MA Harvard University Press, 1957.

26. Rear Admiral Raja Menon, *Maritime Strategy and Continental Power*, London: Frank Cass, 1998, p. 2.

27. For the traditional assumption that a professional officer corps is apolitical, see Pavel K. Baev, *The Russian Army in a Time of Troubles*, London: Sage, 1996, p. xi.

28. William C. Fuller Jr, *Civil-Military Conflict in Imperial Russia: 1881-1914*, Princeton: Princeton University Press, 1985, pp. 28-9.

29. V.R. Berghahn, *Militarism: The History of an International Debate, 1861-1979*, Leamington Spa: Berg, 1981, pp. 38-9.

30. For a historical analysis of Fiscal-Military State characterized by fiscal-militarism refer to John Brewer, *The Sinews of Power: War, Money and the English State*, London: Unwin Hyman, 1989, pp. 25-134, 250-1; Douglas Peers, *Between Mars and Mammon: Colonial Armies and the Garrison State in India, 1819-1835*, London: I.B. Tauris: 1995.

31. Srikanth Kondapalli, *China's Military: The PLA in Transition*, New Delhi: Knowledge World, 1999, pp. 14, 163.

32. Colonel Peng Guangqian, 'Deng Xiaoping's Strategic Thought', and General Zhao Nanqi, 'Deng Xiaoping's Theory of Defence Modernization', in Michael Pillsbury (ed.), *Chinese Views of Future Warfare*, New Delhi: Lancer, 1998, pp. 7, 15; Jacques van Doorn, 'Political Change and the Control of the Military', and P. Zihlin, 'The Armed Forces of the Soviet State: Fifty Years of Experience in Military Construction', in Doorn (ed.), *Military Profession and Military Regimes: Commitments and Conflicts*, The Hague and Paris: Mouton, 1969, pp. 19-31, 167.

33. R.G. Matthews, 'The Development of India's Defence-Industrial Base', *Journal of Strategic Studies* (hereafter *JSS*), no. 4, 1989, pp. 405-30; Raju G.C. Thomas 'Arms Procurement in India: Military Self-Reliance versus

Technological Self-Sufficiency', in Eric Arnett (ed.), *Military Capacity and the Risk of War: China, India, Pakistan and Iran*, Oxford: Oxford University Press, 1997, pp. 114-15; Chris Smith, *India's Ad Hoc Arsenal: Direction or Drift in Defence Policy*, Oxford: Oxford University Press, 1994, p. 96; R. Ramachandran, 'India and the US', *Frontline*, 12 February 1999, pp. 103-4.

34. Air Vice Marshal Samir K. Sen, *Military Technology and Defence Industrialisation: The Indian Experience*, New Delhi: Manas, 2001, p. 46.

35. Yezid Sayigh, 'Arms Production in Pakistan and Iran: The Limits of Self Reliance', in Arnett, *Military Capacity*, p. 164.

36. Shirin Tahir Kehli, 'The Military in Contemporary Pakistan', *Armed Forces and Society*, vol. 6, no. 4, 1980, pp. 641, 645, 650.

37. T.A. Heathcote, *The Military in British-India: The Development of British Land Forces in South Asia, 1600-1947*, Manchester: Manchester University Press, 1995, p. 241.

38. Yacov Vertzberger, 'India's Strategic Posture and the Border War Defeat of 1962: A Case Study of Miscalculation', *JSS*, vol. 5, no. 3, 1982, p. 382.

39. Rahul Roy-Chaudhuri, *Sea Power and Indian Security*, London: Brassey's, 1995, pp. 33, 144.

40. Irmgard Steinisch, 'Different Paths to War: A Comparative Study of Militarism and Imperialism in the United States and Germany, 1871-1914', in R. Chickering, et al. (eds.), *Anticipating Total War: The German and American Experiences, 1871-1914*, Washington D.C.: Cambridge University Press, 1999, pp. 34, 39.

41. John Keegan, *War and Our World*, 1998, rpt, London: Pimlico, 1999, pp. 9-10.

42. Leena Parmar, 'Resettlement of Ex-Servicemen in India: Problems of Army Socialization and Adjustment', in idem (ed.), *Military Sociology: Global Perspectives*, New Delhi: Rawat Publications, 1999, p. 448; Shantanu Guha Ray, 'The Army Wants You', *Outlook*, 21 June 1999, p. 50.

43. George Tanham, 'Indian Strategic Thought: An Interpretative Essay', and 'Indian Strategy in Flux', in Kanti P. Bajpai and Amitabh Mattoo (eds), *Securing India: Strategic Thought and Practice*, New Delhi: Manohar, 1996, pp. 29-133.

44. For an account of Nehru's foreign policy see Sarvepalli Gopal, *Jawaharlal Nehru: A Biography, 1947-56*, vol. 2, 1979, rpt, Delhi: Oxford University Press, 1988, pp. 50-65, 166-95.

45. Mohammad Ayub Khan, *Friends Not Masters*, Lahore: Oxford University Press, 1967, pp. 202-3; Pamela Constable, 'Pakistan's Army Faces Islamic Challenge', *Times of India*, 24 June 2000, p. 9.

46. Benazir Bhutto interviewed by Sharbani Basu, *Sunday*, 1-7 August 1999, pp. 18-9.

47. Field-Marshal Viscount Montgomery of Alamein, *A History of Warfare*, London: Collins, 1968, p. 138; Philip Mason, *A Matter of Honour: An Account of the Indian Army, Its Officers and Men*, 1974, rpt, Dehra Dun: EBD Publishers, 1988, pp. 126, 529.

48. Paul A.C. Koistinen, 'The Political Economy of Warfare in America, 1865-1914', and Gerald D. Feldmann, 'Hugo Stinnes and the Prospect of War before 1914', in Chickering, *Anticipating Total War*, pp. 57-71, 92-3.

49. This is known as the Contingency Theory of Organization. J. Galbraith, *Designing Complex Organizations*, Reading: Mass, 1973, quoted in Martin Van Creveld, *Command in War*, Cambridge, MA: Harvard University Press, 1985, pp. 318-9; Williamson Murray, 'Innovation: Past and Future', in idem, and Alan R. Millett (eds), *Military Innovation in the Interwar Period*, Cambridge: Cambridge University Press, 1996, pp. 302-3.

50. Cohen, *The Indian Army*, pp. 21-2, 24-6.

51. Peter Paret, 'Armed Forces and the State: The Historical Essays of Otto Hintze', in Brian Bond and I. Roy (eds), *War and Society: A Yearbook of Military History*, vol. 2, London: Croom Helm, 1977, p. 156.

52. Lorne J. Kavic, *India's Quest for Security: Defence Policies, 1947-1965*, Berkeley and Los Angeles: University of California Press, 1967, pp. 145-6; Jaswant Singh, *Defending India*, Chennai: Macmillan, 1999, pp. 108-9.

53. Lieutenant General K.P. Candeth, *The Western Front: The Indo-Pakistan War, 1971*, New Delhi: Allied, 1984, pp. 179-80; Lieutenant General Depinder Singh, *Field Marshal Sam Manekshaw: Soldiering with Dignity*, Dehra Dun: Natraj Publishers, 2002, p. 204.

54. For a hagiographic account of the IAS in the functioning of the MoD see P.R. Chari, 'Civil-Military Relations in India', *Armed Forces and Society*, vol. 4, no. 1, 1977, pp. 7-26.

55. Major General D.K. Palit, *War in High Himalaya*, New Delhi: Lancer International, 1991, pp. 420-1.

56. B.N. Mullick, *My Years with Nehru: 1948-1964*, Bombay: Allied, 1972, pp. 68-82, 107-31, 215-23; idem, *The Chinese Betrayal*, Bombay: Allied, 1971, pp. 500-1.

57. Tahir-Kheli, 'The Military', pp. 641, 645, 650; Ross Masood Husain, 'Threat Perception and Military Planning in Pakistan: The Impact of Technology, Doctrine and Arms Control', in Arnett, *Military Capacity*, pp. 130-1.

58. Ranjit Bhushan, 'Still Buttoned Up', *Outlook*, 25 October 1999, p. 56.

59. C.E. Bosworth, 'The Army of the Ghaznavids', in Jos J.L. Gommans and Dirk H.A. Kolff (eds), *Warfare and Weaponry in South Asia: 1000-1800*, New Delhi: Oxford University Press, 2001, pp. 153-66.

60. David Ayalon, 'The Mamluks of the Seljuks: Islam's Military Might at the Crossroads', *Journal of Royal Asiatic Society*, Series 3, vol. 6, no. 3, 1996, pp. 308-9.
61. Nirad C. Chaudhuri, 'The Martial Races of India', *Modern Review*, vol. XLIX, no. 1 (1931) pp. 67-8; Lieutenant Colonel Gautam Sharma, *Nationalization of the Indian Army: 1885-1947*, New Delhi: Allied, 1996, p. 105; C.H. Enloe, 'Ethnicity in the Evolution of Asia's Armed Bureaucracies', in idem, and DeWitt C. Ellinwood (eds), *Ethnicity and the Military in Asia*, New Brunswick and London: Transaction Books, 1981, Preface, pp. 1-17.
62. J. Ellen, *Red Army and Society: A Sociology of the Soviet Military*, Boston: Allen & Unwin, 1985, pp. 138-91, 187-8.
63. Stephen P. Cohen, 'The Military and Indian Democracy', in Atul Kohli (ed.), *India's Democracy: An Analysis of Changing State-Society Relations*, 1988, rpt, New Delhi: Orient Longman, 1991, pp. 103, 105; Apurba Kundu, *Militarism in India: The Army and Civil Society in Consensus*, New Delhi: Viva, 1998, pp. 170, 177, 181.
64. Sandy Gordon, 'Indian Security Policy and the Rise of the Hindu Right', *South Asia*, Special issue, vol. 17, 1994, pp. 202-3.
65. Stephen P. Cohen, *The Pakistan Army*, 1984, rpt, Karachi: Oxford University Press, 1993, pp. 42, 44, 54; Brian Cloughley, *A History of the Pakistan Army: Wars and Insurrections*, Karachi: Oxford University Press, 1999, p. 139; Mohammad Ashgar Khan, *Generals in Politics: Pakistan, 1958-1982*, London: Croom Helm, 1983, pp. 28-31; Ayesha Jalal, *The State of Martial Rule: The Origins of Pakistan's Political Economy of Defence*, 1990, rpt, New Delhi: Foundation Books, 1992, p. 139; Benazir Bhutto, *Daughter of the East: An Autobiography*, London: Hamish Hamilton, 1988, pp. 47-8.
66. Cynthia H. Enloe, *Ethnic Soldiers: State Security in Divided Societies*, Harmondsworth: Penguin, 1980, pp. 130-1.
67. Ayesha Jalal, 'State-Building in the Post-War World: Britain's Colonial Legacy, American Futures and Pakistan', in S. Bose (ed.), *South Asia and World Capitalism*, New Delhi: Oxford University Press, 1990, pp. 300-1.
68. Veena Kukreja, *Civil-Military Relations in South Asia: Pakistan, Bangladesh and India*, New Delhi: Sage, 1991, pp. 39-40; Lieutenant General Gul Hassan Khan, *Memoirs*, Karachi: Oxford University Press, 1993, pp. 235-73.
69. Sun Tzu, *The Art of War*, in Caleb Carr (ed.), *The Book of War*, Introduced by Ralph Peters, New York: Modern Library, 2000, p. 80.
70. Di Hua, 'Threat Perception and Military Planning in China: Domestic Instability and the Importance of Prestige', in Arnett, *Military Capacity*, p. 37.

71. Stephen Biddle and Robert Zirkle, 'Technology, Civil-Military Relations, and Warfare in the Developing World', *JSS*, vol. 19, no. 2, 1996, pp. 172-89.

72. 'Armed forces to get Chief of Staff', *Statesman*, 28 March 2001, p. 1.

73. Paul Bracken, *Fire in the East: The Rise of Asian Military Power and the Second Nuclear Age*, New Delhi: HarperCollins, 1999, pp. 77-80.

74. For an overview of the institutional and occupational militaries, see Editor's Note and Charles C. Moskos' essay titled, 'The Military: Institution or Occupation', in Parmar, *Military Sociology*, pp. 11-15, 35-47. For the turnover in the US army, see Roger A. Beaumont and William P. Snyder, 'Combat Effectiveness: Paradigms and Paradoxes', and Lewis Sorley, 'Prevailing Criteria: A Critique', in Sam C. Sarkesian (ed.), *Combat Effectiveness: Cohesion, Stress, and the Volunteer Military*, Beverly Hills and London: Sage, 1980, pp. 26, 30, 38, 78-9.

75. For the theory that military institutions change only due to maverick politicians or the fear of foreign aggression, see Barry R. Posen, *The Sources of Military Doctrine: France, Britain and Germany between the World Wars*, Ithaca: Cornell University Press, 1984, pp. 225-6.

76. B.R. Srikanth and Sunil Narula, 'Sparring in the Thin Air', *Outlook*, 26 April 1999, p. 38.

77. For the Information Revolution, see Alvin and Heidi Toffler, *War and Anti-War: Survival at the Dawn of the 21st Century*, 1993, rpt, London: Warner, 1994.

78. For the anti-Western attitude of the officer corps, see Ahmar Mustikhan and D. Vijayamohan, 'General Discontent', *Week*, 24 October 1999, p. 44.

CONCLUSION

The Future of the Fourth Horseman of the Apocalypse

> If thy soul finds rest in me, thou shalt overcome all dangers by my grace; but if thy thoughts are on thyself, and thou will not listen, thou shalt perish. If thou wilt not fight thy battle of life because in selfishness thou art afraid of the battle, thy resolution is in vain: nature will compel thee. Because thou art in the bondage of Karma, of the forces of thine own past life; and that which thou, in thy delusion, with a good will dost not want to do, unwillingly thou shalt have to do.
>
> *Bhagavad Gita*[1]

As the *Bhagavad Gita* tells us, despite our unwillingness the challenges posed by warfare need to be tackled. Otherwise, as history shows us, foreigners will rule over India. From the dawn of civilization in the Indian subcontinent, floods, famines, and disease have killed more human beings than the engines of war. However, in case of a nuclear confrontation in the future, not only one-fourth of the earth as the Book of Revelation tells us but the whole planet would be destroyed.

Throughout the tortuous ride of the fourth horseman of the Apocalypse in India, we have seen that *bitvas* (big battles which involved a great deal of slaughter) like Hydaspes, the Second Battle of Tarain, were an important imperative behind altering the trajectory of South Asia's evolution. Hence, the assertion of some Western historians that decisive encounter battles were a European exclusivity and were unknown among the Asians is erroneous.[2] Frederick the Great's statement: 'War is decided only by battles and is not finished except by them'[3] holds true for the entire history of India's military experience, from Hydaspes to Kargil. The claim of some recent Western historians and political analysts that large-scale warfare and especially battles have no future[4] remains merely a fond hope. For the Indian case, Kargil and for the Western world, Desert Storm should put a nail in the coffin of such wishful thinking. The fourth horseman's ride is yet to be finished.

Our voyage through the centuries has shown that one of the principal factors behind the survival of the state was its capacity to conduct war. War between the polities assumed a competitive character.[5] The process of innovation and amalgamation of various elements from the spheres of military theory, tactics, and technology for constructing a combat-effective army is termed as military synthesis. And this crucial ingredient of warfare also assumed a competitive character. Different polities compete with each other for engineering, in the quickest possible time, a successful military synthesis. The relative failure of a particular polity to synthesize the proper elements of warfare at the right time and at the right place sounded its death knell. As we have seen, in the sixteenth century the failure of the Delhi Sultanate to synthesize gunpowder weapons within the military format compared with the relative success of the Chaghtai Turks under Babur to amalgamate artillery with the steppe model of warfare resulted in Mughal victory. And this competitive nature of military synthesis is seen even today.

The nature of the constituents of a military synthesis determined the nature of the army for a particular type of warfare. Manoeuvre warfare emphasizing mobility had more or less been successful against positional warfare focusing on static defence.[6] One of the principal reasons behind the military collapse of the 1857 rebels was their failure to initiate mobile warfare against the East India Company's troops. Even for the information age warfare of twenty-first century, manoeuvre warfare in its various forms will remain dominant.

After the lapse of some time, the very elements constituting a particular type of military synthesis require to be updated in the light of changing conditions and circumstances. Blindly imitating the organization of advanced armies with their sophisticated technology was never an adequate step. This was because of varied regional and local demands. And this trend will continue in the future. For example, a nuclear weapons-equipped digitalized army may be an essential requirement for the USA with her global commitments but not for India. This is because, unlike the US army, the Indian army's chief challenges come from the terrorists equipped and backed by the neighbouring foreign governments. Hence, military synthesis continues to be a dynamic and context-specific complex of various elements.

NOTES

1. *The Bhagavad Gita*, tr. from Sanskrit with an Introduction by Juan Mascaro, London: Penguin, 1962, p. 84.
2. Geoffrey Parker writes that the Western Way of Warfare was characterized by an emphasis on technology and decisive set-piece encounter battles (invented by the Greeks) and its evolution culminated in the two industrial World Wars. His implicit assumption is that the Asians had nothing to contribute to this process, as they were engaged in ritualized combats, i.e. 'flower wars'. Parker, 'Introduction: The Western Way of War', in idem (ed.), *The Cambridge Illustrated History of Warfare*, Cambridge: Cambridge University Press, 1995, pp. 2-9.
3. Brigadier General Thomas R. Phillips (ed.), *Roots of Strategy: A Collection of Military Classics*, 1940, rpt, Dehra Dun: Natraj, 1989, p. 391.
4. John Keegan, *The Face of Battle: A Study of Agincourt, Waterloo and the Somme*, 1976, rpt, Harmondsworth, Middlesex: Penguin, 1978, pp. 331-43; Robert L. O'Connell, *Ride of the Second Horseman: The Birth and Death of War*, 1995, rpt, New York and Oxford: Oxford University Press, 1997, pp. 223-42.
5. W.B. Gallie, *Understanding War*, London: Routledge, 1991, pp. 32, 53.
6. Lieutenant General Francis Tuker, in *The Pattern of War*, London: Cassell, 1948, argues, somewhat incoherently, that manoeuvre warfare has always been successful against positional warfare in human history.

Bibliography

MANUSCRIPT SOURCES AT THE NATIONAL
ARCHIVES OF INDIA, NEW DELHI

Digest of Services of the 44th Merwara Infantry: 1818-1916.
General Orders by the Commander-in-Chief, 23 November 1857.
Military Department Proceedings, January, February, and August 1860.
Military Despatches from the Secretary of State to the Governor General,
February 1860-1.
Proceedings of the Board of Ordnance, Military Department, November
1775.

PARLIAMENTARY PAPERS

*Minutes of Evidence taken before the Commissioners appointed to inquire
into the Organization of the Indian Army, Parliamentary Papers*,
Cd 2515, 1859.
*Papers connected with the Reorganization of the Army in India,
Supplementary to the Report of the Army Commission, Parliamentary
Papers*, Cd 2541.
Report of Major General H. Hancock of the Bombay Army, Cd 2516,
Parliamentary Papers, 1859.

BOOKS AND ARTICLES

Alam, Muzaffar, *The Crisis of Empire in Mughal North India: Awadh and
Punjab, 1707-1748*, New Delhi: Oxford University Press, 1986.
Alavi, Seema, *The Sepoys and the Company: Tradition and Transition in
Northern India, 1770-1830*, Delhi: Oxford University Press, 1995.
Alexander, Martin S., 'The Fall of France, 1940', in John Gooch (ed.),
Decisive Campaigns of the Second World War, London: Frank Cass,
1990.
Ali, Ameer, *A Short History of the Saracens*, London: Macmillan, 1949.

Ali, Athar M., *The Apparatus of Empire: Awards of Ranks, Offices and Titles to the Mughal Nobility, 1574-1678*, New Delhi: Oxford University Press, 1985.

———, 'Organization of the Nobility: Mansab, Pay, Conditions of Service', in Jos J.L. Gommans and Dirk H.A. Kolff (eds), *Warfare and Weaponry in South Asia: 1000-1800*, New Delhi: Oxford University Press, 2001.

Allchin, Bridget and Allchin, Raymond, *The Birth of Indian Civilization: India and Pakistan before 500 BC*, Harmondsworth, Middlesex: Penguin, 1968.

Allen, Charles, *Soldier Sahibs: The Men Who Made the North-West Frontier*, London: John Murray, 2000.

Ambashthya, B.P., *The Decisive Battles of Sher Shah*, Patna: Janaki Prakashan, 1977.

Amitai-Preiss, Reuven, *Mongols and Mamluks: The Mamluk-Ilkhanid War, 1260-1281*, Cambridge: Cambridge University Press, 1995.

Anand, Brigadier Vinod, 'India's Military Response to the Kargil Aggression', *Strategic Analysis*, vol. 23, no. 7, 1999.

———, 'Future Battlespace and Need for Jointmanship', *Strategic Analysis*, vol. 23, no. 10, 2000.

Andreski, Stanislav, *Military Organization and Society*, 1954, rpt, Berkeley: University of California Press, 1968.

Arnett, Eric, 'Military Research and Development', in *Sipri Yearbook 1998: Armaments, Disarmament and International Security*, Oxford: Oxford University Press, 1998.

Arnold, Thomas, *The Renaissance at War*, London: Cassell, 2001.

Arrian, *The Campaigns of Alexander*, tr Aubrey De Selincourt, 1958, rpt, Harmondsworth, Middlesex: Penguin, 1976.

Athar, Ali, 'Military Exercise and Training in the Sultanate of Delhi during the 13th and 14th Centuries', *Journal of the Asiatic Society*, vol. 37, no. 1, 1995.

———, 'The Role of Piyadah in the Sultanate of Delhi', *Journal of the Asiatic Society*, vol. 37, no. 2, 1995.

———, 'The Ministry of War in the Delhi Sultanate', *Journal of the Asiatic Society*, vol. 37, no. 3, 1995.

———, 'Military Hierarchy and Designations under the Sultans of Delhi (13th-14th Centuries)', *Journal of the Asiatic Society*, vol. XLII, nos 1-2, 2000.

Ayalon, David, 'The Mamluks of the Seljuks: Islam's Military Might at the Crossroads', *Journal of Royal Asiatic Society*, Series 3, vol. 6, no. 3, 1996.

Aziz, Abdul, *The Mansabdari System and the Mughal Army*, Delhi: Idarah-i-Adabiyat, 1972.

Baark, Erik, 'Military Technology and Absorptive Capacity in China and India: Implications for Modernization', in Eric Arnett (ed.), *Military*

Capacity and the Risk of War: China, India, Pakistan and Iran, Oxford: Oxford University Press, 1997.

Babur *Padshah Ghazi,* Zahir–ud-din Muhammad, *Babur-Nama,* vols 1 & 2, tr A.S. Beveridge, 1921, rpt, Delhi: Saeed International, 1989.

Bachrach, Bernard S., 'Logistics in Pre-Crusade Europe', in John A. Lynn (ed.), *Feeding Mars: Logistics in the Western World from the Middle Ages to the Present,* Boulder: Westview Press, 1993.

_____, 'On Roman Ramparts', in Geoffrey Parker (ed.), *The Cambridge Illustrated History of Warfare: The Triumph of the West,* Cambridge: Cambridge University Press, 1995.

Badsey, Stephen, 'Coalition Command in the Gulf War', in G.D. Sheffield (ed.), *Leadership and Command: The Anglo-American Military Experience Since 1861,* London: Brassey's, 1997.

Baev, Pavel K., *The Russian Army in a Time of Troubles,* London: Sage, 1996.

Bajwa, Fauja Singh, *Military System of the Sikhs during the Period 1799-1849,* Delhi: Motilal Banarasidas, 1964.

Ballance, Edgar O', *The Red Army,* London: Faber & Faber, 1964.

Bandopadhyay, Durgadas, *Amar Jivancharit,* in Bengali, 1925, rpt, Calcutta: Ananya Prakashan, n.d.

Banerjee, A.C., *Peshwa Madhav Rao I,* 1943, rpt, Calcutta: A. Mukherjee, 1968.

_____, *The State and Society in Northern India: 1206-1526,* Calcutta: K.P. Bagchi, 1982.

Baoxiu, Colonel Hong, 'Deng Xiaoping's Theory of War and Peace', in Michael Pillsbury (ed.), *Chinese Views of Future Warfare,* New Delhi: Lancer, 1998.

Bar-Kochva, B., *The Seleucid Army: Organization and Tactics in the Great Campaigns,* Cambridge: Cambridge University Press, 1978.

Barnett, Correlli, *Britain and her Army: 1509-1970, A Military, Political and Social Survey,* London: Penguin, 1970.

Barua, Pradeep, 'Military Developments in India: 1750-1850', *Journal of Military History,* vol. 58, no. 4, 1994.

Baumgart, Winfred, *The Crimean War: 1853-1856,* London: Arnold, 1999.

Bayly, C.A. (ed.), Eric Stokes, *The Peasant Armed: The Indian Revolt of 1857,* Oxford: Oxford University Press, 1986.

Beaumont, Roger A. and Snyder, William P., 'Combat Effectiveness: Paradigms and Paradoxes', in Sam C. Sarkesian (ed.), *Combat Effectiveness: Cohesion, Stress, and the Volunteer Military,* Beverly Hills and London: Sage, 1980.

Beevor, Antony, *Stalingrad: The Fateful Siege, 1942-1943,* 1998, rpt, Harmondsworth, Middlesex: Penguin, 1999.

Begum, Gul Badan, *Humayun Nama,* tr. A.S. Beveridge, 1901, rpt, New Delhi: Atlantic Publishers, 1989.

Bennell, A.S., 'The Anglo-Maratha War of 1803-1805', *Journal of the Society for Army Historical Research*, Autumn 1985.

Berghahn, V.R., *Militarism: The History of an International Debate, 1861-1979*, Leamington Spa: Berg, 1981.

Bhadra, Gautam, 'Two Frontier Uprisings in Mughal India', in Ranajit Guha (ed.), *Subaltern Studies*, vol. 2, Delhi: Oxford University Press, 1983, rpt, 1986.

Bhakari, Major S.K., *Indian Warfare: An Appraisal of Strategy and Tactics of War in Early Medieval Period*, New Delhi: Munshiram Manoharlal, 1981.

Bhandarkar, D.R., *Asoka*, Calcutta: University of Calcutta, 1932.

Bhandarkar, R.G., *Early History of Dekkan down to the Mahomedan Conquest*, 1895, rpt, Calcutta: Chakravarty, Chatterjee & Co. Ltd, 1928.

Bhutto, Benazir, *Daughter of the East: An Autobiography*, London: Hamish Hamilton, 1988.

Biddle, Stephen and Zirkle, Robert, 'Technology, Civil-Military Relations, and Warfare in the Developing World', *Journal of Strategic Studies*, vol. 19, no. 2, 1996.

Bidwell, Shelford, *Swords for Hire: European Mercenaries in Eighteenth Century India*, London: John Murray, 1971.

Bird, Lieutenant Colonel W.D., 'The Assaye Campaign', *Journal of the United Service Institution of India*, vol. XLI, no. 187, 1912.

Black, Jeremy, *A Military Revolution? Military Change and European Society, 1550-1800*, London: Macmillan, 1991.

_____, *Cambridge Illustrated Atlas of Warfare: Renaissance to Revolution, 1492-1792*, Cambridge: Cambridge University Press, 1996.

Blomfield, David (ed.), *Lahore to Lucknow: The Indian Mutiny Journal of Arthur Moffatt Lang*, London: Leo Cooper, 1992.

Blumenson, Martin, 'The Development of the Modern Military', *Armed Forces and Society*, vol. 6, no. 4, 1980.

Bopegamage, A., 'Caste, Class and the Indian Military: A Study of the Social Origins of Indian Army Personnel', in Jacques van Doorn (ed.), *Military Profession and Military Regimes: Commitments and Conflicts*, The Hague and Paris: The Mouton, 1969.

Bosworth, A.B., *Conquest and Empire: The Reign of Alexander the Great*, 1988, rpt, Cambridge: Canto, 1993.

Bosworth, C.E., 'The Army of the Ghaznavids', in Jos J.L. Gommans and Dirk H.A. Kolff (eds), *Warfare and Weaponry in South Asia: 1000-1800*, New Delhi: Oxford University Press, 2001.

Bowden, Hugh, 'Hoplites and Homer: Warfare, Hero Cult, and the Ideology of the Polis', in John Rich and Graham Shipley (eds), *War and Society in the Greek World*, 1993, rpt, London: Routledge, 1995.

Boxer, C.R., 'Asian Potentates and European Artillery in the 16th-18th Centuries: A Footnote to Gibson-Hill', *Journal of the Malaysian Branch of the Royal Asiatic Society*, vol. 38, no. 208, 1966.

Bracken, Paul, *Fire in the East: The Rise of Asian Military Power and the Second Nuclear Age*, New Delhi: HarperCollins, 1999.

Brady, Ciaran, 'The Captains' Games: Army and Society in Elizabethan Ireland', in Thomas Bartlett and Keith Jeffrey (eds), *A Military History of Ireland*, 1996, rpt, Cambridge: Cambridge University Press, 1997.

Brett-James, Antony (ed.), *Wellington at War: 1794-1815, A Selection of His Wartime Letters*, London: Macmillan, 1961.

Brewer, John, *The Sinews of Power: War, Money and the English State*, London: Unwin Hyman, 1989.

Broughton, T.D., *Letters Written in a Maratha Camp during the Year 1809*, 1892, rpt, New Delhi: Asian Educational Services, 1995.

Bruce, George, *Six Battles for India: The Anglo-Sikh Wars, 1845-46, 1848-49*, Calcutta: Rupa, 1969.

_____, *The Burma Wars: 1824-1886*, London: Hart-Davis, 1973.

Bryant, G.J., 'The Cavalry Problem in the Early British Indian Army, 1750-85', *War in History*, vol. 2, no., 1, 1995.

Bullock, Brigadier Humphrey, *History of the Army Service Corps: 1760-1857*, vol. 1, New Delhi: Sterling Publishers, 1976.

Burton, Captain R.G., 'Battles of the Deccan', *Journal of the United Service Institution of India*, vol. 20, no. 84, 1891.

_____, 'Argaum', *Journal of the United Service Institution of India*, vol. 28, 1899.

Burton-Page, J., 'A Study of Fortification in the Indian Subcontinent from the Thirteenth to the Eighteenth Century A.D.', *Bulletin of the School of Oriental and African Studies*, vol. 23, 1960.

Butalia, Brigadier R.C., *The Evolution of Artillery in India: From the Battle of Plassey to the Revolt of 1857*, New Delhi: Allied, 1998.

Callahan, Raymond, *The East India Company and Army Reform: 1793-98*, Cambridge, MA: Harvard University Press, 1972.

Callwell, Colonel C.E., *Small Wars: A Tactical Textbooks for Imperial Soldiers*, 1896, rpt, London: Greenhill, 1990.

Campbell, Brian, 'War and Diplomacy: Rome and Parthia, 31 BC-AD 235', in John Rich and Graham Shipley (eds), *War and Society in the Roman World*, 1993, rpt, London: Routledge, 1995.

Candeth, Lieutenant General K.P., *The Western Front: The Indo-Pakistan War, 1971*, New Delhi: Allied, 1984.

Cardew, Lieutenant F.G., *A Sketch of the Services of the Bengal Native Army to the Year 1895*, 1903, rpt, New Delhi: Today & Tomorrow's Publishers, 1971.

Caroe, Olaf, *The Pathans: 500 BC-AD 1957*, London: Macmillan, 1958.

Chakravarti, P.C., *The Art of War in Ancient India*, 1941, rpt, Delhi: Low Price Publications, 1989.

Chaliand, Gerard (ed.), *The Art of War in World History: From Antiquity to the Nuclear Age*, Berkeley: University of California Press, 1994.

Chander, Ramesh, 'Sultan Mahmud of Ghazni and the Khukhrain Kshatriyas of the Punjab', *Punjab Past and Present*, vol. 15, no. 29, 1981.

Chandra, Bipan et al., *India's Struggle for Independence*, 1988, rpt, New Delhi: Penguin, 1990.

Chandra, Satish, *Parties and Politics at the Mughal Court*, 1959, rpt, New Delhi: New Age, 1979.

Chari, P.R., 'Civil-Military Relations in India', *Armed Forces and Society*, vol. 4, no. 1, 1977.

Chattopadhyay, Brajadulal, *Aspects of Rural Settlements and Rural Society in Early Medieval North India*, Calcutta: K.P. Bagchi, 1990.

Chaudhuri, Nirad C., 'The Martial Races of India', *Modern Review*, vol. XLIX, no. 1, 1931.

Chaudhuri, S.B., *Ethnic Settlements in Ancient India*, Part-1, *Northern India*, Calcutta: General Printer & Publishers, 1955.

Childe, Gordon, *What Happened in History*, 1942, rpt, Harmondsworth, Middlesex: Penguin, 1946.

Clausewitz, General Carl von, *On War*, tr. Colonel J.J. Graham with Introduction and Notes by Colonel F.N. Maude, vol. 3, London and Boston: Routledge & Kegan Paul, 1968.

_____, *On War*, ed. with an Introduction by Anatol Rapoport, 1968, rpt, London: Penguin, 1982.

_____, *On War*, ed. and tr. Michael Howard and Peter Paret, 1976, rpt, Princeton: Princeton University Press, 1984.

_____, *On War*, in Caleb Carr (ed.), *The Book of War*, New York: Modern Library, 1993.

Cloughley, Brian, *A History of the Pakistan Army: Wars and Insurrections*, Karachi: Oxford University Press, 1999.

Cohen, Stephen P., *The Indian Army: Its Contribution to the Development of a Nation*, 1971, rpt, Delhi: Oxford University Press, 1991.

_____, *The Pakistan Army*, 1984, rpt, Karachi: Oxford University Press, 1993.

_____, 'The Military and Indian Democracy', in Atul Kohli (ed.), *India's Democracy: An Analysis of Changing State-Society Relations*, 1988, rpt, New Delhi: Orient Longman, 1991.

Coker, Christopher, *Waging War Without Warriors? The Changing Culture of Military Conflict*, Boulder, Colorado: Lynne Rienner, 2002.

Collins, L.J.D., 'The Military Organization and Tactics of the Crimean Tatars, 16th–17th Centuries', in V.J. Parry and M.E. Yapp (eds), *War, Technology and Society in the Middle East*, London: Oxford University Press, 1975.

Compton, Herbert, *A Particular Account of the European Military Adventurers of Hindustan from 1784 to 1803*, 1892, rpt, Karachi: Oxford University Press, 1976.

Connell, Robert L. O', *Of Arms and Men: A History of War, Weapons and Aggression*, New York: Oxford University Press, 1989.

———, *Ride of the Second Horseman: The Birth and Death of War*, New York: Oxford University Press, 1995.

Contamine, Philippe, *War in the Middle Ages*, tr. Michael Jones, 1984, rpt, Oxford: Blackwell, 1996.

Cook, Hugh, *The Sikh Wars: The British Army in Punjab, 1845-49*, New Delhi: Thomson Press, 1975.

Cooper, Randolf G.S., 'Wellington and the Marathas', *International History Review*, vol. 11, no. 1, 1989.

Creveld, Martin Van, *Supplying War: Logistics from Wallenstein to Patton*, 1977, rpt, Cambridge: Cambridge University Press, 1980.

———, *Command in War*, Cambridge, MA: Harvard University Press, 1985.

———, *Technology and War: From 2000 B.C. to the Present*, London: Brassey's, 1991.

———, 'Technology and War II: Postmodern War?', in Charles Townshend (ed.), *The Oxford Illustrated History of Modern War*, Oxford: Oxford University Press, 1997.

Crosbie-Weston, R., 'The Huns' in James Lawford (ed.), *Cavalry*, New York: Crescent Books, 1976.

Crowell, Lorenzo M., 'Military Professionalism in a Colonial Context, circa 1832', *Modern Asian Studies*, vol. 24, no. 2, 1990.

Dasgupta, Sanjay, 'Command and Control in the Nuclear Era', in Maroof Raza (ed.), *Generals and Governments in India and Pakistan*, New Delhi: Har-Anand, 2001.

Dawson, Doyne, *The First Armies*, London: Cassell, 2001.

De, Barun, 'The Ideological and Social Background of Haidar Ali and Tipu Sultan', in Irfan Habib (ed.), *Resistance and Modernization under Haidar Ali and Tipu Sultan*, New Delhi: Tulika, 1999.

Devahuti, D., *Harsha: A Political Study*, Oxford: Oxford University Press, 1970.

Digby, Simon, 'Dreams and Reminiscences of Dattu Sarvani: A Sixteenth Century Indo-Afghan Soldier', *Indian Economic and Social History Review*, vol. 2, nos 1 & 2, 1965.

———, *War Horse and Elephant in the Delhi Sultanate*, Karachi: Oxford University Press, 1971.

———, 'The Problem of Military Ascendancy of the Delhi Sultanate', in Jos J.L. Gommans and Dirk H.A. Kolff (eds), *Warfare and Weaponry in South Asia: 1000-1800*, New Delhi: Oxford University Press, 2001.

———, *Sufis and Soldiers in Aurangzeb's Deccan*, New Delhi: Oxford University Press, 2001.

Dikshitar, V.R. Ramachandra, *War in Ancient India*, 1944, rpt, Delhi: Motilal Banarasidas, 1987.

Dirom, Major, *A Narrative of the Campaign in India which terminated the War with Tipu Sultan in 1792*, 1793, rpt, New Delhi: Asian Educational Services, 1997.

Divine, Albert, 'Alexander the Great', in General John Hackett (ed.), *Warfare in the Ancient World*, London: Sidgwick & Jackson, 1989.

Dodge, Colonel Theodore Ayrault, *Alexander*, 1890, rpt, New York: Da Capo, 1996.

_____, *Great Captains: Hannibal*, vol. 1, 1891, rpt, New Delhi: Lancer International, 1992.

_____, *Caesar*, 1892, rpt, New York: Da Capo, 1997.

Doorn, Jacques van 'Political Change and the Control of the Military', in idem (ed.), *Military Profession and Military Regimes: Commitments and Conflicts*, The Hague and Paris: Mouton, 1969.

Duff, James Grant, *History of the Marathas*, 3 vols combined, 1863, rpt, Delhi: Low Price Publications, 1990.

Duffy, Christopher, *The Military Experience in the Age of Reason*, London: Routledge & Kegan Paul, 1987.

_____, *Red Storm on the Reich: The Soviet March on Germany, 1945*, 1991, rpt, New York: Da Capo, 1993.

Dunbar, Janet (ed.), *Tigers, Durbars and Kings: Fanny Eden's Indian Journals, 1837-38*, London: John Murray, 1988.

Dunlop, Robert Henry Wallace, *Service and Adventure with the Khakee Ressalah or Meerut Volunteer Horse during the Mutinies of 1857-58*, 1858, rpt, Allahabad: Legend Publications, 1974.

Dupuy, Trevor N., *The Evolution of Weapons and Warfare*, 1984, rpt, New York: Da Capo, 1990.

Edwardes, Michael, *Clive: The Heaven Born General*, London: Hart-Davis, 1977.

Ellen, J., *Red Army and Society: A Sociology of the Soviet Military*, Boston: Allen & Unwin, 1985.

Elting, Colonel John R., *Swords around a Throne: Napoleon's Grande Armee*, 1988, rpt, New York: Da Capo, 1997.

Engels, Donald W., *Alexander the Great and the Logistics of the Macedonian Army*, Berkeley: University of California Press, 1978.

Enloe, Cynthia H., *Ethnic Soldiers: State Security in Divided Societies*, Harmondsworth: Penguin, 1980.

_____, 'Ethnicity in the Evolution of Asia's Armed Bureaucracies', in idem, and DeWitt C. Ellinwood (eds), *Ethnicity and the Military in Asia*, New Brunswick and London: Transaction Books, 1981.

Fazl, Abul, *The Akbar Nama*, 3 vols, tr H. Beveridge, 1903, rpt, New Delhi: Saeed International, 1989.

Featherstone, Donald, *At Them with the Bayonet: The First Sikh War*, London: Jarrolds, 1968.

Feldmann, Gerald D., 'Hugo Stinnes and the Prospect of War before 1914', in Roger Chickering, et al., *Anticipating Total War: The German and American Experiences, 1871-1914,* Cambridge: Cambridge University Press, 1999.

Ferrill, Arthur, *The Origins of War: From the Stone Age to Alexander the Great,* 1985, rpt, London: Thames & Hudson, 1986.

Fisher, Michael H., 'The Office of Akhbar Nawis: The Transition from Mughal to British Forms', *Modern Asian Studies,* vol. 27, no. 1, 1993.

Forrest, G.W. (ed.), *The Indian Mutiny: 1857-58, Selections from the Letters, Despatches and other State Papers preserved in the Military Department of the Government of India,* vol. 3, 1902, rpt, Delhi: D.K Publishers, 2000.

Forster, George, *A Journey from Bengal to England through the Northern part of India, Kashmir, Afghanistan, and Persia and into Russia, by the Caspian Sea, 1782-84,* vol. 1, 1798, rpt, New Delhi: Munshiram Manoharlal, 1997.

Foucault, Michel, *Politics, Philosophy, Culture: Interviews and Other Writings, 1977-1984,* ed. and with an Introduction by Lawrence D. Kritzman, 1988, rpt, New York: Routledge, 1990.

France, John, *Victory in the East: A Military History of the First Crusade,* Cambridge: Cambridge University Press, 1994.

Fraser, James, *The History of Nadir Shah,* MDCCXLII, rpt, New Delhi: Mohan Publications, 1973.

Fraser, John, 'Captain Clifford Henry James', *Journal of the Society for Army Historical Research,* no. 243, Autumn 1982.

Freemantle, Major General F.L., *Fred's Foibles,* New Delhi: Lancer, 2000.

From Surprise to Reckoning: The Kargil Review Committee Report, New Delhi: Sage, 2000.

Friedman, Wendy, 'Arms Procurement in China: Poorly Understood Processes and Unclear Results', in Eric Arnett (ed.), *Military Capacity and the Risk of War: China, India, Pakistan and Iran,* Oxford: Oxford University Press, 1997.

Fuller, Major General, J.F.C., *The Second World War: 1939-1945,* 1954, rpt, New York: Da Capo, 1993.

_____, *A Military History of the Western World: From the Earliest Times to the Battle of Lepanto,* vol. 1, 1954, rpt, New York: Da Capo, 1987.

_____, *A Military History of the Western World: From the Defeat of the Spanish Armada to the Battle of Waterloo,* vol. 2, 1955, rpt, New York: Da Capo, 1987.

_____, *The Generalship of Alexander the Great,* 1960, rpt, New York: Da Capo, 1989.

_____, *The Conduct of War: 1789-1961,* 1961, rpt, London: Methuen, 1971.

Fuller Jr, William C., *Civil-Military Conflict in Imperial Russia: 1881-1914,* Princeton: Princeton University Press, 1985.

Gabriel, Richard A. and Savage, Paul L., *Crisis in Command: Mismanagement in the Army*, 1978, rpt, New Delhi: Himalayan Books, 1986.

Gallie, W.B., *Understanding War*, London: Routledge, 1991.

Ganguly, D.C. (ed.), *Select Documents of the British Period of Indian History*, Calcutta: The Trustees of Victoria Memorial, 1958.

Gat, Azar, *The Origins of Military Thought: From the Enlightenment to Clausewitz*, Oxford: Clarendon Press, 1989.

Gaylor, John, *Sons of John Company: The Indian and Pakistan Armies, 1903-91*, 1992, rpt, New Delhi: Lancer, 1993.

Glantz, David M., *The Soviet Conduct of Tactical Maneuver: Spearhead of the Offensive*, London: Frank Cass, 1991.

Gommans, Jos J.L., 'Indian Warfare and Afghan Innovation during the Eighteenth Century', *Studies in History*, New Series, vol. 11, no. 2, 1995.

_____, *The Rise of the Indo-Afghan Empire: c. 1710-80*, Leiden: E.J. Brill, 1995.

_____, *Mughal Warfare: Indian Frontiers and High Roads to Empire, 1500-1700*, London and New York: Routledge, 2002.

_____ and Dirk Kolff, 'Introduction' in Gommans and Kolff (eds), *Warfare and Weaponry in South Asia: 1000-1800*, New Delhi: Oxford University Press, 2001.

Gooch, John, 'Introduction', in John Gooch (ed.), *Decisive Campaigns of the Second World War*, London: Frank Cass, 1990.

Gopal, Sarvepalli, *Jawaharlal Nehru: A Biography, 1947-56*, vol. 2, 1979, rpt, Delhi: Oxford University Press, 1988.

Gordon, Sandy, 'Indian Security Policy and the Rise of the Hindu Right', *South Asia*, vol. 17, special issue, 1994.

Gordon, Stewart, 'The Limited Adoption of European-Style Military Forces by Eighteenth Century Rulers in India', *Indian Economic and Social History Review*, vol. 35, no. 3, 1998.

Gough, Charles and Innes, Arthur, *The Sikhs and the Sikh Wars: The Rise, Conquest and Annexation of the Punjab State*, 1897, rpt, Delhi: Gian Publishing, 1986.

Grewal, J.S. and Banga, Indu (eds), *Civil and Military Affairs of Maharaja Ranjit Singh*, Amritsar: Guru Nanak Dev University, 1988.

Grey, C., *European Adventurers of Northern India: 1785-1849*, edited by H.L.O. Garrett, 1929, rpt, New Delhi: Asian Educational Services, 1993.

Grove, Eric, 'Maritime Forces and Stability in Southern Asia', in Eric Arnett (ed.), *Military Capacity and the Risk of War: China, India, Pakistan and Iran*, Oxford: Oxford University Press, 1997.

Guangqian, Colonel Peng, 'Deng Xiaoping's Strategic Thought', in Michael Pillsbury (ed.), *Chinese Views of Future Warfare*, New Delhi: Lancer, 1998.

Guha, Ranajit (ed.), *Subaltern Studies: Writings on South Asian History and Society*, vol. 1, 1982, rpt, Delhi: Oxford University Press, 1986.

Gupta, Pratul Chandra, *Nana Sahib and the Rising at Kanpur*, Oxford: Clarendon Press, 1963.

_____, 'John Macleod's Private Journal during the Maratha War, 1817-18', *Bengal Past and Present*, vol. C, no. 190, 1981.

Gupta, Rajni Kant, *Military Traits of Tatya Tope*, New Delhi: Sultan Chand, 1987.

Habib, Irfan, 'Changes in Technology in Medieval India', *Studies in History*, vol. 2, no. 1, 1980.

_____, *An Atlas of Mughal Empire: Political and Economic Maps with Detailed Notes*, 1982, rpt, Delhi: Oxford University Press, 1986.

_____, 'Non-Agricultural Production and Urban Economy', in Dharma Kumar and Tapan Raychaudhuri (eds), *The Cambridge Economic History of India: c. 1200- c. 1750*, vol. 1, 1982, rpt, New Delhi: Orient Longman in association with Cambridge University Press, 1991.

_____, 'Introduction: An Essay on Haidar Ali and Tipu Sultan', in Irfan Habib (ed.), *Confronting Colonialism: Resistance and Modernization under Haidar Ali and Tipu Sultan*, New Delhi: Tulika, 1999.

Habib, Mohammad, *Sultan Mahmud of Ghaznin*, Aligarh: Aligarh Muslim University, 1927.

_____, 'The Urban Revolution in Northern India', in Jos J.L. Gommans and Dirk H.A. Kolff (eds), *Warfare and Weaponry in South Asia: 1000-1800*, New Delhi: Oxford University Press, 2001.

Habibullah, A.B.M., *The Foundation of Muslim Rule in India*, 1961, rpt, Allahabad: Central Book Depot, 1976.

Hackett, General John, *The Profession of Arms*, 1983, rpt, London: Sidgwick & Jackson, 1984.

Hall, Bert S. and Vries Kelly De, 'Essay Review—The "Military Revolution" Revisited', *Technology and Culture*, vol. 31, no. 3, 1990.

Hamilton, Colonel W.G., 'Ochterlony's Campaign in the Simla Hills: 1814-15', *Journal of the United Service Institution of India*, vol. XLI, no. 187, 1912.

_____, 'Ochterlony's Campaign in the Simla Hills—Some Further Notes On', *Journal of the United Service Institution of India*, vol. XLI, no. 189, 1912.

Handel, Michael I., *Masters of War: Classical Strategic Thought*, 1992, rpt, London: Frank Cass, 1996.

Hanson, Victor Davis, 'The Ideology of Hoplite Battle, Ancient and Modern', in idem (ed.), *Hoplites: The Classical Greek Battle Experience*, 1991, rpt, London: Routledge, 1993.

Haq, S. Moinul (ed.), *Memoirs of Hakim Ahsanullah Khan*, Karachi: Pakistan Historical Society, 1958.

Heathcote, T.A., *The Indian Army: The Garrison of British Imperial India, 1822-1922*, Newton Abbot: David & Charles, 1974.

_____, *The Military in British India: The Development of British Land Forces in South Asia, 1600-1947*, Manchester: Manchester University Press, 1995.

Heng, Gao, 'Future Military Trends', in Michael Pillsbury (ed.), *Chinese Views of Future Warfare*, 1997, rpt, New Delhi: Lancer, 1998.

Hill, James Michael, 'The Distinctiveness of Gaelic Warfare: 1400-1750', *European History Quarterly*, vol. 22, no. 3, 1992.

Hiranandani, Vice Admiral G.M., *Transition to Triumph: History of the Indian Navy, 1965-1975*, New Delhi: Lancer, 2000.

History of the Indian Ordnance and Clothing Factories, Simla: Government of India Press, 1938.

History of the Regiment of Artillery Indian Army, Published under the authority of the Director of Artillery, Army Headquarters, Dehra Dun: Palit & Palit, 1971.

Hitti, Philip, *History of the Arabs*, London: Macmillan, 1937.

Hodder, Reginald, 'The Sikhs and the Sikh Wars', *Panjab Past and Present*, vol. 4, no. 1, 1970.

Homer, *The Iliad*, tr E.V. Rieu, 1950, rpt, Harmondsworth, Middlesex: Penguin, 1986.

Hooper, Nicholas and Bennett, Matthew, *The Cambridge Illustrated Atlas of Warfare: The Middle Ages, 768-1487*, Cambridge: Cambridge University Press, 1996.

Howard, Michael, *War in European History*, 1976, rpt, Oxford: Oxford University Press, 1977.

Hua, Di, 'Threat Perception and Military Planning in China: Domestic Instability and the Importance of Prestige', in Eric Arnett (ed.), *Military Capacity and the Risk of War: China, India, Pakistan and Iran*, Oxford: Oxford University Press, 1997.

Huaqin, General Liu, 'Defence Modernization in Historical Perspective', in Michael Pillsbury (ed.), *Chinese Views of Future Warfare*, 1997, rpt, New Delhi: Lancer, 1998.

Hughes, Major General B.P., 'Siege Artillery in the Nineteenth Century', *Journal of the Society for Army Historical Research*, no. 243, Autumn 1982.

Hunter, William Wilson, *The Marquess of Dalhousie and the Final Development of the Company's Rule*, Oxford: Clarendon Press, MDCCCXCV.

Huntington, Samuel, *The Soldier and the State*, Cambridge, MA: Harvard University Press, 1957.

Husain, Iqbal, *The Ruhela Chieftaincies: The Rise and Fall of Ruhela Power in India in the Eighteenth Century*, New Delhi: Oxford University Press, 1994.

Husain, Ross Masood, 'Threat Perception and Military Planning in Pakistan: The Impact of Technology, Doctrine and Arms Control', in Eric Arnett (ed.), *Military Capacity and the Risk of War: China, India, Pakistan and Iran*, Oxford: Oxford University Press, 1997.

Hutchinson, Lester, *European Freebooters in Moghul India*, Bombay: Asia Publishing, 1964.

Inalcik, Halil, 'The Socio-Political Effects of the Diffusion of Firearms in the Middle East', in V.J. Parry and M.E. Yapp (eds), *War, Technology and Society in the Middle East*, London: Oxford University Press, 1975.

Indian Voices of the Great War: Soldiers' Letters, 1914-18, Selected and Introduced by David Omissi, London: Macmillan, 1999.

Indra, *Ideologies of War and Peace in Ancient India*, Hoshiarpur: Vedic Research Institute, 1957.

Irvine, William, *Later Mughals*, 2 vols, rpt, New Delhi: Taj Publications, -1989.

_____, *The Army of the Indian Mughals: Its Organization and Administration*, 1903, rpt, Delhi: Low Price Publication, 1994.

Irwin, Major General Alistair, 'The Buffalo Thorn: The Nature of the Future Battlefield', *Journal of Strategic Studies*, vol. 19, no. 4, 1996.

Jackson, Peter, *The Delhi Sultanate: A Political and Military History*, Cambridge: Cambridge University Press, 1999.

Jalal, Ayesha, 'State-Building in the Post-War World: Britain's Colonial Legacy, American Future and Pakistan', in S. Bose (ed.), *South Asia and World Capitalism*, New Delhi: Oxford University Press, 1990.

_____, *The State of Martial Rule: The Origins of Pakistan's Political Economy of Defence*, 1990, rpt, New Delhi: Foundation Books, 1992.

Jauhri, R.C., *Firoz Tughluq*, 1968, rpt, Jalandhar: ABS Publication, 1990.

Jeffrey, Keith, 'Colonial Warfare: 1900-1939', in Colin McInnes and G.D. Sheffield (eds), *Warfare in the Twentieth Century: Theory and Practice*, London: Unwin Hyman, 1988.

Jespersen, Knud J.V., 'Social Change and Military Revolution in Early Modern Europe: Some Danish Evidence', *Historical Journal*, vol. 26, no. 1, 1983.

Jones, Major H. Helsham, 'The Campaigns of Lord Lake against the Marathas: 1804-6', *Journal of the Royal Engineers*, vol. 8, 1882.

Joshi, Akshay, 'A Holistic View of the Revolution in Military Affairs (RMA)', *Strategic Analysis*, vol. 22, no. 11, 1999.

Joshi, P.C., '1857 in Our History', in P.C. Joshi (ed.), *Rebellion 1857: A Symposium*, 1957, rpt, Calcutta: K.P. Bagchi, 1986.

Juvaini, Ata-Malik, *Genghis Khan: The History of the World Conqueror*, tr and ed. J.A. Boyle with an Introduction by David O. Morgan, 1958, rpt, Manchester: Manchester University Press, 1997.

Kaegi, Walter E., 'Byzantine Logistics: Problems and Perspectives', in John A. Lynn (ed.), *Feeding Mars: Logistics in the Western World from the Middle Ages to the Present*, Boulder: Westview Press, 1993.

Kantak, M.R., *The First Anglo-Maratha War: 1774-1783, A Military Study of the Major Battles*, Bombay: Popular Prakashan, 1993.

Kar, Lieutenant Colonel H.C., *Military History of India*, Calcutta: Firma KLM Pvt. Ltd., 1980.

Karim, Major General Afsir, 'Airborne Forces: AB Division in Its Classic Role', Part II, *Indian Defence Review*, January 1992.

Kautilya. *The Arthashastra*, tr, ed. and Rearranged by L.N. Rangarajan, 1987, rpt, New Delhi: Penguin, 1992.

Kavic, Lorne J., *India's Quest for Security: Defence Policies, 1947-1965*, Berkeley and Los Angeles: University of California Press, 1967.

Keegan, John, *The Face of Battle: A Study of Agincourt, Waterloo and the Somme*, 1976, rpt, Harmondsworth, Middlesex: Penguin, 1978.

_____, *Six Armies in Normandy: From D-Day to the Liberation of Paris*, 1982, rpt, London: Pimlico, 1992.

_____, *The Mask of Command*, 1987, rpt, Harmondsworth, Middlesex: Penguin, 1988.

_____, *A History of Warfare*, New York: Vintage, 1993.

_____, *War and Our World*, 1998, rpt, London: Pimlico, 1999.

Kehli, Shirin Tahir, 'The Military in Contemporary Pakistan', *Armed Forces and Society*, vol. 6, no. 4, 1980.

Kennedy, Paul, *The Rise and Fall of British Naval Mastery*, 1976, rpt, London: Fontana, 1991.

_____, *The Rise and Fall of the Great Powers: Economic Change and Military Conflict from 1500 to 2000*, 1988, rpt, London: Fontana, 1990.

Khan, Lieutenant General Gul Hassan, *Memoirs*, Karachi: Oxford University Press, 1993.

Khan, Hussain, 'The Genesis of Roh (The Medieval Homeland of the Afghans), *Journal of Asiatic Society of Pakistan*, vol. 15, no. 3.

Khan, Iqtidar Alam, 'Origin and Development of Gunpowder Technology in India: AD 1250-1500', *Indian Historical Review*, vol. 4, no. 1, 1977.

'Coming of Gunpowder and the Response of Indian Polity', Unpublished Paper (Lecture delivered at the Centre for Studies in Social Sciences, Calcutta, 1983).

_____, 'The *Tazkirat ul-Muluk* by Rafi'uddin Ibrahim Shirazi: As a Source on the History of Akbar's Reign', *Studies in History*, vol. 2, no. 1, 1980.

_____, 'Early Use of Cannon and Musket in India: AD 1442-1526', in Jos J.L. Gommans and Dirk H.A. Kolff (eds), *Warfare and Weaponry in South Asia: 1000-1800*, New Delhi: Oxford University Press, 2001.

Khan, Mohammad Ashgar, *Generals in Politics: Pakistan, 1958-1982*, London: Croom Helm, 1983.

Khan, Mohammad Ayub, *Friends Not Masters*, Lahore: Oxford University Press, 1967.

Khan, Saqi Mustad, *Maasir-i-Alamgiri*, tr. Jadunath Sarkar, 1947, rpt, Calcutta: Asiatic Society, 1990.

Khan, Yusuf Ali, *The Tarikh-i-Mahabatjangi*, tr. Abdus Subhan, Calcutta: Asiatic Society, 1982.

Khanna, D.D. (ed.), *The Second Maratha Campaign, 1804-05: Diary of James Young, Officer of Bengal Horse Artillery*, New Delhi: Allied, 1990.

Kiernan, V.G., *European Empires from Conquest to Collapse: 1815-1960*, Bungay, Suffolk: Fontana, 1982.

Kincaid, David, *Shivaji: The Founder of Maratha Empire*, rpt, New Delhi: Discovery Publishing House, 1984.

Kiszely, John, 'The British Army and Approaches to Warfare since 1945', *Journal of Strategic Studies*, vol. 19, no. 4, 1996.

Koistinen, Paul A.C., 'The Political Economy of Warfare in America, 1865-1914', in Eric Arnett (ed.), *Military Capacity and the Risk of War: China, India, Pakistan and Iran*, Oxford: Oxford University Press, 1997.

Kolff, Dirk H.A., 'End of an *Ancien Regime*: Colonial War in India, 1798-1818', in J.A. De Moor and H.L. Wesseling (eds), *Imperialism and War: Essays on Colonial Wars in Asia and Africa*, Leiden: E.J. Brill, 1989.

_____, *Naukar, Rajput and Sepoy: The Ethnohistory of the Military Labour Market in Hindustan, 1450-1850*, Cambridge: Cambridge University Press, 1990.

Kondapalli, Srikanth, 'China's Naval Structure and Dynamics', *Strategic Analysis*, vol. 23, no. 7, 1999.

_____, 'China's Naval Equipment Acquisition', *Strategic Analysis*, vol. 23, no. 9, 1999.

_____, *China's Military: The PLA in Transition*, New Delhi: Knowledge World, 1999.

_____, 'China's Naval Training Programme', *Strategic Analysis*, vol. 23, no. 8, 2000.

_____, 'Chinese Navy's Political Work and Personnel', *Strategic Analysis*, vol. 23, no. 10, 2000.

Kukreja, Veena, *Civil-Military Relations in South Asia: Pakistan, Bangladesh and India*, New Delhi: Sage, 1991.

Kundu, Apurba, *Militarism in India: The Army and Civil Society in Consensus*, New Delhi: Viva, 1998.

Laffin, John, *Brassey's Battles: 3,500 Years of Conflict, Campaigns and Wars from A-Z*, 1986, rpt, London: Brassey's, 1995.

Lafont, Jean Marie, 'Military Activities of French Officers of Maharaja Ranjit Singh', *Journal of Sikh Studies*, vol. 9, no. 1, 1982.

_____, *Indika: Essays in Indo-French Relations, 1630-1976*, New Delhi: Manohar, 2000.

Laird, M.A. (ed.), *Bishop Heber in Northern India: Selections from Heber's Journal*, Cambridge: Cambridge University Press, 1971.

Lal, K.S., The Striking Power of the Army of the Sultanate', *Journal of Indian History*, Part II, vol. LV, August 1977.

Lane-Poole, Stanley, *The Emperor Babur*, 1899, rpt, New Delhi: Sunita Publications, 1988.

Latham, J.D., 'Note on Mamluk Horse-Archers', *Bulletin of the School of Oriental and African Studies*, vol. 32, 1969.

Lattimore, Owen, *Inner Asian Frontiers of China*, 1940, rpt, Oxford: Oxford University Press, 1988.

Lawford, James, 'Origins', in James Lawford (ed.), *Cavalry*, New York: Crescent Books, 1976.

Lawford, James P., *Clive, Proconsul of India: A Biography*, London: George Allen, 1976.

Lazenby, John, 'Hoplite Warfare', in General John Hackett (ed.), *Warfare in the Ancient World*, London: Sidgwick & Jackson, 1989.

_____, 'The Killing Zone', in Victor Davis Hanson (ed.), *Hoplites: The Classical Greek Battle Experience*, 1991, rpt, London: Routledge, 1993.

Lee, Captain F.R., 'An Ancient Weapon of India', *Journal of the United Service Institution of India*, vol. XLI, no. 187, 1912.

Lewis, Colonel, 'Campaign on the Sutlej: 1845-46', *Journal of the Royal Engineers*, vol. XLIX, 1849.

Liddell Hart, Captain B.H., *Great Captains Unveiled*, 1927, rpt, New York: Da Capo, 1996.

_____, *Strategy*, New York: Frederick A. Praeger, 1954.

Linder, Rudi Paul, 'Nomadism, Horses and Huns', *Past and Present*, no. 92, August 1981.

Livesey, Anthony, *Battles of the Great Commanders*, 1987, rpt, London: Tiger Books, 1990.

Llewellyn, Alexander, *The Siege of Delhi*, London: Macdonald & Jane's, 1977.

Longer, V., *Red Coats to Olive Green: A History of the Indian Army, 1600-1947*, Bombay: Allied, 1974.

Lunt, James (ed.), *From Sepoy to Subedar being the Life and Adventures of Subedar Sita Ram*, 1970, rpt, London: Macmillan, 1988.

Lynn, John A., 'Food, Funds, and Fortresses: Resource Mobilization and Positional Warfare in the Campaigns of Louis XIV', in John A. Lynn (ed.), *Feeding Mars: Logistics in Western Warfare from the Middle Ages to the Present*, Boulder: Westview, 1993.

_____, 'Medieval Introduction', and 'Early Modern Introduction', in John A. Lynn (ed.), *Feeding Mars: Logistics in the Western World from the Middle Ages to the Present*, Boulder: Westview, 1993.

_____, 'A Quest for Glory: The Formation of Strategy under Louis XIV', in Williamson Murray, MacGregor Knox and Alvin Bernstein (eds), *The Making of Strategy: Rulers, States and War*, Cambridge: Cambridge University Press, 1994.

Macgregor, Lieutenant Colonel Douglas M., *Breaking the Phalanx: A New Design for Landpower in the 21st Century*, Westport, CT.: Praeger, 1997.

Machiavelli, Niccolo, *The Art of War*, Introduction by Neal Wood, 1965, rpt, New York: Da Capo, 1990.

Mackenzie, S.P., *Revolutionary Armies in the Modern Era: A Revisionist Approach*, London: Routledge, 1997.

MacMunn, Lieutenant General George, *Vignettes from Indian War*, 1901, rpt, Delhi: Low Price Publications, 1993.

———, *The Indian Mutiny in Perspective*, 1931, rpt; Delhi: Sunita Publications, 1985.

Majumdar, Bimal Kanti, *The Military System in Ancient India*, Calcutta: Firma KLM Pvt. Ltd., 1960.

Majumdar, R.C., Raychaudhuri, H.C. and Datta, Kalikinkar, *An Advanced History of India*, 1946, rpt, Madras: Macmillan, 1991.

Malik, Arjan Dass, *An Indian Guerrilla War: The Sikh Peoples War, 1699-1768*, New Delhi: Wiley, 1975.

Malleson, Colonel G.B., *The Decisive Battles of India: 1746-1849*, 1885, rpt, Jaipur: Aavishkar Publisher, 1986.

Manucci, Niccolao, *A Pepys of Mogul India: 1653-1708*, tr M.L. Irvine, rpt, New Delhi: Srishti, 1999.

Manz, Beatrice Forbes, *The Rise and Rule of Tamerlana*, 1989, rpt, Cambridge: Canto, 1999.

Marcellinus, Ammianus, *The Later Roman Empire: A.D. 354-378*, Selected and tr. Walter Hamilton and with an Introduction and Notes by Andrew Wallace-Hadrill, 1986, rpt, London: Penguin, 1988.

Marshall, Christopher, *Warfare in the Latin East: 1192-1294*, Cambridge: Cambridge University Press, 1992.

Marxism and the Science of War, ed. with an Introduction by Bernard Semmel, Oxford: Oxford University Press, 1981.

Mason, Philip, *A Matter of Honour: An Account of the Indian Army, Its Officers and Men*, 1974, rpt, DehraDun: EBD Publishers, 1988.

Matthews, R.G., 'The Development of India's Defence-Industrial Base', *Journal of Strategic Studies*, no. 4, 1989.

McKnight, Sean, 'Cannae 216 BC-The Double Envelopment', in Richard Holmes, et al., *The Hutchinson Atlas of Battle Plans: Before and After*, Oxford: Helicon Publishing, 1998.

M'Crindle, J.W. (ed.), *The Invasion of India by Alexander the Great*, 1896, rpt, New Delhi: Cosmo, 1983.

Menezes, Lieutenant General S.L., *Fidelity and Honour: The Indian Army from the Seventeenth to the Twenty-First Century*, New Delhi: Viking, 1993.

Menon, Rear Admiral Raja, *Maritime Strategy and Continental War*, London: Frank Cass, 1998.

M'Gregor, W.L., *The History of the Sikhs*, vols. 1 & 2, 1846, rpt, Allahabad: R.S. Publishing House, 1979.

Mills, Arthur, *India in 1858*, 1858, rpt, Delhi: Gian Publishing House, 1986.

Moienuddin, Mohammad, 'Role of Tipu Sultan in the Progress of Mysore State', in Aniruddha Ray (ed.), *Tipu Sultan and his Age: A Collection of Seminar Papers*, Calcutta: The Asiatic Society, 2002.

Montgomery of Alamein, Field Marshal Viscount, *A History of Warfare*, London: Collins, 1968.

Mookerji, R.K., *Chandragupta Maurya and His Times*, 1943, rpt, Delhi: Motilal Banarasidas, 1960.

Moreman, T.R., *The Army in India and the Development of Frontier Warfare: 1849-1947*, London: Macmillan, 1998.

Moskos, Charles C., 'The Military: Institution or Occupation', in Leena Parmar (ed.), *Military Sociology: Global Perspectives*, New Delhi: Rawat Publications, 1999.

Muhammad, Ghulam (ed.), *The History of Haidar Ali and Tipu Sultan: A Contemporary History*, by MMDLT, General of the Mughal Army, 1855, rpt, Delhi: Cosmo, 1976.

Mukherjee, Rudrangshu, *Awadh in Revolt: 1857-1858, A Study of Popular Resistance*, New Delhi: Oxford University Press, 1984.

Mullick, B.N., *The Chinese Betrayal*, Bombay: Allied, 1971.

_____, *My Years with Nehru: 1948-1964*, Bombay: Allied, 1972.

Murray, Williamson, 'Innovation: Past and Future', in Williamson Murray and Alan R. Millett (eds), *Military Innovation in the Interwar Period*, Cambridge: Cambridge University Press, 1996.

Nair, Brigadier Vijai K., 'Employment of Military Helicopters: The Indian Experience and Compulsions', Part II, *Indian Defence Review*, January 1992.

Nanqi, General Zhao, 'Deng Xiaoping's Theory of Defence Modernization', in Michael Pillsbury (ed.), *Chinese Views of Future Warfare*, 1997, rpt, New Delhi: Lancer, 1998.

Naveh, Shimon, *In Pursuit of Military Excellence: The Evolution of Operational Theory*, 1997, rpt, London: Frank Cass, 2000.

Neill, Robert O', 'US and Allied Leadership and Command in the Korean and Vietnam Wars', in G.D. Sheffield (ed.), *Leadership and Command: The Anglo-American Military Experience Since 1861*, London: Brassey's, 1997.

New International Version of the Holy Bible Containing the Old Testament and the New Testament, 1973, rpt, Colorado Springs: International Bible Society, 1984.

Newell, Clayton R., *The Framework of Operational Warfare*, London: Routledge, 1991.

Nicolle, David, *The Armies of Islam: 7th-11th Centuries*, London: Osprey, 1982.

Nijjar, B.S., *Anglo-Sikh Wars: 1845-1849*, New Delhi: K.B. Publications, 1976.

Ning, Colonel Fang, 'Defence Policy in the New Era', in Michael Pillsbury (ed.), *Chinese Views of Future Warfare*, 1997, rpt, New Delhi: Lancer, 1998.

Nizami, K.A. (ed.), *Politics and Society during the Early Medieval Period: Collected Works of Mohammad Habib*, vol. 2, New Delhi: People's Publishing House, 1981.

Nizami, Taj ud Din Hasan, *Taj ul Ma'Athir*, tr Bhagwat Saroop, Delhi: Said Ahmad Dehlavi, 1998.

Ohlmeyer, Jane H., 'The Wars of Religion: 1603-1660', in Thomas Bartlett and Keith Jeffrey (eds), *A Military History of Ireland*, 1996, rpt, Cambridge: Cambridge University Press, 1997

Palit, Major General D.K., *War in High Himalaya*, New Delhi: Lancer International, 1991.

Paret, Peter, 'Armed Forces and the State: The Historical Essays of Otto Hintze', in Brian Bond and I. Roy (eds), *War and Society: A Yearbook of Military History*, vol. 2, London: Croom Helm, 1977.

Parker, Geoffrey, *The Military Revolution: Military Innovations and the Rise of the West, 1500-1800*, Cambridge: Cambridge University Press, 1988.

———, 'The "Military Revolution, 1560-1660"—A Myth?', in Clifford J. Rogers (ed.), *The Military Revolution Debate: Readings on the Military Transformation of Early Modern Europe*, Boulder: Westview, 1995.

———, 'Introduction: The Western Way of War', in Geoffrey Parker (ed.), *The Cambridge Illustrated History of Warfare*, Cambridge: Cambridge University Press, 1995.

Parmar, Leena, 'Resettlement of Ex-servicemen in India: Problems of Army Socialization and Adjustment', in Leena Parmar (ed.), *Military Sociology: Global Perspectives*, New Delhi: Rawat Publications, 1999.

Parry, V.J. and Yapp, M.E., 'Introduction', in Parry and Yapp (eds), *War, Technology and Society in the Middle East*, London: Oxford University Press, 1975.

———, 'La maniere de combattre', in V.J. Parry and M.E. Yapp (eds), *War, Technology and Society in the Middle East*, London: Oxford University Press, 1975.

Patterson, John, 'Military Organization and Social Change in the later Roman Republic', in John Rich and Graham Shipley (eds), *War and Society in the Roman World*, 1993, London: Routledge, 1995.

Peers, Douglas, *Between Mars and Mammon: Colonial Armies and the Garrison State in India, 1819-1835*, London: I.B. Tauris: 1995.

———, 'Introduction', in Douglas Peers (ed.), *Warfare and Empires: Contact and Conflict between European and Non-European Military and Maritime Forces and Cultures*, Aldershot: Variorum, 1997.

Pemble, John, *The Invasion of Nepal: John Company at War*, Oxford: Clarendon Press, 1971.

———, 'Resources and Techniques in the Second Maratha War', *Historical Journal*, vol. 19, no. 2, 1976.

Petrovic, Djurdjica, 'Fire-arms in the Balkans on the eve and after the

Ottoman Conquests of the Fourteenth and Fifteenth Centuries', in V.J. Parry and M.E. Yapp (eds), *War, Technology and Society in the Middle East*, London: Oxford University Press, 1975.

Phillips, Brigadier General Thomas R. (ed.), *Roots of Strategy: A Collection of Military Classics*, 1940, rpt, Dehra Dun: Natraj, 1989.

Piggott, Stuart, *Prehistoric India to 1000 BC*, Harmondsworth, Middlesex: Penguin, 1950.

Pinch, William R., 'Who was Himmat Bahadur? Gosains, Rajputs and the British in Bundelkhand, ca. 1800', *Indian Economic and Social History Review*, vol. 35, no. 3, 1998.

Polier, Antoine Louis Henry, *Shah Alam II and his Court*, ed. and with an Introduction, Notes and Appendices by P.C. Gupta, Calcutta: S.C. Sarkar & Sons Ltd., 1947.

Posen, Barry R., *The Sources of Military Doctrine: France, Britain and Germany between the World Wars*, Ithaca: Cornell University Press, 1984.

Prasad, Rajiv Nain, *Raja Man Singh of Amber*, Calcutta: World Press, 1966.

Preston, Richard A. and Wise, F. Sydney, *Men in Arms: A History of Warfare and its Interrelationships with Western Societies*, 1956, rpt, New York: Holt, Rinehart & Winston, 1979.

Qaisar, A. Jan, 'Horseshoeing in Mughal India', *Indian Journal of History of Science*, vol. 27, no. 2, 1992.

Qifen, Major General Yu, 'The International Military Situation in the 1990s', in Michael Pillsbury (ed.), *Chinese Views of Future Warfare*, New Delhi: Lancer, 1998.

Quanyou, General Fu, 'Future Logistics Modernization', in Michael Pillsbury (ed.), *Chinese Views of Future Warfare*, New Delhi: Lancer, 1998.

Rabie, Hassanein, 'The Training of the Mamluk Faris', in V.J. Parry and M.E. Yapp (eds), *War, Technology and Society in the Middle East*, London: Oxford University Press, 1975.

Raghavan, T.R., 'Admiral Kanjoji Angre', in K.K.N. Kurup, *India's Naval Tradition*, New Delhi: Northern Book Centre, 1997.

Ralston, David B., *Importing the European Army: The Introduction of European Military Techniques and Institutions into the Extra-European World, 1600-1914*, Chicago: University of Chicago Press, 1990.

Ram, Moti (ed.), *Two Historic Trials in Red Fort*, New Delhi: Roxy Printing Press, n.d..

Rao, Narayan et al., 'The Art of War under the Nayakas', in Jos J.L. Gommans and Dirk Kolff, *Warfare and Weaponry in South Asia: 1000-1800*, New Delhi: Oxford University Press, 2001.

Ray, Jogesh Chandra, 'Fire-Arms in Ancient India: Parts II & III', *Indian Historical Quarterly*, vol. 8, nos 2 & 3, 1932.

Raychaudhuri, Hemchandra, *Political History of Ancient India: From the*

Accession of Parikshit to the Extinction of the Gupta Dynasty, 1927, rpt, Calcutta: University of Calcutta, 1972.

Raychaudhuri, Tapan, 'The Mughal Empire', in Tapan Raychaudhuri and Dharma Kumar (eds), *The Cambridge Economic History of India*: c. 1200-c. 1750, vol. 1, Delhi: Orient Longman in association with the Cambridge University Press, 1982.

Reid, Brian Holden, 'Introduction', in Brian Holden Reid and Major General J.J.G. Mackenzie (eds), *The British Army and the Operational Level of War*, New Delhi and London: Lancer in association with Tri Service Press, 1989.

_____, 'The Italian Campaign, 1943-45: A Reappraisal of Allied Generalship', in John Gooch (ed.), *Decisive Campaigns of the Second World War*, London: Frank Cass, 1990.

_____, 'Introduction', *Journal of Strategic Studies*, vol. 19, no. 4, 1996.

_____, 'Introduction', in Brian Holden Reid (ed.), *Military Power: Land Warfare in Theory and Practice*, London: Frank Cass, 1997.

Rich, John, 'Introduction', in John Rich and Graham Shipley (eds), *War and Society in the Roman World*, 1993, rpt, London: Routledge, 1995.

Richards, John F., 'The Seventeenth-Century Crisis in South Asia', *Modern Asian Studies*, vol. 24, no. 4, 1990.

Roberts, Field Marshal Lord, *Forty-One Years in India: From Subaltern to Commander-in-Chief*, vol. 1, London: Richard Bentley & Sons, 1897.

_____, *Letters Written during the Indian Mutiny*, 1923, rpt, New Delhi: Lal Publishers, 1979.

Rogers, Clifford J., 'The Military Revolutions of the Hundred Years War', in idem (ed.), *The Military Revolution Debate: Readings on the Military Transformation of Early Modern Europe*, Boulder: Westview, 1995.

Rosen, Stephen Peter, *Societies and Military Power: India and Its Armies*, New Delhi: Oxford University Press, 1996.

Ross, Steven T., *From Flintlock to Rifle: Infantry Tactics, 1740-1866*, 1979, rpt, London: Frank Cass, 1996.

Roy, Kaushik, 'The Historiography of the Colonial Indian Army', *Studies in History*, New Series, vol. 12, no. 2, 1996.

_____, 'Netaji's Military Strategy', *Asian Studies*, vol. 17, no. 2, 1999.

_____, 'Mars in Indian History', *Studies in History*, New Series, vol. 16, no. 2, 2000.

Roy, M.P., *Origin, Growth and Suppression of the Pindaris*, New Delhi: Sterling, 1973.

Roy-Chaudhuri, Rahul, *Sea Power and Indian Security*, London: Brassey's, 1995.

_____, 'The Limits to Naval Expansion', in Kanti P. Bajpai and Amitabh Mattoo (eds), *Securing India: Strategic Thought and Practice*, New Delhi: Manohar, 1996.

Roy, Tapti, *The Politics of a Popular Uprising: Bundelkhand in 1857,* New Delhi: Oxford University Press, 1994.

Roy, Udai Narain, 'Fortifications of Cities in Ancient India', *Indian Historical Quarterly,* vol. 30, no. 3, 1954.

Runciman, Steven, *The Fall of Constantinople: 1453,* 1965, rpt, Cambridge: Canto, 1990.

Sachdev, Captain A.K., 'Modernisation of the Chinese Air Force', *Strategic Analysis,* vol. 23, no. 6, 1999.

_____, 'Media Related Lessons From Kargil', *Strategic Analysis,* vol. 23, no. 10, 2000.

Saggs, Harry, 'Seleucus I', in John Canning (ed.), *100 Great Lives of Antiquity,* London: Methuen, 1985.

Salim, Ghulam Hussain, *Riyaz-us-Salatin,* tr Abdus Salam, 1903, rpt, Delhi: Idarah-i Adabiyat, 1975.

Sarkar, Jadunath, *Studies in Aurangzeb's Reign,* 1912, rpt, Calcutta: Orient Longman, 1989.

_____, *Studies in Mughal India,* Calcutta, 1913.

_____, *Anecdotes of Aurangzeb,* 1912, rpt, Calcutta: Orient Longman, 1978.

_____, *History of Aurangzeb,* vol. 5, 1924, rpt, New Delhi: Orient Longman, 1974.

_____, *A Short History of Aurangzeb,* 1930, rpt, New Delhi: Orient Longman, 1979.

_____, *Shivaji,* 1919, rpt, Calcutta: M.C. Sarkar, 1961.

_____, *House of Shivaji,* 1940, rpt, New Delhi: Orient Longman, 1978.

_____, *Fall of the Mughal Empire: 1739-1754,* vol. 1, 1932, rpt, New Delhi: Orient Longman, 1988.

_____, *Fall of the Mughal Empire: 1754-1771,* vol. 2, 1934, rpt, New Delhi: Orient Longman, 1991.

_____, *Fall of the Mughal Empire: 1771-1778,* vol. 3, 1938, rpt, New Delhi: Orient Longman, 1991.

_____, *Fall of the Mughal Empire: 1780-1803,* vol. 4, 1950, rpt, New Delhi: Orient Longman, 1992.

_____, *Military History of India,* 1960, rpt, Bombay: Orient Longman, 1970.

_____, 'Haidar Ali's Invasion of the Eastern Carnatic: 1780', in Irfan Habib (ed.), *Confronting Colonialism: Resistance and Modernization under Haidar Ali and Tipu Sultan,* New Delhi: Tulika, 1999.

Sarkar, Jagadish Narayan, *The Military Despatches of a Seventeenth Century Indian General,* Calcutta: Scientific Book, 1969.

_____, *The Life of Mir Jumla: The General of Aurangzeb,* 1951, rpt, New Delhi: Rajesh Publications, 1979.

_____, 'Aspects of Military Policy in Medieval India', *Proceedings of the Indian History Congress,* 36th Session, Aligarh, 1975.

_____, *The Art of War in Medieval India,* New Delhi: Munshiram Manoharlal, 1984.

Saunders, J.J., *The History of the Mongol Conquests*, London: Routledge & Kegan Paul, 1971.

Sawyer, Ralph D., *The Seven Military Classics of Ancient China*, Boulder: Westview, 1993.

Sayigh, Yezid, 'Arms Production in Pakistan and Iran: The Limits of Self Reliance', in Eric Arnett (ed.), *Military Capacity and the Risk of War: China, India, Pakistan and Iran*, Oxford: Oxford University Press, 1997.

Scott, Harriet Fast and Scott, F. William, *The Armed Forces of the USSR*, 1979, rpt, Boulder: Westview, 1984.

Secunda, Nick, 'Hellenistic Warfare', in General John Hackett (ed.), *Warfare in the Ancient World*, London: Sidgwick & Jackson, 1989.

_____, 'The Persians', in General John Hackett (ed.), *Warfare in the Ancient World*, London: Sidgwick & Jackson, 1989.

Selth, Andrew, 'Burma and the Strategic Competition between China and India', *Journal of Strategic Studies*, vol. 19, no. 2, 1996.

Sen, Air Vice Marshal Samir K., *Military Technology and Defence Industrialization: The Indian Experience*, New Delhi: Manas, 2000.

Sen, S.N., *The Military System of the Marathas*, 1928, rpt, Calcutta: K.P. Bagchi, 1979.

Sensarma, Major P., *The Military Profile of Sher Shah Sur*, Calcutta: Naya Prokash, 1976.

_____, *The Military History of Bengal*, Calcutta: Naya Prakash, 1977.

_____,Shakespear, Colonel L.W., 'The War with Nepal: Operations in Sirmoor, 1814-15', *Journal of the United Service Institution of India*, vol. XLII, no. 193, 1913.

Sharma, Lieutenant Colonel Gautam, *Indian Army Through the Ages*, Bombay: Allied, 1979.

_____, *Nationalization of the Indian Army: 1885-1947*, New Delhi: Allied, 1996.

Shaw, Stanford J., 'The Origins of Ottoman Military Reform: The Nizam-i-Cedid Army of Sultan Selim III', *Journal of Modern History*, vol. 37, no. 3, 1963.

Sheffield, G.D., 'Blitzkrieg and Attrition: Land Operations in Europe, 1914-45', in idem and Colin McInnes (ed), *Warfare in the Twentieth Century: Theory and Practice*, London: Unwin Hyman, 1988.

_____, 'Introduction: Command, Leadership and the Anglo-American Experience', in G.D. Sheffield (ed.), *Leadership and Command: The Anglo-American Military Experience Since 1861*, London: Brassey's, 1997.

Sheng-Wu, Yu and Chen-Kun Chang, 'China and India in the Mid-19th Century', in P.C. Joshi (ed.), *Rebellion 1857: A Symposium*, 1957, rpt, Calcutta: K.P. Bagchi & Company, 1986.

Shipley, Graham, 'Introduction: The Limits of War', in Graham Shipley and

John Rich (eds), *War and Society in the Greek World*, 1993, rpt, London: Routledge, 1995.

Simon, Lieutenant Colonel Rufus, *Their Formative Years: History of the Corps of Electrical and Mechanical Engineers*, vol. 1, Vikas: New Delhi, 1977.

Sinclair, Lieutenant Colonel H.M., 'Second Sikh War: 1848-49', *Journal of the United Service Institution of India*, vol. 28, 1899.

Sindhu, Waheguru Pal Singh, 'Of Oral Traditions and Ethnocentric Judgements', in Kanti P. Bajpai and Amitabh Mattoo (eds), *Securing India: Strategic Thought and Practice*, New Delhi: Manohar, 1996.

Singh, Lieutenant General Depinder, *Field Marshal Sam Manekshaw: Soldiering with Dignity*, Dehra Dun: Natraj, 2002.

Singh, Ganda, 'Colonel Polier's Account of the Sikhs', *Panjab Past and Present*, vol. 4, August 1970.

———, 'Colonel Mouton's Account of the First Sikh War: 1845-46', *Panjab Past and Present*, vol. 15, no. 29, 1981.

Singh, Lieutenant General Harbakhsh, *In the Line of Duty: A Soldier Remembers*, New Delhi: Lancer, 2000.

Singh, Jasjit, 'Pakistan's Fourth War for Kashmir', *Asian Strategic Review*, 1998-99, New Delhi: IDSA, 1999.

———, 'Strategic Framework for Defence Planners: Air Power in the 21st Century', *Strategic Analysis*, vol. 22, no. 12, 1999.

Singh, Jaswant, *Defending India*, Chennai: Macmillan, 1999.

Singh, Khushwant, *Ranjit Singh, Maharajah of Punjab: 1780-1839*, London: George Allen & Unwin, 1962.

Singh, Nagendra, *The Theory of Force and Organization of Defence in Indian Constitutional History: From Earliest Times to 1947*, Bombay: Asia Publishing, 1969.

Singh, Sarva Daman, *Ancient Indian Warfare with Special Reference to the Vedic Period*, 1965, rpt, Delhi: Motilal Banarasidas, 1989.

Singh, Swaran, 'China's Doctrine of Limited Hi-Tech War', *Asian Strategic Review, 1998-99*, New Delhi: IDSA, 1999.

———, 'Continuity and Change in China's Maritime Strategy', *Strategic Analysis*, vol. 23, no. 9, 1999.

Sinha, B.K., *The Pindaris: 1798-1818*, Calcutta: Bookland, 1971.

Sinha, B.P., 'Art of War in Ancient India (600 BC-AD 300)', in Guy S. Metraux and Francois Crouzet (eds), *Studies in the Cultural History of India*, Agra: Shiva Lal Agarwal, 1965.

Sinha, N.K., *Ranjit Singh*, 1933, rpt, Calcutta: Niva Mukherjee, 1975.

———, *Rise of the Sikh Power*, 1936, rpt, Calcutta: University of Calcutta, 1946.

———, *Haidar Ali*, 1941, rpt, Calcutta: A. Mukherjee & Company, 1969.

Smail, R.C., *Crusading Warfare: 1097-1193*, 1956, rpt, Cambridge: Cambridge University Press, 1995.

Smith, Chris, *India's Ad Hoc Arsenal: Direction or Drift in Defence Policy*, New York: Oxford University Press, 1994.

Smith, Major Lewis Ferdinand, *A Sketch of the Rise, Progress, and*

Termination of the Regular Corps ... of the Native Princes of India with the Principal Events and Actions of the Late Maratha War, Calcutta: J. Greenway & Harkaru Press, 1804.

Smith, Vincent, *Akbar: The Great Mogul, 1542-1605*, rpt, Delhi: S. Chand, 1962.

Sorley, Lewis, 'Prevailing Criteria: A Critique', in Sam C. Sarkesian (ed.), *Combat Effectiveness: Cohesion, Stress, and the Volunteer Military*, Beverly Hills and London: Sage, 1980.

Spaulding Oliver Lyman, Jr, Nickerson, Hoffman and Wright, Womack John *Warfare: A Study of Military Methods from the Earliest Times*, London: George G. Harrap & Co. Ltd., 1924.

Spence, I.G., *The Cavalry of Classical Greece: A Social and Military History*, 1993, rpt, Oxford: Oxford University Press, 1995.

Stanley, Peter, '"Dear Comrades": Barrack Room Culture and the "White Mutiny" of 1859-60', *Indo-British Review*, vol. 21, no. 2, 1996.

_____, *White Mutiny: British Military Culture in India, 1825-1875*, London: Hurst & Company, 1998.

Steinbach, Henry, *The Country of the Sikhs*, 1846, rpt, New Delhi: KLM Book House, 1978.

Steinisch, Irmgard, 'Different Paths to War: A Comparative Study of Militarism and Imperialism in the United States and Germany, 1871-1914', in R. Chickering et al. (eds), *Anticipating Total War: The German and American Experiences, 1871-1914*, Washington, D.C.: Cambridge University Press, 1999.

Stokes, Eric, 'Rural Revolt in the Great Rebellion of 1857 in India: A Study of the Saharanpur and Muzaffarnagar Districts', *Historical Journal*, vol. 12, no. 4, 1969.

Strachan, Hew, *European Armies and the Conduct of War*, 1983, rpt, London: Routledge, 1993.

Streusand, Douglas E., *The Formation of the Mughal Empire*, New Delhi: Oxford University Press, 1989.

Subrahmanyam, Sanjay, 'Warfare and State Finance in Woodeyar Mysore, 1724-25: A Missionary Perspective', *Indian Economic and Social History Review*, vol. 26, no. 2, 1989.

Sundarji, General K., *Of Some Consequence: A Soldier Remembers*, New Delhi: HarperCollins, 2000.

Tallett, Frank, *War and Society in Early Modern Europe: 1495-1715*, 1992, rpt, London: Routledge, 1997.

Tambiah, Stanley J., 'What did Bernier actually say? Profiling the Mughal Empire', in Veena Das et al. (eds), *Tradition, Pluralism and Identity: In Honour of T.N. Madan*, New Delhi: Sage, 1999.

Tanham, George, 'Indian Strategic Thought: An Interpretative Essay', in Kanti P. Bajpai and Amitabh Mattoo (eds), *Securing India: Strategic Thought and Practice*, New Delhi: Manohar, 1996.

_____, Indian Strategy in Flux', in Kanti P. Bajpai and Amitabh Mattoo (eds), *Securing India: Strategic Thought and Practice*, New Delhi: Manohar, 1996.

Taylor, A.J.P., *The First World War: An Illustrated History*, 1963, rpt, Harmondsworth: Penguin, 1985.

Taylor, P.J.O. (General Editor), *A Companion to the 'Indian Mutiny' of 1857*, Delhi: Oxford University Press, 1996.

Terraine, John (ed.), J.F.C. Fuller, *The Decisive Battles of the Western World and Their Influence upon History*, vol. 1, 1954, rpt, London: Granada, 1982.

Thapar, Romila, *Asoka and the Decline of the Mauryas*, 1963, rpt, New Delhi: Oxford University Press, 1989.

_____, *The Past and Prejudice*, 1975, rpt, New Delhi: National Book Trust, 1994.

_____, *From Lineage to State: Social Formations in the Mid-First Millennium BC in the Ganga Valley*, 1984, rpt, New Delhi: Oxford University Press, 1990.

_____, *The Mauryas Revisited*, 1987, rpt, Calcutta: K.P. Bagchi, 1993.

The Bhagavad Gita, tr. from the Sanskrit and with an Introduction by Juan Mascaro, London: Penguin, 1962.

The Book of the Thousand Nights and One Night, vol. 1, tr. into English from the French by Powys Mathers, 1962, rpt, London: Routledge, 1996.

The Holy Quran, English Translation of the Meanings and Commentary, Al-Madinah Al-Munawarah: The Ministry of Hajj and Endowments of Saudi Arabia, 1413 H.

The Marquess of Anglesey (ed.), *Sergeant Pearman's Memoirs ... in India from 1845-53*, London: Jonathan Cape, 1968.

The Rig Veda, tr and Annotated by Wendy Doniger O'Flaherty, 1981, rpt, New Delhi: Penguin, 1994.

The Seven Military Classics of Ancient China, tr Ralph D. Sawyer, Boulder: Westview, 1993.

The Shah Jahan Nama of Inayat Khan, W.E. Begley and Z.A. Desai (eds), tr. A.R. Fuller, New Delhi: Oxford University Press, 1990.

The Tabaqat-i-Akbari of Khwajah Nizamuddin Ahmad, vol. 1, tr. B. De, 1911, rpt, Calcutta: The Asiatic Society, 1973.

The Travels of Marco Polo, tr. William Marsden and with an Introduction by Benjamin Colbert, Ware, Hertfordshire: Wordsworth, 1997.

The Upanishads, tr. from the Sanskrit and with an Introduction by Juan Mascaro, Harmondsworth, Middlesex: Penguin, 1965.

Thomas, Raju G.C., 'Arms Procurement in India: Military Self-Reliance versus Technological Self-Sufficiency', in Eric Arnett (ed.), *Military Capacity and the Risk of War: China, India, Pakistan and Iran*, Oxford: Oxford University Press, 1997.

Thompson, E.W., *The Last Siege of Seringapatam*, 1923, rpt, New Delhi: Asian Educational Service, 1990.

Thornton, John K., 'The Art of War in Angola: 1575-1680', *Comparative Studies in Society and History*, vol. 30, 1988.

Toffler, Alvin and Toffler Heidi, *War and Anti-War: Survival at the Dawn of the 21st Century*, 1993, rpt, London: Warner Books, 1994.

Towle, Philip, 'Air Power in Afghanistan', in Air Commodore E.S. Williams (ed.), *Soviet Air Power: Prospects for the Future*, London: Tri Service Press, 1990.

Treadgold, Warren, *Byzantium and Its Army: 284-1081*, Stanford: Stanford University Press, 1995.

Tuker, Lieutenant General Francis, *The Pattern of War*, London: Cassell, 1948.

Tzu, Sun, *Art of War*, tr. and with a Historical Introduction by Ralph D. Sawyer, Boulder: Westview, 1994.

_____, *The Art of War*, in Caleb Carr (ed.), *The Book of War*, Introduced by Ralph Peters, New York: Modern Library, 2000.

Tzu II, Sun, *The Lost Art of War*, tr. with Commentary by Thomas Cleary, New York: HarperCollins, 1996.

Verma, Amrit, and Verma, H.N., *Decisive Battles of India through the Ages*, vol. 1, California: GIP Books, 1994.

Verma, D.C., *Plassey to Buxar: A Military Study*, New Delhi: K.B. Publications, 1976.

Vertzberger, Yacov, 'India's Strategic Posture and the Border War Defeat of 1962: A Case Study of Miscalculation', *Journal of Strategic Studies*, vol. 5, no. 3, 1982.

Waldron, Arthur, *The Great Wall of China: From History to Myth*, Cambridge: Cambridge University Press, 1990.

Wallace, J.J.A., 'Maneuver Theory in Operations Other Than War', *Journal of Strategic Studies*, vol. 19, no. 4, 1996.

Warren, Alan, *Waziristan: The Faqir of Ipi and the Indian Army, The Northwest Frontier Revolt of 1936-37*, Karachi: Oxford University Press, 2000.

Warry, John, *Warfare in the Classical World*, London: Salamander Books, 1980.

Watkins, Trevor, 'The Beginnings of Warfare', in General John Hackett (ed.), *Warfare in the Ancient World*, London: Sidgwick & Jackson, 1989.

Watson, Bruce, *The Great Indian Mutiny: Colin Campbell and the Campaign at Lucknow*, New York: Praeger, 1991.

Weller, Jac, *Wellington in India*, London: Longman, 1972.

Wellhausen, J., *The Arab Kingdom and its Fall*, tr. Margaret Graham Weir, Calcutta: University of Calcutta, 1927.

Wheatley, Captain G.R.P., 'The Final Campaign against Tipu', *Journal of the United Service Institution of India*, vol. XLI, no. 185, 1912.

Wheeler, Mortimer, *The Cambridge History of India: The Indus Civilization*, Cambridge: Cambridge University Press, 1960.

Wheeler, Mortimer, *My Archaeological Mission to India and Pakistan*, London: Thames & Hudson, 1976.

White Jr., Lynn, 'The Crusades and the Technological Thrust of the West', in V.J. Parry and M.E. Yapp (eds), *War, Technology and Society in the Middle East*, London: Oxford University Press, 1975.

Wiseman, D.J., 'The Assyrians', in General John Hackett (ed.), *Warfare in the Ancient World*, London: Sidgwick & Jackson, 1989.

Yadava, B.N.S., 'Chivalry and Warfare', in Jos J.L. Gommans and Dirk H.A. Kolff (eds), *Warfare and Weaponry in South Asia: 1000-1800*, New Delhi: Oxford University Press, 2001.

Young, Brigadier Peter, 'The Horse in War', in James Lawford (ed.), *The Cavalry*, 1976, rpt, New York: Crescent Books, 1982.

——, *Strategy and Tactics of the Great Generals and their Battles*, London: Bison Books, 1986.

Youzhi, Colonel Yao and Hongson, Colonel Liu, 'Future Security Trends in the Asia-Pacific Region', in Michael Pillsbury (ed.), *Chinese Views of Future Warfare*, New Delhi: Lancer, 1998.

Yule, Captain, 'Some Account of the Passage of the Sutlej by the British Army, in February 1846', *Journal of the Royal Engineers*, vol. XLIX, 1849.

Zaidi, S. Inayat Ali, 'Ordinary Kachawaha Troopers Serving the Mughal Empire: Composition and Structure of the Contingents of the Kachawaha Nobles', *Studies in History*, vol. 2, no. 1, 1980.

——, 'Rozindar Troopers under Sawai Jai Singh of Jaipur (AD 1700-1743)', *Indian Historical Review*, vol. 10, 1983-4.

Zaidi, Sunita, 'The Mughal State and Tribes in Seventeenth Century Sind', *Indian Economic and Social History Review*, vol. 26, no. 3, 1989.

Zihlin, P., 'The Armed Forces of the Soviet State: Fifty Years of Experience in Military Construction', in Jacques van Doorn (ed.), *Military Profession and Military Regimes: Commitments and Conflicts*, The Hague and Paris: The Mouton, 1969.

NEWSPAPERS AND MAGAZINES

Business Week, 20 March 2000.

Far Eastern Economic Review, 13 July and 20 July 2000.

Frontline, 12 February 1999.

India Today, vol. 24, no. 24, 14 June 1999; vol. 24, no. 27, 5 July 1999; vol. 24, no. 28, 12 July 1999.

Outlook, vol. 5, no. 15, 26 April 1999; vol. 5, no. 21, 7 June 1999; vol. 5, no. 24, 21 June 1999, 28 June 1999, 25 Oct. 1999; vol. XL, no. 9, 13 March 2000.

Strategic Digest, vol. 29, no. 12, 1999.

Sunday, vol. 26, 18-24 July 1999, 25-31 July 1999; vol. 26, 1-7 August 1999.

The Statesman, 28 March 2001.

The Telegraph, 5 July 2000.

The Times of India, 24 June 2000.

The Week, 24 October 1999; 11 June 2000; 9 July 2000.

Time, vol. 152, no. 21, 30 November 1998.

Index